The timing for this book is perfect. As healthcare moves from caring predominantly for the sick to the Triple Aim—better care, improved health for our communities, and lower costs—we need new perspectives and skills to lead the transformation. This book is the perfect guide to building the leadership and governance systems we'll need to get there. Gabow's wonderful definition of what women leaders bring to these challenges is inspirational and practical. She defines the unique approaches used by many women leaders, including seeing across the whole system, building multi-generational and multiprofessional teams, including all parts of the community and more. The book is filled with helpful advice for women in healthcare and for those who mentor them. A must-read for all in healthcare leadership today!

Maureen Bisognano
President Emerita and Senior Fellow, Institute for Healthcare Improvement

Patricia Gabow offers a new and unique perspective on leadership for women in healthcare. As a physician and CEO of a major safety net health system, Dr. Gabow provides a view of leadership that women in healthcare rarely see. She does this in a way that is extremely approachable, authentic, often humorous, and always practical. Dr. Gabow recognizes the obstacles confronting women who aspire to lead and importantly, remains optimistic. She gives clear examples and guidance for those who are navigating the path towards leadership, those transitioning into leadership roles, and has words of wisdom for senior leaders too. Chapter 6, entitled, "Now You are a Leader," offers a playbook and is essential reading for all as they enter new leadership roles. Dr. Gabow, always inclusive, rounds out her guidance by including and synthesizing the observations of women in health leadership across the U.S. The book offers many important insights and lessons and reminds us that as healthcare leaders we must lead with our values and always place our commitment to the patient first.

Carrie L. Byington, M.D.
Executive Vice President, University of California Health
Past (held concurrently) Jean and Thomas McMullin Professor and Dean of the
College of Medicine
Senior Vice President for Health Sciences and Vice Chancellor for Health Services,
Texas A&M University

Leadership, especially for women, starts with taking the next right action. Dr. Patricia Gabow's insightful and well-written book will inspire any leader, and especially women leaders, to do those things that matter: for their own personal growth, their organizations, and healthcare nationally. Whether you're aspiring to be a physician leader, a corporate leader, or want to chart your own course as an entrepreneur, *TIME'S NOW for Women Healthcare Leaders* will give you the confidence and wisdom to help you achieve the success you want.

Halee Fischer-Wright, M.D., MMM, FAAP, FACMPE
President & CEO, Medical Group Management Association

I wish I had *TIME'S NOW for Women Healthcare Leaders* early in my career. Dr. Gabow is master-ful at laying out why more women are needed in healthcare leadership and breaking down how women can make it happen—including the critical path to be successful once in a leadership role. Her use of thought exercises challenges each of us to not just read but to take action no matter where we are on our individual journey.

Evon Holladay, MBA
Past Vice President, Catholic Health Initiatives

TIME'S NOW for Women Healthcare Leaders successfully navigates many topics pertinent to women leaders, starting from developing a vision and values all the way to managing a board.

We all know that the characteristics of women being more collaborative and better communicators are factors that support an organization's success, including financially. *TIME'S NOW* helps individual women, as well as organizations, understand how to leverage these characteristics into a winning effort. *TIME'S NOW* provides the reader with an understanding of the critical skills women need that can make them successful leaders as well as the weaknesses that can hold them back. What I enjoyed the most in *TIME'S NOW* is when Dr. Gabow, in particular, and the other women leaders, shared real-life examples of their successes and failures. Dr. Gabow is a pioneer in leading large healthcare organizations. In this book, she paints an "end to end" experience for aspiring women leaders: from knowing "who's your boss" to "making the trains run on time" to spelling out many of the early steps a woman needs to pursue before she moves into senior leadership. I wish I had this book before I started on my leadership journey.

Donna Lynne, DrPH
CEO ColumbiaDoctors and COO, Columbia University Medical Center
Past Lt Governor of the State of Colorado
VP Kaiser Foundation Health Plans

In its opening pages, the book *TIME'S NOW for Women Healthcare Leaders* eloquently describes the imperative for transformational change in the U.S. healthcare system and the compelling need for women's leadership skills and voices to help drive the necessary change. The book is more than an anthem for female empowerment. It is a carefully researched and powerfully constructed business case for why women need to be at the leadership table. It is, therefore, worthwhile reading for both women and men interested in improving healthcare in America. Dr. Patricia Gabow is a nationally recognized healthcare leader. She acknowledges that the glass ceiling still exists but "there are stairways to the top even if some of them seem hidden or hazardous." Dr. Gabow then proceeds to identify and clarify the important skills and steps of a woman's professional journey to leadership, influence, and impact. Along the way, she engages the reader in a series of thought exercises designed to encourage the reader to reflect more deeply on how the issues discussed define their personal and institutional perspectives and reality.

TIME'S NOW is filled with practical and philosophical insights and advice for both aspiring and experienced women leaders. It is worth reading not only once, but again to absorb the complex and nuanced observations offered by Dr. Gabow and further enriched by the perspectives and wisdom of a dozen successful women healthcare leaders who were interviewed. All of these women were unified in the belief that successful leadership is not about the acquisition of power and title but the ability to use one's power and influence to make a difference and have a positive impact on the health and lives of others.

Lilly Marks
Vice President for Health Affairs, University of Colorado Anschutz Medical Campus

TIME'S NOW is an important addition to our growing literature on leadership. Patricia Ann Gabow M.D. is an American academic physician, researcher, consultant, and, for two decades, the highly successful Chief Executive Officer of Denver Health, transforming it into a model of financially secure community service. This eminently readable book is aimed at a particularly underserved niche—women leaders in healthcare—but the lessons described apply to all organizations interested in doing well by doing good.

Dr. Gabow's conversational style, coupled with her wisdom and humility, allow the reader to readily imagine successfully using the tools and techniques she discusses in other arenas. Her real-world vignettes bring home the realization that every physician must lead. She doesn't shy away from the difficult issues of managing sexual harassment and outdated management practices that stifle women. The use of personal stories and comments from other prominent women in healthcare, and the distillation of the pertinent points into self-help questions, is particularly effective.

TIME'S NOW should be required reading for all women in healthcare leadership—as well as all the men who work with women.

Barbara L. McAneny M.D., FASCO, MACP
Past President, American Medical Association

Patty Gabow is a giant among healthcare, public health and community leaders. She has inspired many to take on the challenging role of leadership and has brought inspiration and guidance for many of us who have followed in her footsteps. Now she has taken time to put down in writing much of her personal philosophy and experience. This book combines the topics of women's advancement and leadership in an individualized approach that allows thoughtful preparation and helpful guidance for those in leadership. If you know Dr. Gabow, read this book, if you don't know Dr. Gabow read this book and learn from a master.

Janis M. Orlowski, M.D., MACP
Chief Healthcare Officer, AAMC

TIME'S NOW for Women Healthcare Leaders could not have arrived at a more urgent and yet promising time in the pursuit of gender equity in healthcare. Patricia Gabow's book not only lays out the ethical, business and performance cases for gender equity in healthcare leadership, but also provides insight into the barriers women face, first-hand accounts of the challenges and successes of women leaders, and steps that women can take in pursuit of leadership roles in healthcare. This is a must-read for all who seek the best outcomes for our American healthcare system.

Nancy Spector, M.D.
Professor of Pediatrics
Executive Director, Executive Leadership in Academic Medicine
Associate Dean of Faculty Development
Drexel University College of Medicine

Dr. Gabow has written another valuable book, this one with a timely focus on what women bring to executive roles in healthcare and how we could use more of that! Using direct quotes from women leaders, national data on current trends, and her own voice of experience, she covers the personal to the political. I strongly recommend this book to women who now lead or who aspire to healthcare leadership.

Nanette Santoro, M.D.
Professor and E. Stewart Taylor Chair of Obstetrics & Gynecology
University of Colorado School of Medicine

TIME'S NOW for Women Healthcare Leaders

TIME'S NOW for Women Healthcare Leaders

A Guide for the Journey

Patricia A. Gabow, M.D., MACP

Routledge
Taylor & Francis Group

A PRODUCTIVITY PRESS BOOK

First published 2020
by Routledge
52 Vanderbilt Avenue, New York, NY 10017
and by Routledge
2 Park Square, Milton Park, Abingdon, Oxon, OX14 4RN

Routledge is an imprint of the Taylor & Francis Group, an informa business

Library of Congress Cataloging-in-Publication Data

Names: Gabow, Patricia A., author.
Title: Time's now for women healthcare leaders : a guide for the journey / Patricia A. Gabow.
Description: New York, NY : Routledge, 2020. | Includes bibliographical references and index.
Identifiers: LCCN 2019056527 (print) | LCCN 2019056528 (ebook) | ISBN 9781138365582 (hardback) | ISBN 9780429430671 (ebook)
Subjects: MESH: Health Facility Administrators | Women, Working | Leadership | Administrative Personnel | Vocational Guidance | Women's Rights | United States
Classification: LCC RA564.85 (print) | LCC RA564.85 (ebook) | NLM WX 155 | DDC 362.1082--dc23
LC record available at https://lccn.loc.gov/2019056527
LC ebook record available at https://lccn.loc.gov/2019056528

ISBN: 978-1-138-36558-2 (hbk)
ISBN: 978-0-429-43067-1 (ebk)

Typeset in Garamond
by Deanta Global Publishing Services, Chennai, India

To the generations of women in my family—my great grandmother, great aunt, grandmother, mother, and daughter—for their strength, resilience, great kindness, and inspiration.

Contents

Foreword

Time's Now for Women Healthcare Leaders is an important book and a welcome addition to the healthcare debate. And Dr. Patty Gabow is uniquely qualified to write this volume, since she is one of the most successful woman health leaders in America.

No one has to be convinced that healthcare is a critical issue for most Americans. Our political debate is saturated with healthcare discussions, most Americans know and agree that costs are too high and care is too often mediocre, and America is losing ground as a healthy nation compared to other developed countries, with shorter life spans, more chronic disease, and more uninsured people within our borders.

The issue that hasn't often been a focus of this dialogue is the role that women play in the healthcare system. As a majority of the population, women are the majority of patients. Since we live longer than men and often have fewer resources later in life, we often face additional health challenges in our senior years.

Women perform the majority of caregiving work for ourselves, our children, and aging family members, so the majority of healthcare decisions are made by women. And women comprise the largest share of the healthcare workforce, EXCEPT in leadership positions.

This is the focus that Dr. Gabow exposes and explores in this book. After laying out some well-known issues with the American healthcare delivery system, she writes about the paucity of women leaders and what that means to the system. But most important, she provides some ideas about how to change the current structure, and how women in healthcare can prepare themselves for leadership positions.

Some of what Dr. Gabow discusses as barriers to women's advancement in healthcare are found in any workplace in America: the "motherhood penalty," limited access to paid parental leave, sexual harassment and gender bias, and pay equity issues. But there are also some distinct challenges for leadership positions in medicine and medical research, like the so-called imposter syndrome, difficulty accessing research grants, less attention to the health needs of women, and more controversy around women's reproductive health, which is often treated as a political debate instead of a healthcare issue.

Dr. Gabow was CEO of the Denver Health and Hospital Authority for 20 years. I know Patty and her work—she was legendary in the advocacy community—and had the opportunity to both study her results at Denver Health and visit her facility when I served as Secretary of HHS.

I went to Denver to try to get a first-hand view of how Dr. Gabow achieved such high-quality care results and ran a profitable health system with a patient population that was almost entirely uninsured or on Medicaid, which is often considered the most challenging health population in the country. Her team consisted of a high number of women leaders, and their collaborative style of patient care, measuring results, and holding themselves accountable for outcomes was a beacon for those of us searching for successful models.

But this book doesn't rely just on Patty's experiences and background, as impressive as they might be. She has included the insights of 12 other women healthcare leaders, as well as very practical steps that the women who comprise almost 80% of the healthcare workforce can do to "lead where they stand."

Management experts have long identified that companies and financial entities with women leaders and women board members produce better results. While I have never seen a study focused only on women in health leadership, perhaps because they are so few, it's hard to believe that the results wouldn't be similar.

As we search for various solutions to our current American healthcare challenges, where we spend too much to achieve mediocre health outcomes, *TIME'S NOW for Women Healthcare Leaders* identifies a problem that has received far too little focus—the small number of women in healthcare leadership. And following some of Dr. Gabow's ideas for a more balanced health system could improve the overall health and well-being of our country.

Kathleen Sebelius
21st U.S. Secretary of Health and Human Services

Acknowledgments

My first thank you must go to Denver Health and the University of Colorado School of Medicine. These institutions, especially Denver Health, provided me with the opportunity to be a leader and to interact with colleagues who inspired and taught me. These experiences enabled me to write this book.

I am grateful to Secretary Kathleen Sebelius who graciously agreed to write the Foreword to this book. Her leadership roles, especially as Secretary of Health and Human Services, give her a unique perspective from which to view this book.

The amazing women leaders who enthusiastically agreed to be interviewed deserve special thanks: Nancy Agee, Kim Bimesterfer, Evalina Burger, Linda Burnes Bolton, Carrie Byington, Karen DeSalvo, Leah Devlin, Halee Fischer-Wright, Risa Lavizzo-Mourey, Donna Lynne, Lilly Marks, and Nanette Santoro (their titles and positions are in Table 11.1). They added valuable perspectives from their different life journeys, professions, and the components of the healthcare system that they led. Their input not only added richness to the book, but they inspired me in its writing.

The women leaders from the Denver Health Executive staff have been with me on my leadership journey for many years, some for decades: Kathy Boyle, Peg Burnette, Darlene Ebert, Paula Herzmark, Stephanie Thomas, and Elbra Wedgeworth (their titles are listed in Chapter 1). They were instrumental in creating Denver Health's success. I appreciate their sharing their insights into that leadership experience and the contributions that women healthcare leaders can make.

I thank the male physician Directors of Service who shared their perspective on the influence of a predominantly female Executive staff on them and Denver Health: Richard Albert, M.D.; John Christopher Carey, M.D.; Robert House, M.D.; Paul Melinkovich, M.D.; and Ernest Moore, M.D. (their titles are listed in Chapter 1). They underscored that women's journeys to leadership will be facilitated by men like them who accept women as leaders.

The views of early and mid-career women from medicine, nursing, and research offered important insights on the ongoing challenges women face. I thank them for their openness in sharing: Mona Abaza, M.D., M.S. (Dept. of Otolaryngology-Head and Neck Surgery, University of Colorado School of Medicine (UCSOM), Anschutz Medical Campus (AMC)); Katie Bakes, M.D. (Dept. of Emergency Medicine, Denver Health and UCSOM); Marisha Burden, M.D. (Hospital Medicine, UCSOM,

AMC); Lilia Cervantes, M.D. (Dept. of Medicine, Denver Health and UCSOM); Melanie Cree-Green, M.D., Ph.D. (Pediatric Endocrinology, Children's Hospital of Colorado and UCSOM, AMC); Debra Gardner, MSN, RN,NE-BC (Nursing, Denver Health); Tracy Johnson, Ph.D. (Ambulatory Care Services, Denver Health and CO School of Public Health), Nicole Stafford, MBA, MSN, RN, NEA-BC (Nursing, Denver Health); Sarah Stella, M.D. (Dept. of Medicine, Denver Health and UCSOM); Elaine Stickrath, M.D.(Dept. of Obstetrics and Gynecology, Denver Health and UCSOM); Thida Thant, M.D. (Dept. of Psychiatry, UCSOM, AMC); Jennifer Whitfield, M.D. (Dept. of Emergency Medicine, Denver Health and UCSOM), and Florence Wu, M.D. (Dept. of Pediatrics, Denver Health and UCSOM). They not only provided a relevant perspective, but they also demonstrated that this new generation of women has the capacity to make our healthcare system focus on doing what is good and right.

Finally, I want to thank my family—those who I am blessed to still have with me and those who are gone. My grandparents, parents, and many uncles and aunts started me on the right path in life with love and guidance. My children, Tenaya and Aaron, give me joy and added balance to my work life. My husband Hal of 48 years has supported me in every step of my life and career with love and encouragement.

The many individuals to whom I owe thanks underscores an important lesson of leadership—none of us can make the journey alone.

Author

Patricia A. Gabow, M.D., MACP is a national leader in healthcare delivery innovation and the care of vulnerable populations. She served as CEO of Denver Health and Hospital Authority (DHHA), an integrated safety net healthcare system for 20 years, before retiring in 2012. Under her leadership, Denver Health was transformed from a struggling city/county healthcare system to an independent entity that became a national model. It was the first healthcare entity in the world to earn the Shingo Bronze Medallion for Operational Excellence.

Dr. Gabow began her career as an academic practitioner and medical researcher in nephrology, focusing on acid-base disorders and polycystic kidney disease. She is the author of more than 130 articles, 36 book chapters, and two books. *The Lean Prescription: Powerful Medicine for Our Ailing Healthcare System* received the Shingo Institute Research and Professional Publication Award. Her awards include the American Medical Association Nathan Davis Award for Outstanding Public Servant, the National Healthcare Leadership Award, the David E. Rogers Award from the Association of American Medical Colleges, the Ohtli Award from the Mexican Government, the Health Quality Leader Award from the National Committee for Quality Assurance, the University of Colorado Florence Rena Sabin Award, the Distinguished Graduate Award from the University of Pennsylvania School of Medicine, and the Gustav O. Lienhard Award from the National Academy of Medicine. She was a founding member of the federal Medicaid and CHIP Payment and Access Commission (MACPAC). She currently serves on the Robert Wood Johnson Foundation Board of Trustees and the Lown Institute Board. She was elected to the Association for Manufacturing Excellence Hall of Fame and the National Academy of Social Insurance. She has been granted honorary degrees by the University of Colorado School of Medicine and the University of Denver.

Dr. Gabow graduated from Seton Hill University and the University of Pennsylvania School of Medicine. She is Professor Emerita of the University of Colorado School of Medicine and a Master of the American College of Physicians.

Introduction

The time is now for women in healthcare to step into leadership. There is an increased awareness that American healthcare is desperately in need of change. There is also growing acknowledgment that women, who have been excluded from the tables of healthcare leadership, have valuable perspectives, talents, and skills to facilitate that change. This offers women an unprecedented opportunity. Women must be ready and willing to meet the challenges, grasp the opportunity, and shine.

The purpose of this book is to clearly articulate those challenges, provide a guide for overcoming them, and share insights for succeeding as a woman healthcare leader. It captures the journeys of those who have walked the boulder-strewn road and become successful leaders. The book has three major components, reflecting both documented observations and learnings from personal experiences. The first three chapters provide extensive information on the current state of American healthcare, the journey and current state of women healthcare professionals, and the challenges and obstacles that still exist for women in healthcare. Chapters 4 through 10 delve into the foundations, preparation, and execution of healthcare leadership. Chapter 11 offers the insights and guidance of twelve senior women leaders.

Healthcare and a leadership journey were an unlikely path for me. I grew up in an Italian immigrant family in rural Pennsylvania. My father was killed in WWII when I was a baby. My mother and I lived with my grandparents and an uncle until my mother remarried years later. These adults gave me support, guidance, and direction. The stories of my grandparents and great grandparents who as young people journeyed from Italy to America to start a new life were an inspiration. My maternal grandfather shared many old-country sayings filled with wisdom. Two guided my life: "If you have a gift and you don't use it, no confessor on earth can absolve you" and "If you get an education in America, there is nothing you can't do." He acted on the latter, sending my mother and her two brothers to college during the Depression. They and my stepfather were all schoolteachers. They embraced the benefit of education for men and women and encouraged my journey. But how I veered from teaching to medicine was a mystery to both them and me.

I started on the path to healthcare leadership as one of six women in my medical school class and the only woman in my internship and fellowship group. When

I joined the Department of Medicine at Denver Health and the University of Colorado School of Medicine, I was the only woman. Role models, mentors, and sponsors helped me move around or through the barriers and enabled me to persist. At Denver Health I found an institution with a noble mission and dedicated colleagues who inspired me (see Appendix). My journey led to my being a successful academician and CEO of a major healthcare system for twenty years, transforming it from a struggling safety net to a national model.

On this journey I have seen and experienced much and gained an understanding of our healthcare system and of the qualities and practices of leadership. At this moment of opportunity for women I want to pay forward my learnings and help other women become tomorrow's leaders. I realize I have only one perspective. Part of that view is of a white woman who has not experienced the same journey as a minority woman. But I believe much of these learnings are valuable to any woman (or man) who aspires to leadership. To broaden the perspective in this book I have interviewed other women leaders and up-and-coming women healthcare professionals from medicine, nursing, and research.

In becoming leaders, we need to be clear-eyed about the myriad problems of American healthcare before we can provide new directions. American healthcare must change—expenditures must come down and access and quality must improve. But change will not come without a new vision and different people at the tables of healthcare leadership.

As women we have unique talents to bring to these tables. The book provides evidence of those talents. We are the child-bearers and we are the care givers. This gives us a unique perspective on the healthcare system. We are motivated by doing good and serving others. Our leadership presence in organizations improves performance in multiple dimensions. Yet, we are not equitably represented at the tables of healthcare leadership. Women compose almost 80 percent of the healthcare workforce but only 13 percent of the healthcare CEOs. The barriers that are blocking the path to leadership are myriad: lack of equitable policies, bias, harassment, burnout, and the self-doubt that these barriers produce. This book presents these issues and their solutions.

Despite the barriers and challenges, there is a path for women not only to be leaders but to be great leaders. Great leadership is grounded in values—values which women embrace and exemplify. Women's leadership can come alive in relationships, communication, decision-making, the hard work of delivering operational excellence, and a vision for the future. The book details the perspectives, processes, and skills that facilitate what women can bring to each of these key leadership elements.

At its core this book is a call to action. Women can and should lead. We can make a difference—a needed difference.

Chapter 1

Why Should Women Lead?

"What changes when a woman leads business—Everything."

Goldman Sachs Ad New York Times October 7, 2018

There are three short, straight-forward answers to the question, "Why should women lead?" The first is that fairness demands women have equal representation in healthcare leadership. The second is that in not achieving gender equality in healthcare leadership we are failing to utilize all the available talent. The third is that healthcare has myriad problems and women leaders can bring a new and needed perspective to the solutions. These answers are based on a series of general and healthcare-specific facts:

- Women are 50.8 percent of the United States population.
- Women constitute 47 percent of the American workforce (74.6 million civilian workers).
- Women's presence in the workforce accounts for 25 percent of GDP.
- Women make up 75 to 80 percent of the healthcare workforce but less than 15 percent of the top leadership positions.
- Women make 80 percent of the healthcare buying and use decisions.
- Women are 75 percent of the family caregivers.
- Women bring unique perspectives and skills to leadership.

If the Goldman Sachs' declaration above is true, and I believe it is, then women must answer the call to become healthcare leaders. Moreover, if women constitute the majority of the healthcare workforce, why should men primarily develop and oversee policies, conditions, and goals in the system? Women need to be equally represented among healthcare leaders not solely, or even most importantly, for their own benefit, but for what they will bring to health and healthcare. If, as women, we succeed in achieving fair and equal leadership representation throughout healthcare, but our presence does not drive major transformation, the full promise of women's healthcare leadership will not have been achieved.

Men have almost exclusively led all the components of our society that have shaped American healthcare: physicians, health systems, insurance companies, pharmaceutical and device industries, and government. This is not to say that male leaders are the cause of our healthcare system's problems. But it is to say that we need a different outcome and if we are to achieve that outcome, we need different voices at the table—women and men, people of color and white individuals, and the young and old.

American Healthcare

While American healthcare has achieved amazing breakthroughs in some areas, it is failing in many aspects and is not delivering population health, both objectively, and in comparison to other developed countries. If women are to play a pivotal role in the solutions, we must clearly see the failures before we can address them. We cannot sing from the old song sheet that America has the best healthcare system in the world. We need to be clear that although the system is exceptionally good in some ways, it is exceptionally bad in others. We must preserve and build on what is good and minimize or eliminate what is bad.

Thought Exercise

What do you see as the major issues in our healthcare system? How do we compare in outcomes with other high-income countries (HIC)?

In assessing the performance of our healthcare system, we need to look at how American healthcare performs in the areas of cost, coverage, access, quality, and disparity/equity. We are currently spending almost 18 percent of nation's GDP, or $3.5 trillion on healthcare—twice as much as other high-income countries and over the years our costs have risen faster than in any other HIC (National Health Expenditure Data, 2018; Anderson et al., 2019).

Given the complexity of American healthcare, it is not surprising that the causes of this exaggerated healthcare expenditure are myriad:

■ Prices
■ Salaries
■ Care fragmentation
■ Administrative complexity

- Overuse and misuse of therapies
- Waste

When asked why American healthcare is so expensive, the well-known health economist, Uwe Reinhardt, famously declared, "It's the prices, stupid" (Anderson et al., 2003). This central role of prices has recently been confirmed (Papanicolas et al., 2018; Anderson et al., 2019). This work underscores the major contributions of products, including pharmaceuticals, procedures, and people to our sky-high costs. The annual per capita cost of pharmaceuticals in the United States is $1443 compared to a mean of $749 in other HIC (Papanicolas et al., 2018)—$700 per person creates quite a stack of money at the end of the year! This price differential becomes shocking for some high-cost drugs. For example, the average price of Humira in the United States is 96 percent higher than in the United Kingdom (Kamal and Cox, 2018). We have higher costs of high-margin, high-volume procedures. For example, the average cost of a total knee replacement is over $28,000 in the United States and can reach more than $60,000 in some healthcare systems compared to about $18,000 in the United Kingdom (Millman, 2015; Kamal and Cox, 2018). No wonder healthcare tourism has emerged.

We pay more for components of the American healthcare workforce than do other HIC. Physicians, both primary care doctors and specialists, earn almost double that of other HIC. These wages are higher even after correcting for purchasing power and for the average medical school debt of American physicians (Papanicolas et al., 2018). Although there is variability in nurse salaries, hospital-based nurses earn almost $20,000 per year more in the United States than in other HIC (Anderson et al, 2019). The salary differential is more surprising for health system administrators. The highest hospital administrator's yearly earnings in the United Kingdom in 2015 was a record £340,000, about $430,000 in United States dollars (Donnelly, 2016). The four highest salaries for healthcare system administrators in the United States ranged from $10 million for the CEO of Kaiser Permanente to over $17 million for the CEO of HCA, and 17 hospital administrators in the United States earned over $5 million per year (Knowles, 2018).

The care of patients is often fragmented due to lack of a primary care physician, use of emergency departments for care amenable to ambulatory care, and inadequate communication between providers and systems of care. The fragmentation and complexity are compounded by myriad insurance coverages, all with different benefits and rules. Even at the federal level, there is coverage via Medicare (with its multiple alphabet components), Medicaid (with a version for every state and territory), the Child Health Plan (with state variations), the Veterans Health Administration, the military services health system, and the Federal Employees Health-Benefits Plan. If this wasn't enough, there are hundreds of health insurance companies. Because of the fragmentation and complexity, administrative costs in the United States are about 8 percent of total healthcare expenses compared to 3 percent in other HIC (Papanicolas et al., 2018). These administrative complexities have human costs in burdening providers and patients as well as financial costs to the system.

Despite spending a great deal more than other HIC, unlike these other countries, we do not provide health insurance coverage for everyone. In 2013 there were 44 million Americans who were uninsured (Kaiser Family Foundation, 2018). By 2016, with the implementation of the Affordable Care Act (ACA), that number had fallen to 26 million—much better, but still not zero. However, by 2017 the number of uninsured had increased by 700,000 people (Kaiser Family Foundation, 2018). These numbers will likely continue to grow as the federal government and many states seek to significantly alter the ACA and Medicaid coverage. With the advent of high-deductible plans, even the insured are often substantially underinsured.

In America insurance matters. In 2017, the uninsured were four times more likely than those with Medicaid or private insurance to lack a usual source of care, and these patients were much more likely to postpone care, go without care, or not fill a prescription because of cost—hardly a path to well-being (Kaiser Family Foundation, 2018). Those of us who take care of patients understand that as important as health insurance is as a ticket to healthcare, it does not guarantee access. Recent access problems with long waiting times for care within the Veterans Health Administration dramatically underscored this reality. Access, especially to specialty care and dental care, is also a problem for Medicaid patients, as some physicians and health systems either limit their numbers or do not take them.

Even when individuals get access to care, they do not always receive the appropriate preventive care or care that is indicated. In fact, 10 to 30 percent of the care they do receive is either not indicated or harmful (McGlynn et al., 2003). In 2018 the Medicare Payment and Advisory Commission (MedPAC) noted, "there is substantial use of low value care—the provision of a service that has little or no clinical benefit or care in which the risk of harm from the service outweighs its potential benefit" (Medicare Payment and Advisory Commission, 2018). This low value care cost Medicare as much as $6.5 million in 2014 (Medicare Payment and Advisory Commission, 2018).

You would think that since we spend twice as much as other HIC on healthcare, the outcomes for Americans would be significantly better than that in these other countries. Sadly, this is not the case. One commonly used measure of care is life expectancy, as most of us desire a long life, and it is an unambiguous endpoint with reliable data. The United States has the lowest life expectancy of all HIC—more than three years less on average (Gonzales et al., 2019). That might not seem like much, unless it is you or your family. Not only is our life expectancy lower; it has fallen for three successive years for the first time since 1915–1918, when the First World War and the Spanish flu were taking their toll (Dyer, 2018). This shortened life expectancy starts from birth. The United States has the highest infant mortality of all HIC.

There are several ways to look at this decreased life expectancy, which are surprising, if not shocking. One way is to compare life expectancy against healthcare spending. For almost all countries, spending more on healthcare increases life expectancy—not so for the United States. We are an outlier, spending more and getting less (OECD, 2018). Another way to look at this is to see where the United States ranks in life expectancy across all ages compared to 17 other HIC. Given that it is often stated, "We have the best healthcare system in the world," one might expect that we would be number one or at least two or three across the board— far from it. We never rank above 15th out of 17 countries until age 75, and we achieve the highest life expectancy among 95-year-olds, when most of us are dead (Figure 1.1) (Institute of Medicine and National Research Council, 2013)! In a range of other quality measures, we underperform compared to other HIC, including having a higher mortality for conditions amenable to healthcare.

Within America, there is considerable variability in coverage, access, and outcome by race, socioeconomic group, and geography. African Americans, Native Americans/Alaskan Natives, and Hispanics are less likely to have insurance coverage, and they attain lower health status and poorer outcomes. African Americans fared worse than whites in 24 of 29 measures, Native Americans/Alaskan natives on 20 of 29 measures and Hispanics on 11 of 29 measures (Artiga et al., 2016). There is marked geographic variability across the states, within counties in states, and even within a single city. Generally, health is poorer in the southeastern part

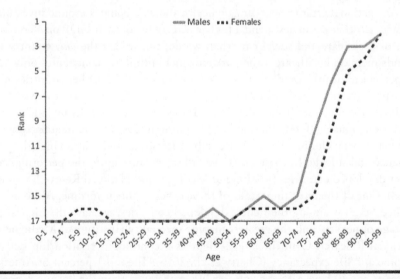

Figure 1.1 Ranking of U.S. mortality rates by age group among 17 peer countries. Number 1 is the top ranking with the lowest death rate and number 17 is the lowest ranking with the highest death rate. (Source: Institute of Medicine and National Research Council. 2013. U.S. Health in International Perspective: Shorter Lives, Poorer Health. https://doi.org/10.17226/13497. Reproduced with permission from the National Academy of Sciences, Courtesy of the National Academic Press, Washington, D.C.)

of the United States than the rest of the country (Radley et al., 2018). Health outcomes vary across counties in every state (County Health Rankings and Roadmap, 2019). The variation within a given city is jaw-dropping. In our nation's capital the difference in life expectancy between a few subway stops is almost 30 years (VCU Center on Society and Health, 2018). This geographic variability has led many healthcare leaders to conclude that your zip code is more important to your health than your genetic code. The only possible good news in this statement is that it should be easier to alter the factors that produce the zip code effect than to alter the genetic code.

All current and aspiring healthcare leaders should look at these data and ask two questions:

Why do we spend more money on healthcare and get less health?
Is it acceptable to allow this performance of American healthcare to persist?

The Institute of Medicine did ask that first question. Their study, "U.S. Health in Perspective: Shorter Lives, Poorer Health," concluded "A major reason lies in the fact that the foci of our attention, our resources, and our incentives are too narrow … our investments are primarily directed to biomedical (focus) …" (Institute of Medicine and National Research Council, 2013).

As a national priority, spending on health and well-being is a sound investment. In fact, 11 other countries spend a higher percentage of their GDP on a combination of healthcare and social care than we do, but we are the *only* country that spends more on healthcare—the portion which ultimately contributes only 10 to 15 percent to health (Bradley et al., 2016; Magnan, 2017). Other countries make a greater investment in social care, which has a greater impact on the well-being of the population (Bradley et al., 2016). These social care factors include income, education, housing, food, qualities of the communities, environmental exposures, and behaviors including diet, exercise, substance abuse, and injuries including gun violence and suicide. In these areas, we fail to measure up to the performance of other developed countries (Institute of Medicine and National Research Council, 2013). One of the most important of these other factors is income. Although the United States is among the richest developed countries, we have the highest percentage of poverty and the greatest income inequality (Institute of Medicine and National Research Council, 2013). There is a continuous relationship between income and life expectancy (Chetty et al., 2016). The top 1 percent of American males at age 40 have a 15-year greater life expectancy than the bottom 1 percent of American males, whose survival is equal to that of similarly aged men in Sudan (Chetty et al., 2016).

A number of groups are beginning to ask the second question "Should these shortcomings be allowed to persist?" Although there is no national answer to this question yet, it seems obvious that there can be no compelling reason to continue a system that costs so much more and delivers so much less than it should.

What Women Bring

The performance of our healthcare system and the health of Americans cannot be ignored. The data present two pivotal and related questions from a gender equality perspective:

Can these problems be solved by only having men, especially white men, who have been the principal developers and benefactors of our current system at the table?

Can women healthcare leaders provide new and needed perspectives that will lead to better outcomes?

There are persuasive reasons to answer "no" to the first question and "yes" to the second. Humans have been evolving for over 200,000 years. In that process, women emerged differently than men genetically, biologically, physiologically, and culturally. In large part because women are the mothers, they developed different roles and different skills. For much of history these differences were not viewed as strengths. They were used to keep women "in their place" which was at the kitchen table not at any leadership table. For centuries no one would have even thought to ask the question, "Did sitting at that kitchen table result in women developing a set of skills and approaches to problem-solving that are unique, important, and valuable?" Finally, we have started to ask these questions. There is a growing body of data that women do bring different skills to leadership. Women make teams function better and they produce better outcomes in a variety of dimensions. These differences matter.

Obviously, these findings are nuanced. Men and women do share many common traits and attributes. Great leaders, regardless of their gender, have much in common. Moreover, not all women are the same, just as not all men are the same. Some women are concerned that calling out differences between men and women may encourage continued bias and discrimination. This would be true if the posited differences conveyed some lesser abilities or talents, but that is not the case.

Thought Exercise

What unique characteristics and talents do you think women bring to leadership roles?

Korn Ferry, a management consulting firm, elicited the views of 38 current and 19 former female CEOs at Fortune 1000 or similarly sized companies (Korn Ferry Institute, 2017). Thirty-eight of these women were assessed using Korn Ferry's Executive psychometric assessment tool and their scores were compared to the Korn Ferry's CEO benchmark scores (Korn Ferry Institute, 2017). Purpose, mission, and a positive organizational culture were strong drivers for women. These women were motivated by a belief that their company could have a positive influence on their community or even the world. The women scored similarly to the benchmark "in persistence, need to achieve, curiosity, focus, assertiveness, risk-taking and empathy." The scores with the greatest difference were the scores on humility, with women scoring significantly higher, and the scores on confidence, with women scoring slightly lower. The investigators interpreted the humility score as a lack of self-absorption, an appreciation of others, and a willingness to note the role of others in their success. The confidence scores reflect women's belief that they are not in complete control. The study also demonstrated that women sought out difficult work and challenges. They did not place a high value on the predictability of the work—not surprising given women's lives! These women CEOs were committed to being authentic. They led with integrity and were not willing to compromise their values even if it meant turning down a promotion. While these were not healthcare leaders, the women leaders I interviewed reflected the same commitment to authenticity and integrity and had the traits of humility, giving credit to others, being motivated by mission, and seeking challenges (see below and Chapter 11). The study concluded that women were "exceptionally motivated to build something new, take risks, to deliver results, and to make a difference" (Korn Ferry Institute, 2017). This bodes well for women leaders bringing needed change to healthcare.

Zenger/Folkman, a leadership development firm, conducted a study that compared over 7000 men (64 percent) and women (36 percent) managers and Executives from high performing American companies (64 percent of the individual participants) and international companies for a group of leadership competencies based on a 360-degree assessment (Zenger/Folkman, 2012). Their data showed that on the "overall leadership effectiveness index females were rated more positively than males." Women scored significantly more positively on 36 of 49 survey items and men scored more positively on two. Women were rated more positively on 12 of the 16 competencies. "The competencies with the largest differences between males and females, with females scoring significantly higher, were taking initiative, practicing self-development, integrity/honesty and driving for results." While these were the areas with the biggest difference, women also scored significantly higher in developing others, inspiring and motivating others, building relationships, collaboration and teamwork, establishing stretch goals, and being champions of change. "While men excel in the technical and strategic arenas, women clearly have the advantage in the extremely important areas of people relationship and communication." Quite an impressive set of traits and skills. The women I interviewed reinforced these findings, believing that women were more engaged in building relationships, were more collaborative, and more willing and able to work in teams (see below and Chapter 11). This study concluded, "It is a well-known fact that women are under-represented at senior level management. Yet the data suggests that by adding more women the overall effectiveness of the leadership team would go up." Let us hope that this advice is heeded.

Do these differences translate to different and more desirable outcomes? There are convincing data that having women in leadership roles influences companies' financial performance. Catalyst performed a large, well-designed study of 353 Fortune 500 companies across 11 industries during the 1990s (Catalyst, 2004). The Return on Investment (ROI) and Total Return to Shareholders (TRS) was substantially higher in companies with the highest percentage of women as corporate officers compared to those with the lowest percentage. The study showed that healthcare overall and the pharmaceutical industry in particular were among those industries with the highest percentage of women and they were also those with the highest financial rewards. Similar conclusions on the positive financial impact of women in corporations emerged from a study by Noland et al. for the Peterson Institute for International Economics. They examined financial data from over 21,000 firms in 91 countries (Noland et al., 2016). Of note, "almost 60 percent of these firms had no female Board members and just over half had no female C-suite Executives and less than five percent had a female CEO." Nonetheless, there was a positive correlation between the firm's performance and the percentage of women in upper management. "A profitable firm at which 30 percent of the leaders are women could expect to add more than one percentage point to its net margin compared with an otherwise similar firm with no female leaders." This represents a remarkable 15 percent improvement over the benchmark profitability. This work also underscores the role of a range of country characteristics that influence women being able to achieve leadership positions.

S&P Global conducted a large, comprehensive, long-term study of Russell 3000 companies from May 2002 to May 2019 (Sandberg, 2019). During this time period there were 578 female Executive appointments to CEO or CFO among 5825 new Executive appointments. Shockingly, the male to female ratio for CEOs was 19:1 and 6.5:1 for CFOs. Both female CEOs and CFOs outperformed the market average and their male counterparts on aspects of financial performance. "In the 24 months post-appointment, female CEOs saw a 20 percent increase in stock price momentum and female CFOs saw a six percent increase in profitability and eight percent larger stock return" (Sandberg, 2019). In addition, over the first 24 months of the appointment of a female CEO, the percent of women on the Boards increased. In fact, "Boards with female CEOs have twice as many female Board members, compared to the market average (23% vs. 11%)." A detailed examination of the Executive biographies revealed that "the average female Executive has characteristics in common with the most successful male Executives. The attributes that correlate with success among male Executives were found more often in female Executives." This may be a good news, bad news story—women leaders financially outperform male leaders, but they have to have more stellar credentials than a man to be appointed to those positions.

While these data are important in demonstrating the contribution that women make to a business's financial success, they raise other relevant questions that should be answered:

■ Is there a percentage of women leaders in a company that creates a tipping point at which they begin to influence organizational priorities?

■ Are there critical leadership roles (e.g., CEO) that matter more than overall leadership percentages?

■ Do the observations of the positive effect of women in industry apply to American healthcare?

■ Can the improvement women bring go beyond finances to improvement in healthcare and health?

■ Can women in healthcare leadership change the focus from profit to the patient and the population?

■ Can women in healthcare leadership create positive societal change?

Most of these questions remain unanswered, but their answers are critical for the future of healthcare, as well as for the other aspects of the society that are the major contributors to health. Some data are beginning to emerge in the clinical arena and across a societal spectrum, which suggests positive answers to some of these questions.

For example, there are a number of studies demonstrating that women physicians have a more positive outcome than men on patient communication, preventive care, and survival (Chapter 3). We do not know if women in leadership can translate these individual patient outcomes to a population. But it seems likely that the perspective and skills demonstrated with patients would carry over to populations.

We are seeing the impact of women in American politics. Record numbers of women were elected at all levels of government in 2018 (Chapter 3). Women appear to accomplish more in that arena. Women legislators sponsor more bills than do their male counterparts (Aguilar, 2019). Their presence will likely create more and better-informed legislation in the broad array of health and healthcare issues. For example, in 2019, 45 percent of the Colorado state legislature and a majority of the House were women. In that session, the legislature passed a broad array of healthcare legislation including a mandate to explore a public option, a cap on insulin prices, increased hospital price transparency, the provision of dental benefits in Medicaid for pregnant women, comprehensive sex education, and all-day kindergarten, some of which were measures that had repeatedly failed before.

The subtitle of Melinda Gates' book, *The Moment of Lift*, emphasizes this broad impact of women— "How Empowering Women Changes the World" (Gates, 2019). This book is filled with examples of empowering women as a critical force for positive health and societal change. One amazing example is how giving sex workers in India a voice prevented a catastrophic AIDS epidemic in that country (Gates, 2019). There is emerging data from randomized studies of village councils led by women and men in India and Afghanistan that show a positive relationship between women leaders and improved physical, social, and economic situations for women in those communities (Javadi et al., 2016).

Studies from India, Nepal, and South America show the benefit of women's participation on water, as well as fishery and forest resource management (Leisher et al., 2016; Lima and Barnes, 2019; UN-Water, 2006). Certainly, women have been the stewards of resources in their homes for centuries. Gates connects these types of improvement to better outcomes for children and families (Gates, 2019).

The power of women to bring change at a societal level is demonstrated by the thousands of women whose protests brought down the Sudanese President Omar al-Bashir in 2019 (Sadek, 2019). There is a remarkable positive impact of having a significant number of women as part of peace negotiations in regions of conflict, including a greater likelihood of success and a long-lasting agreement (Council on Foreign Relations, 2019).

Women standing up and calling for change is not only a phenomenon in the developing world. There are young American women on the opposite side of the economic spectrum who are calling out issues of wealth and income disparities—factors that are critical aspects of health. Abigail Disney, the granddaughter of Roy Disney, called the $65 million compensation of the Disney CEO, which is 1424 times the average Disney worker as "naked indecency" (Sherman, 2019).

What is even more astounding is the power of girls in leading substantial change. What better example could there be for the power of the female voice than Malala Yousafzai who was awarded the Nobel Peace Prize at age 17 for her heroic stance on the right of all children, including girls, to have an education. These voices of girls are not just rising from third world countries. There is Greta Thunberg, a 16-year-old Swedish girl, and Alexandria Villasenor, a 13-year-old American girl, who are organizing their generation around climate change, which has and will have a substantial influence on population health.

This abundance of examples of the positive effect of women and girls across a range of industries, circumstances, and outcomes forcefully underscores why women must lead.

What Leaders Told Me

While studies and examples illustrate the unique contributions women can make, the voices of women themselves offer a valuable perspective of their lived experience. To provide that perspective I interviewed three groups of women in healthcare: current women leaders, women who served on the Executive staff at Denver Health, and aspiring women leaders. There is also value in hearing the voices of men. For that perspective I interviewed five male physician leaders who reported to the Denver Health Executive team.

Perspective of Other Women Leaders

I conducted interviews with 12 senior women leaders whose different backgrounds and roles are provided in Chapter 11. They underscored the unique perspective and skills that women bring to leadership. Their extensive comments are Chapter 11, but a selection of those provide valuable insights into why women should lead.

- ■ "Over our lifetime we see the good and the bad in healthcare from [different] perspectives. That gives us a unique way of solving the problems of the healthcare system" (Risa Lavizzo-Mourey).
- ■ "Women have an important view of the care pathways and where those pathways get interrupted" (Lilly Marks).
- ■ "Women are care givers and care takers in the family. They bring that perspective to healthcare" (Evalina Burger).
- ■ "Women believe in health maintenance more than men do" (Nanette Santoro).
- ■ "Women have developed a team approach to help them juggle their many priorities" (Leah Devlin).
- ■ "Women are particularly good at relationship building" (Nancy Agee).
- ■ "They skillfully navigate different interests" (Halee Fischer-Wright).
- ■ "We find common ground" (Karen DeSalvo).

These women also underscored the data gleaned in the more formal studies which detailed what motivates women to become leaders.

- ■ "I wanted to make things better" (Karen DeSalvo).
- ■ "I had a passion to make things better and improve lives" (Evalina Burger).
- ■ "I was driven to be of use to others" (Linda Burnes Bolton).
- ■ "I sought to leverage my talents to do good" (Nanette Santoro).
- ■ "I wanted to accomplish more than I could one patient at a time" (Nancy Agee).

Women's leadership motivations suggest that they will provide new directions in healthcare.

Denver Health Women Leaders

The Denver Health experience could be an example of both the financial and healthcare outcomes that result from a high percentage of women in the C-suite. Seventy percent of Denver Health's population were from minority communities and the majority were uninsured or covered by Medicaid. From 1992 to 2012 (my tenure as CEO) Denver Health was in the black, despite the unsponsored healthcare increasing from $100 million to over $400 million with almost unchanged city financial support of $27 million for this care.

Despite a vulnerable population, during this period Denver Health achieved outstanding clinical outcomes, including the lowest observed-to-expected mortality of all academic health centers in the University Healthsystem Consortium.

These data reflect both extraordinary and sustained commitment to vulnerable populations and highly credible management skills. While it cannot be proven that this reflects women's leadership, it can be said that both the number of women in the C-suite and this performance for a safety net institution were remarkable.

During my tenure as CEO, the C-suite had women in the positions of COO, CFO, CNO, General Counsel, Chief Communications Officer, Chief Government Relations Officer, Executive Director of the Health Plan, and Executive Director of the Foundation. I interviewed the following leaders:

Kathy Boyle, Ph.D., RN, CNO
Peg Burnette, B.S., CPA, CFO
Darlene Ebert, J.D., Retired, General Counsel
Paula Herzmark, M.A., Retired, Executive Director of the Foundation
Stephanie Thomas, MBA, Retired, COO
Hon. Elbra Wedgeworth, B.A., Chief Government Relationship Officer

I have included some of their comments related to women in leadership here, and some others where relevant in other chapters.

These women Executives believed that having this cadre of women in leadership made a difference in the organization. "If you look at the results [during our leadership] compared to other groups that came before and after [the results the organization achieved] were not a flash in the pan. They were sustained for years."

In addition to believing that women made a demonstrable difference in the outcomes, these women affirmed the unique skills that women have, especially in building relationships.

■ "Women are willing to spend more time building relationships. I don't think men put the time in the same way that women do. Women are more inclined to listen ... and hearing what it is the other [person] needs and wants" (Paula Herzmark).
■ "We take time to communicate with people. You learn their family situation and background and ... how it shapes how they communicate and their priorities. Men aren't concerned with that" (Darlene Ebert).
■ "Women are adept at operating within a team environment. In our ... *Lean* journey we were learning that. We said check your badge at the door. My female [colleagues] were more open to that. [They] didn't need credit; it was for the good of the organization. Denver Health felt like a family, more so than any other hospital. People who came from the outside commented because it was so palpable" (Stephanie Thomas).
■ "[The family feeling] came as a surprise to me when I came to Denver Health and saw that. I didn't expect that in such a large organization. Women are very good at multi-tasking" (Kathy Boyle).

■ "I think it was advantageous to have women in leadership roles because we bring empathy and a work ethic that benefits in many ways. We give more thought to how programs and services affect patients and … the community. At times, men do not bring that to the table. We get more done, because as women we are always in a position of having to prove ourselves. Women are more [likely to be] caretakers … so we want to take care of people" (Elbra Wedgworth).

■ "Women are good at picking the right team. Women know the potential of other women. Women tend to pay more attention to details that men think are unimportant. Typically, I don't see men operating at that level … [they think] that is something that someone else can do. In reality these details can be quite important" (Peg Burnette).

Aspiring Women Leaders

I also met with a group of 14 younger women. This group included practicing physicians, physician and Ph.D. researchers, and nurses. Some had recently finished their training, others were mid-career, and a few were in a position of some leadership. They shared the barriers they faced and the opportunities they perceived as they pursued their careers. But they did not wish to be directly quoted. This in itself makes a statement about the barriers women face. I have included their reasons for aspiring to leadership roles here. A number of the other comments from this group are noted in other chapters where they are relevant. Their goals for leadership were to benefit others:

■ "I feel like [leadership] is an opportunity … to take the incredible privilege I was born into and pay that forward. I want to be in a position to be impactful for people who don't have that voice."

■ "I am following my moral compass. As a leader I can impact the well-being of vulnerable patients."

■ "I am driven to provide excellent care to poor kids."

■ "Be an advocate for the people who you know are doing the best work. I want to make sure their voices are heard."

■ "I [want to] match my skill set with things that make a difference. I can [be a bridge]. I want to pull things together and I see so much that isn't together."

■ "I love taking care of patients, but I feel that I need to do something about the social problems that we see every day. About giving people a voice and being a connector."

■ "Advocating for women's health and for women including women in my profession. I saw many examples of what not to do."

■ "I am tired of people not doing the things that they could be doing to impact more people. It is frustrating when people who are making the rules are doing things wrong, not considering the values we care about."

- "If it's broken, I want to fix it; if it doesn't exist, I want to create it. I would suffer trying to fix something [rather] than sit on the sidelines."
- "The world is increasingly small, and I am trying to change the world."
- "It is about making the system different so that my daughter may have better opportunities."

They were inspiring in that not one was interested in leadership for money, prestige, a C-suite position, or increasing the profitability of the component they might lead. While I have worked with many men at Denver Health who embrace these goals, the unanimity among these women in their goal of helping others supports the belief that women will bring to healthcare a major change in focus and direction if they are given the opportunity to lead.

Thought Exercise

Why do you want a leadership role in healthcare?

Male Physician Leaders

I also interviewed five physicians who were Denver Health Clinical Department Chiefs (Directors of Service) during the time that I was CEO. I asked them if they thought that there was a difference in having women leaders in contrast to male leaders. Those interviewed were:

Richard Albert, M.D., Medicine
John Christopher (Chris) Carey, M.D., Obstetrics and Gynecology
Robert House M.D., Psychiatry
Paul Melinkovich, M.D., Community Health Services
Ernest (Gene) Moore, M.D., Surgery

The interviews underscored the importance of positive experiences they all had with strong women including their mothers, spouse, mentors, their colleagues, and previous bosses, in how they perceived women leaders (Paul Melinkovich, Robert House, Chris Carey). A number of them never thought about whether there were differences between women and men leaders before I asked them the question (Paul Melinkovich, Robert House, Rick Albert, Gene Moore). However, upon reflection all of them identified differences and these differences were positive attributes of women's leadership:

"I never really thought about it until you asked me. There was no gender bias in this institution. Since we were a safety net institution that was fair to everyone, it was easier for women to become leaders without anyone thinking about it. Women leaders probably promoted equity and fairness. That helped [the organization] mature and succeed. The attitude was we are all at the table, we are all the same, and we all have needs; let's figure out how to make it work. Women facilitated that. Women probably collect more facts and try to look at both sides before making a decision" (Gene Moore).

"Until you went down the list of women on the Executive staff, it never registered. I think it's the people in those [leadership] positions that change the organization. I think it is hard to separate good leadership skills from gender-related determinants of those skills. I can say this. After we started the hospitalist program, it became very apparent that the way the women related to their patients was different than the way the men related to their patients and I do think that was a gender-related issue, not a person-related issue. They had closer connections to their patients as people" (Richard Albert).

"A lot of people in my life ... were strong women. I never thought of [women in leadership] as unusual. I never found it unusual to be in the minority. I never thought a lot about are they doing things differently than a man would do? If I could pick anything out about working with women, maybe they are more direct and more willing to say it like it is and deal with [issues] that are emotionally charged. As I think about our leadership team in Community Health where it was a mixed group, the women were more willing to call out something they thought was wrong even though they knew it wasn't going to sit well with the group where some of the men would shy away from that. Having many women Executives at Denver Health allowed young women at Denver Health to recognize their potential and that they would be listened to. It gave them a voice" (Paul Melinkovich).

"My mother was the nurse leader on a surgical service at a naval hospital. I came from a background were women were a little more assertive. In my residency ... there was a woman psychoanalyst who was brilliant. Before she went to medical school, she joined the women's army and she flew bombers. [My women mentors] showed me that compassion worked. So, coming to Denver Health didn't seem like a major cultural shift. Women give clear, specific direction. It seems women are more transparent. When I was at Denver Health as an intern and resident there was a lot of chaos, and when I came [back as faculty] it was organized and there was a different ambiance. It was the friendliest place I had ever been ... I don't know if that came from [the women in] administration. There is this culture of equity. The sense of mission is really strong. This is mutually reinforcing—women in leadership and equity and mission" (Robert House).

"I have spent a lot of my life thinking about gender as a scientific and as a cultural issue. Gender is critical to the interactions we have ... perceived gender and gender roles. In our society we expect different behaviors from men and women, and these are mostly learned behaviors. These behaviors have to be adapted in a professional environment. There has been more modeling for men. There have been a lot more men over the last couple hundred years in leadership societies that taught young men how to be a leader. I don't think there are as many role models for women. For almost 20 years, I reported to women, and it is different to report to a woman than a man. I prefer dealing with women. There are differences. Denver Health has been committed to taking care of the most vulnerable. This is a mothering type behavior. Having many women in leadership roles is both a reflection of that and an influence on that. The culture of Denver Health promotes women in leadership and women in leadership promote the culture of Denver Health. Women seem to have a good sense of what is important. When there were times when that wasn't as prominent, we weren't doing as well" (Chris Carey).

The connection between women's leadership and the safety net mission, the cultural environment of these institutions, and women's commitment to this mission suggests that changing the focus of healthcare institutions will promote more women in leadership and they in turn will change the focus of the institutions, creating a virtuous cycle.

Taken together, the need for fairness, women's unique perspectives and skills, and the contributions that women can make to healthcare and health, require that women equitably share the leadership of all the groups that influence health. We cannot and should not be the only voice, but we must be a meaningfully represented voice. We need to add women in roles and numbers that give us a real place in addressing the myriad issues in American healthcare. If this is to happen, women need to step up. We cannot wait to be invited. We know the answer to the question, "Why should women lead?" Because we can make a difference.

Chapter 2

Lay of the Land

Knowing the lay of the land is important on any journey. To reach your destination you should know what progress has been made and how much further there is to go. The journey to women's healthcare leadership is no exception. Viewing the landscape of women in healthcare is less like seeing a still-life picture and more like seeing a varied tapestry being woven over many decades with different strands coming together to show the past, the present, and leaving space for the future. It depicts the path of women pioneers, women's many roles in health and healthcare, and the emergence of women leaders. Healthcare over decades, even centuries, has offered women rewarding professions that benefit them and society. However, in many of these professions, the acceptance of women, their equal and equitable treatment, and their achieving leadership roles has been very slow. Meaningful progress has been made, but more barriers must be removed from the roads that remain to be traveled before women can achieve the positions they deserve and in which they can make significant contributions.

Examining the lay of the land for women in healthcare reveals the large swath of terrain in which women have a significant impact, as well as those areas that impact them. The women who came before us laid important groundwork. They opened doors but some doors remain only ajar. Women are the primary caregivers for their families, but this comes with not only joy, but also with burdens and penalties. Their role as child-bearers creates unique health needs for them, and this plays a pivotal role in the health of the next generation. Yet, as health researchers and as subjects, they have been under-represented. They fill substantial roles across the healthcare professions, but they have not achieved leadership positions or pay equality in these professions. All these domains should be understood by women in healthcare, especially those who aspire to leadership. These are discussed in this chapter. The obstacles of bias and sexual harassment are discussed in Chapter 3.

Figure 2.1   The difference between equality and equity using a bicycle example. With equality everyone has the same bicycle but because they are all different, only one person can effectively ride. With equity each person has the bicycle that enables him/her to ride. (Reproduced with permission from the Robert Wood Johnson Foundation.)

As we examine the lay of the land for women in healthcare, it is useful to consider both equality and equity. Although these two words are often used interchangeably, they are different, and the difference has relevance to women's leadership journey. Equal means every person is treated the same. Equity means providing each person with the opportunity to achieve the desired outcome. A simple figure conveys how equality and equity are different (Figure 2.1).

Having equal pay for men and women for equal work and the same position would be equality. However, if women have barriers that prevent them from achieving the same positions, equity would require the removal of those barriers. Therefore, without attention to equity, it will be difficult for women to achieve equality.

Women Healthcare Pioneers

Learning about the women pioneers in healthcare serves several purposes. Their stories can inspire us to be pioneers in our own way, in our own times. Learning about the barriers these women had to overcome can put into perspective the barriers that we each face. Their journeys may show us a better path for our own journey. There are many types of women pioneers in health and healthcare and in the battle for equality. They come from many countries and backgrounds. They come from the ranks of scientists (Marie Curie, Rosalind Franklin), physicians (Gertrude Cori, Virginia Apgar), nurses (Florence Nightingale, Dorothy Lynde Dix), lawyers (Sarah Hughes, Myra Bradwell), and public personas (Abigail Adams, Patricia Roberts Harris, Francis Perkins). Many were champions for women beyond the boundaries of healthcare, providing a broad path for equity and equality. Some represent "the first," such as the first woman medical student, the first African American woman physician, or the first woman nursing school Dean. These women pushed open doors that had been closed and left them ajar for other women to come through. Many women, who may not have been among "the firsts," have made seminal contributions to health and healthcare, and their work has benefited society for decades. Some women in healthcare were genuine frontier pioneers. We never heard of them, but in the rough and tumble Wild West they showed that women could not only endure the hardships of living in a rugged territory, but also that they could provide succor for men and women. It is impossible to name every woman healthcare pioneer who deserves our recognition and gratitude. I have picked two American women to highlight in detail, but each of us needs to find our own woman pioneer to inspire us on our journey.

Thought Exercise

Which women healthcare pioneers have inspired you? Why did you pick these women?

A woman physician who had many "firsts," left a legacy, and inspired me and many others at Denver Health was Dr. Florence Sabin (State of Colorado, 1959; Mehnert and Cravedi, 2003). She is one of nine women in Congress's Statuary Hall and the only woman from healthcare. Dr. Sabin was one of Colorado's early citizens, being born in a mining town in 1871. Like every woman healthcare pioneer, she had obstacles on her journey. Her mother died when she was seven, and she and her sister were sent to Chicago to live with an uncle and later attended Vermont Academy and Smith College. After graduating she wanted to be a physician, but there was no money for medical school, so she began work as a schoolteacher (a "women's profession"). She opened many doors, being the first woman to graduate from Johns Hopkins School of Medicine, the first woman to become a Full Professor in a medical school, the first woman lifetime member of the National Academy of Sciences, and the first woman to head a division at the Rockefeller Institute for Medical Research—quite a lot of "firsts" for one woman.

In 1938 she retired to Colorado, probably thinking that there were no more amazing accomplishments ahead. Not so. In 1944 Colorado Governor John Vivian was hunting for someone who would not rock the boat to Chair the health committee in his post-war planning efforts. Someone suggested a retired, 73-year-old woman who wore her hair in a bun. That woman was Florence Sabin—obviously, the recommender had never met her! She spearheaded Colorado's first health laws in 70 years and visited every county in Colorado in support of those bills (not an easy trek in those days), answering every challenge from myriad vested interests. The Colorado legislature passed the Sabin Health Laws in 1947 and these laws governed public health in Colorado until 2008. She then proceeded to transform public health in Denver, tackling rats, garbage, milk pasteurization, and tuberculosis, reducing its rate by 50 percent. Accepting no salary, she became the head of Denver's Department of Health and Charities, which later became Denver Health, a position in which I was honored to follow her 50 years later. She brought public and personal health together in one institution, being decades ahead of her time. She finally retired at age 80, having rocked a good many boats. She saw opportunity in problems, was unstoppable once on a mission, and cared for the most vulnerable. So, not only can women lead, but also it is never too late for us to lead or rock a few boats—a heartening thought for women of my age!

Any list of American women healthcare pioneers must include Clara Barton (Wikipedia a, Clara Barton). This is fitting for at least two reasons. First, nurses compose the single largest group in the healthcare workforce and they often have significant leadership roles. Second, Clara Barton left a legacy with her formation and leadership of the American Red Cross. She was born in Massachusetts in 1821. She began her career as a teacher at age 17, establishing a school in New Jersey, only to have a man replace her as principal and being demoted to his assistant. Although she acquired her nursing training informally, she played a critical role in the care of soldiers in the American Civil War, earning her the title of "Angel of the Battlefield." Her commitment to the soldiers on both sides continued after the war ended with her leading the Office for Missing Soldiers, helping to locate 22,000 missing soldiers. Her experiences in the Civil War equipped her to help set up military hospitals during the Franco-Prussian War. In her visits to Europe she learned about the International Red Cross. She saw the role such an organization could play in peacetime and lobbied two Presidents to establish the American Red Cross. She became its first President in 1881. The role of the American Red Cross in national disasters started with its response to tornados and the Johnstown Flood in 1897. Every disaster victim who has been and will be helped by the American Red Cross can thank Clara Barton. She showed us that you must persevere in your cause even if you have to "bug" not just one, but two U.S. Presidents.

Some of the most important women healthcare pioneers were not even in healthcare, but nonetheless they shaped health policy. Such a person was Eleanor Roosevelt, who, in her role as Chair of the UN Commission on Human Rights, championed healthcare as a human right and equal pay for equal work (Wikipedia b, Eleanor Roosevelt).

Although the contributions of the many women healthcare pioneers were varied, they shared characteristics that are highly relevant to all women leaders:

■ A vision for a better way of doing things
■ A willingness to challenge barriers
■ A goal not for their own self-interest but for the benefit of others

- A deep commitment to improving health and well-being for all
- A long-standing and sustained effort

These guideposts should direct us all on our leadership journeys.

Women's Role in Health and Caregiving
Maternal-Child Health

Women occupy a central role in health and healthcare for their families. Their myriad roles emanate, in part, from being daughters, spouses, partners, and mothers. The healthcare of women before, during, and after pregnancy, as well as the outcome of pregnancies, are of critical importance to women and to population health. It is concerning that as important as this is, maternal and infant mortality have received little focus in the United States. For example, there is no standardized reporting of maternal mortality by states, and more than a decade has passed since the CDC published an official maternal mortality report (Slomski, 2019). We have ignored our poor performance among developed nations in maternal and infant mortality. Why is there this major blind spot? Is it a reflection of the paucity of women leaders in health policy, research, and institutions?

In 1900 in the United States approximately 850 women died in childbirth per 100,000 births (approximately 0.8 percent) and approximately 100 infants died per 1,000 live births (10 percent) (Centers for Disease Control and Prevention, 1999). A current commonly used maternal death rate for the United States is 17.2 per 100,000 live births—an impressive 50-fold improvement from a century earlier (Petersen et al., 2019). But having only one number belies reality. There is marked geographic variability among states and substantial racial differences. The five states with the lowest maternal mortality are California, Massachusetts, Nevada, Connecticut, and Colorado with maternal mortality ranging from 4.0 to 11.5 per 100,000 live births (Unger and Simon, 2018). The five states with the highest maternal mortality are Louisiana, Georgia, Indiana, Arkansas, and New Jersey ranging from 36.2 to 58.1 per 100,000 live births (Unger and Simon, 2018). The highest numbers are roughly equal to the maternal mortality of Vietnam and Jordan (Roser and Ritchie, 2019). Native Americans/Alaska Natives and African American women have 2.5 to 3.3 times the mortality rate of white women, respectively (Petersen et al., 2019). There is similar variability in infant mortality between geographic regions and racial groups (Mathews, 2018). We are far from being the best among developed countries—in fact, we are among the worst (Institute of Medicine and National Research Council, 2013).

Closely related to childbearing is overall reproductive health. Margaret Sanger was a nurse in the early 1900s whose care for women dying from "back alley" abortions led her to be a champion for "birth control" (Wikipedia c, Margaret Sanger). She opened the first birth control clinic in 1916 and was promptly arrested. Her involvement in a series of court cases finally led to the legalization of contraception in the United States in 1965 (for married couples). This, along with the development and commercial availability of birth control pills, enabled women to have control over the timing and spacing of pregnancies. The availability of long-acting contraception and the coverage provided in the ACA added to this control. Contraceptive availability facilitated women's entrance into all professions, including healthcare. Women no longer had to make the choice that many women healthcare pioneers had to make: being married with children or having a professional career. As leaders we must be among those who work to address the inequalities in maternal and infant mortality and to preserve and expand access to reproductive healthcare, not only for ourselves but for all women.

Thought Exercise

What are maternal and infant mortality rates for your state? Is your organization playing a role in addressing these issues?

Women's Role in the Care of the Family

Women play a pivotal role in the health and healthcare of their families. Approximately 75 percent of mothers make the decisions regarding the choice of physicians for their children and take them to their healthcare visits, compared to about 20 percent of fathers (Ranji et al., 2018). Forty percent of mothers stay home from work when a child is sick, losing wages in about half of those occasions compared to 10 percent of fathers (Ranji et al., 2018). Female physician-researchers with a male spouse or partner and children spend 8.5 hours more per week than their male partner on parenting or domestic activities, and they were statistically more likely to be the ones taking time off during disruption of the usual child care arrangement (42.6 vs. 12.4 percent) (Jolly et al., 2014).

Not only do women disproportionately care for their children, they are disproportionately responsible for the care of other family members. Seventy-five percent of family caregivers are women (Family Caregiver Alliance, 2019). This caregiving consumes many hours per week and is largely unpaid, impacting a woman's work life and her lifetime earnings (Family Caregiver Alliance, 2019).

While this involvement in the health and healthcare of American families is of great benefit to society, it places a disproportionate burden on women as they try to develop their careers and it affects their earnings. Policies that acknowledge this differential responsibility between men and women are needed to ameliorate these disparities. Such policies will greatly facilitate gender equity and equality, lessening some of the barriers for women on the path to leadership. These include:

- Job sharing
- Paid time off

- Paid family leave
- Subsidized childcare
- On-site childcare
- On-site care for sick children

Unfortunately, these policies are far from universal, or even widely available, or affordable in the United States or in the healthcare institutions in which women are the primary workforce.

Women in the Healthcare Professions

There are over 18 million people employed in all aspects of healthcare in the United States and nearly 80 percent of these employees are women (National Institute for Occupational Health and Safety, 2017). Women are employed in the array of healthcare roles, institutions, and industries. Among the various healthcare professions there are markedly different female-to-male ratios, extending from nursing at one end of the spectrum with a very high ratio, to surgical specialists on the other end with a low ratio. The mix of women and men is changing in all the healthcare professions, opening opportunities for everyone and enriching the perspectives in each discipline. While women may not want to enter every healthcare profession with the same frequency as men, they should be able to enter any one they wish without barriers, obstacles, or discrimination.

Nursing

Nursing has long been a path open to women, dating back to the earliest centuries of the Current Era. In the early centuries, nursing and care of the sick were often linked to the religious traditions of Christianity, Islam, and Buddhism. In early Western culture many of those engaged in nursing were nuns. Florence Nightingale, an important healthcare pioneer, is credited with developing nursing into its status as a profession. Nursing has flourished both in numbers and in the diversity of opportunities for women. The first American nursing schools opened in 1873 and proliferated in lockstep with the increased numbers of hospitals, many of which were run by religious groups (Penn Nursing, 2018). By the 1960s much of nursing training had moved to colleges and universities (Penn Nursing, 2018). Nurses are now the single largest group of healthcare professionals, numbering approximately 4.2 million, of whom over 800,000 are licensed practical nurses (Kaiser Family Foundation, 2018). Nursing remains primarily a women's profession. In 1970 about 3 percent of registered nurses were men; by 2017 still only 11 percent of nurses were men (U.S. Census Bureau, 2013; Auerbach et al., 2017).

The majority of nurses practice in acute care settings, but the profession spans the disciplines from bedside nursing to public health and school nurses, nurse practitioners, certified nurse anesthetists, nurse midwives, and faculty members in nursing schools. Women outnumber men in all these domains with the smallest gender difference among nurse anesthetists.

Nursing can be a pathway for women to leadership positions. But among many nurses, this may not be an aspect of nursing that has great appeal. In one survey 61 percent of nurses said they would not pursue a leadership position, even at the manager level (AMN Healthcare, 2017). This may be changing as younger nurses had a greater interest in leadership than nurses overall. Related to leadership aspirations is the pursuit of advanced degrees. Only 17 percent of nurses have a master's degree and about 2 percent have a doctoral degree which may limit the path to advancement (American Association of Colleges of Nursing, 2019). Those who do pursue an academic path appear to have achieved major leadership positions. One 2015 survey noted that 28 of the 30 most influential Deans of nursing schools were women (Willis, 2015). There are examples of nurses serving in C-suite positions and as CEOs, but the percentage in these positions is unknown. In order to have a clear picture of this pathway to leadership for women, reliable information on the number and percentage of nurses in a leadership position should be obtained by nursing and other healthcare groups.

Physicians

Physicians are the second largest group of healthcare professionals with over a million active practitioners, 36 percent of whom are women (Kaiser Family Foundation, 2019; Bureau of Labor Statistics, 2019). The journey of women in medicine has been long and arduous, traversing the terrain from entrance into medical schools, through graduate medical education, to attainment of leadership positions.

The first American woman medical student, graduating in 1849, was Elizabeth Blackwell, who faced barriers at every turn, including being rejected for admission by 29 medical schools (Amazing Women in History, 2012). After she pushed open that door, she helped other women by founding the Women's Medical College in New York in 1867. However, the number of women medical students increased at a snail's pace, with only 9.3 percent of the first-year medical students being female by 1965, the year I started medical school (American Association of Medical Colleges (AAMC) Data Book, 2017). I was one of six women in a class of 125 (5 percent). Starting in the mid-1970s there was a dramatic rise in women medical students. By 2002, 49 percent of the first-year medical students were female (AAMC Data Book, 2017). In 2018 the equality barrier was broken, with 50.7 percent of medical students being women (Kirch, 2017). In 53 of the 147 medical schools, the number of women exceeds the number of men, in some instances by a large margin. As the percentage and number of women increased, the absolute number of men in medical school also increased, reflecting the increased number of medical school positions (AAMC Data Book, 2017).

When I began my career at Denver Health in 1973 as Chief of Nephrology, 22 percent of the medical students at the University of Colorado School of Medicine were women; by 1981 when I become Director of Medicine, 40 percent of the medical students were women. In my roles, I interacted daily with medical students and I perceived a marked improvement in overall performance with this representation of women—increasing the number of women enriched the talent.

Forty-six percent of residency positions are now held by women (Brotherton and Etzel, 2016). However, there is still unequal representation of women residents among the medical specialties, particularly in the surgical disciplines (Brotherton and Etzel, 2016).

Despite the dramatic increase in the women in the medical school and graduate medical education pipelines, they are under-represented in leadership positions within academic medicine and as leaders within healthcare institutions. In 2018, 47 percent of Assistant Professors and 25 percent of Full Professors in medical schools were women (AAMC, 2019). A study of 91,073 faculty members found that even with multivariate adjustment for age, years from residency, publications, and funding, women were less likely to be promoted to Full Professor than men (Jena et al., 2015). Twenty-four percent of Basic Science Chairs and 16 percent of Clinical Department Chairs are women (AAMC, 2019). Only 15 percent of Deans are women, and the decanal positions filled by women are most commonly those focusing on education or institutional image, not the top academic leadership position (Schor, 2018).

This steep academic pyramid leaves women out of many important leadership roles (Figure 2.2).

We have solved the pipeline problem for women in medicine, but we are a long way from solving the leadership problem within faculty, who are the teachers and role models of the next generation. This will not be solved without a deliberate and focused approach.

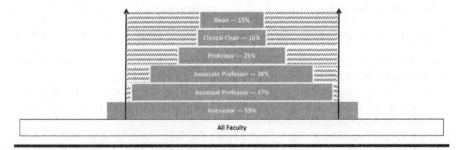

Figure 2.2 Percentage of women in the medical school faculty in each listed category. There is a steep pyramid in academic medicine with women representing 59 percent of the instructors and 25 percent of the Full Professors. The hatch areas represent the percentage of women that would need to be added to achieve equal representation. (Source: AAMC, 2019; Jena et al., 2015; Schor, 2018.)

Other Healthcare Professions

As the clinical provision of healthcare has broadened from the individual practitioner to team-based care, the equal representation of women in myriad other healthcare professions is relevant to the provision of healthcare. The gender distribution across an array of the health disciplines is shown in Table 2.1. Of note, in most of these professions, women are the majority of the providers.

Table 2.1   Number and Gender Distribution of Specific Healthcare Professions

	Number	*Percent Women*
Registered Nurses	3,213,000	86[a]
Physicians	1,094,000	40[a]
Dentists	199,486	32[b]
Physician Assistants	88,604	63[c]
Nurse Practitioners	165,480	88[d]
Nurse Anesthetists / CRNAs	44,000	59[e]
Nurse Midwives	12,218	95[f]
Pharmacists	348,000	63[a]
Psychologists	224,000	76[a]
Physical Therapists	286,000	70[a]
Occupational Therapists	116,000	87[a]
EMTs and Paramedics	214,000	34[a]

[a] Bureau of Labor Statistics. https://www.bls.gov/cps/cpsaat 1 l.htm. Accessed July 7, 2019.

[b] ADA American Dental Association. https://www.ada.org/en/science-research/health-policy-institute/dental-statistics/workforce. Accessed July 6, 2019.

[c] Kaiser Family Foundation. State Health Facts. Total Number of Physician Assistants, by Gender. https://www.Kff.org/other/state-indicator/total physician assistants/. Accessed July 5, 2019.

[d] Kaiser Family Foundation. State Health Facts. Total Number of Nurse Practitioners, by Gender. https://www.Kff.org/other/state-indicator/total-number-of-nurse-practitioners-by-gender/. Accessed July 7, 2019.

[e] Dunn, L. 10 Facts and Statistics about Nurse Anesthetists and CRNAs. Beckers ASC review 2010. https://www.beckersasc.com/anesthesia/10-facts-and-statistics-about-nurse-anesthetists-and-cmas.html. Accessed July 7, 2019.

[f] American College of Nurse Midwives. Accessed July 7, 2019.

An important group of professionals in our system are the administrators. Estimates report 300,000 healthcare administrators from manager level to CEO (ExploreHealthCareers). They work in a broad range of healthcare from physician groups and hospitals to device manufacturers. A 2006 survey by the American College of Healthcare Executives suggests that there is a higher percentage of men than women in general healthcare administration (57 vs. 44 percent) (American College of Healthcare Executives, 2018). Women tend to be in specialized areas such as planning and strategy, marketing, and quality assurance.

Women in Research

Women's role in research is two-fold: first as researchers, and second as subjects in clinical trials. In both these areas, the National Institutes of Health acted to improve the representation of women. Part of this effort was the establishment of the Office on Women's Health within the U.S. Department of Health and Human Services in 1991, which had the following broad mandates:

- Advise the NIH Director and staff on matters relating to research on women's health
- Strengthen and enhance research related to diseases, disorders, and conditions that affect women
- Ensure that research conducted and supported by NIH adequately addresses issues regarding women's health
- Ensure that women are appropriately represented in biomedical and biobehavioral research studies supported by NIH
- Develop opportunities and support for recruitment, retention, re-entry, and advancement of women in biomedical careers
- Support research on women's health issues (National Institutes of Health Office of Research on Women's Health a, 2014)

Women as Investigators

Women are active clinical and basic science researchers and appear critical in advancing the understanding of women's health. At the University of Colorado's Center for Women's Health Research 41 of the 61 investigators are women. The University of Colorado data suggests that in the present research environment, advances in women's health will, in large part, depend on the funding and presence of women investigators. Surprisingly, similar data could not be obtained from NIH without a formal Freedom of Information Request.

A successful research career depends heavily on research support, including grant funding. Despite similar degrees and the prestige of their previous institutions, the median startup package for women PhDs joining basic science faculties is significantly less than that for men (Sege et al., 2015). Given the importance of grant funding and the NIH's pre-eminence in providing that funding, it is important to examine the role of gender in this area. The picture is more gray than black and white. Women are less likely to apply for NIH grants than men (Rockey, 2014; Ginther et al., 2016). This may contribute to only 33 percent of NIH grants being awarded to women in 2018, having increased only 10 percent in 20 years. The failure to apply may be due, in part, to women faculty choosing clinical tracks rather than research tracks, receiving less institutional support, or less mentoring. When they do apply, women are equally likely to receive an initial NIH grant as male applicants, but the grant award is 13 percent smaller (NIH Databook, 2019). However, even this is nuanced. A recent study "found sex differences in the size of NIH funds awarded to comparable first-time female and male PI's even at top research institutions" with men receiving larger awards across a range of types of awards, even when controlled for key factors such as number of articles published (Oliveira et al., 2019). However, for the RO1 awards (the most common first-time awards) the grants for women were larger than for men (Oliveira et al., 2019). Women are slightly less likely to have a successful renewal than male grantees (NIH Databook, 2019). But here again, a major contributor appears to be a failure to reapply (Hechtman et al., 2018). When the resubmission rate is considered, there was no difference in the women's grant survival rate. Hechtman et al. concluded their study of NIH grants by saying,

> Thus, the data tell two very important stories. The first story, a positive one, is that women who have 'made it' in science are having careers of comparable length to men and are sustaining funding to support these careers ... The second—equally important story is that broad gender differences remain, and that thoughtful interventions during key transitions ... could help reduce those differences.

> **(Hechtman et al., 2018)**

There are institutional examples of this type of intervention and their positive impact. In 1996 Harvard Medical School developed a fellowship program that awarded small grants to junior faculty to help in research activity. An assessment of 16 years of the program revealed that a small investment in women instructors resulted in earlier promotion (Connelly et al., 2017). The $1.4 million that the University of Colorado's Center for Women's Health Research invested in women researchers enabled them to obtain $49.9 million in grant funding and advanced the field (Judy Regenstein, personal communication, 2019). Thus, investing in women investigators yields a big pay-off for both the women and science.

Women physicians in academic medicine have fewer total publications and fewer first or last author publications than male physicians (Jena et al., 2015). This may result in women being less likely to be acknowledged as research leaders. For example, they are invited to be guest speakers at academic institutions less often than men (Nittrouer et al., 2018) or as speakers at scientific meetings. However, there are nuances in such findings. A study of speakers at medical conferences with more than 100 attendees in the United States and Canada over a ten-year period starting from 2007 found that there was wide variation in the percentage of women speakers, but overall the percentage has increased over time (Ruzycki et al., 2019). Although women were under-represented, their representation reflected the proportion of women in particular disciplines. There may be a greater under-representation at the larger, more prestigious meetings. This is suggested by Director of the NIH, Dr. Francis Collins' recent pronouncement on this subject: "It is time to end the tradition in science of all male-speaking panels, sometimes wryly referred to as 'manels.' If that attention to inclusiveness is not evident in the agenda, I will decline to take part" (Collins, 2019). These types of clear messages and actions by prestigious male leaders will be both encouraging and essential for meaningful change.

Women can play an active role in advancing our representation as scientists. There is now a group "Request A Women Scientist" with a network of 500 women scientists who can be contacted by a journalist seeking information or an interviewee, or a conference organizer seeking speakers, or another scientist seeking a collaborator (McCullagh et al., 2019). Hopefully, more women will enter their information on this platform.

Women as Research Subjects

Although females compose 50.8 percent of the United States population, they have historically been greatly under-represented in clinical trials (Liu and Dipietro Mager, 2016). Myriad reasons have been given for this disparity. These include concerns regarding human subject abuses in the past, impacts on a fetus in a pregnant woman, hormonal fluxes in pre-menopausal women confounding data interpretation (thus requiring larger study populations to address confounding effects), and lastly, the fact that the investigators were predominantly male. Unfortunately, this exclusion and the failure to analyze sex-specific differences resulted in falsely assuming that study results from a white, male population are transferable to minority and female populations. Moreover, it failed to address diseases and conditions that are more common or unique to women, as well as the difference in physiologic response to the same diseases or therapies. This has had significant implications for a range of health issues, including drug therapies. For example, eight of the ten drugs withdrawn from the market by the FDA from 1997 to 2001 posed a greater risk to women than to men (GAO, 2001). The importance of understanding the difference in drug pharmacokinetics in women and men is underscored by the Ambien story in which the same dose can produce twice the drug level in women, causing morning driving impairment (Liu and Dipietro Mager, 2016). The lack of concern for the effects of sex on outcomes extended to animal and cellular studies as well.

A series of actions and policy updates by Congress and the National Institutes of Health, which began in 1986, require the inclusion of women in late phase clinical research trials. NIH has extended this inclusion to reporting of sex in human, animal, and cellular studies. While overall women now account for about 50 percent of the participants in NIH-supported clinical research, there appears to be substantial variability (Office of Research on Women's Health b, 2017; Tahhan et al., 2018). A recent examination of the inclusion of women in heart failure trials concluded that women represented only 27 percent of the enrollees (Tahhan et al., 2018). A demonstration of the need to recognize the unique health issues of women is represented by a new journal series, *JAMA Clinical Insights: Women's Health* (Crandall and Livingston, 2019).

The federal government, academic institutions, and all healthcare leaders must continue to address the issue of women's representation as investigators, grantees, and speakers, and their equal and adequate participation in all phases of clinical trials, as well as the inclusion of information on sex in all human, animal, and cellular studies. This is both good science and necessary for the health and well-being of over 50 percent of the population.

Gender and Pay

Ideally, a society would pay for professional work based on a range of consideration including the investment made to achieve the profession, the contribution the profession makes to the society and to the employing organization, the risk of performing the profession, the seniority and responsibility of the position, equality and fairness. Clearly, we are a long way from this ideal.

Pay for women in the healthcare professions is part of the broader issue of pay equality. The United Nation's Commission on Human Rights in 1948 and President Kennedy's Commission on the Status of Women in 1961, both chaired by Eleanor Roosevelt, affirmed the right of equal pay for equal work. More than five decades later we still have not reached that goal. Overall, full-time, salaried working women make less than men. In 1979 (the first year for which data were available) women made 62 percent of what men made; by 2016 it was 82 percent—progress, but not yet equal (Bureau of Labor Statistics, 2017). As with a range of other disparities, the gender pay disparity differs by geographic region and is greatest for minority women. The gap between men's and women's pay differs across the healthcare professions.

There is an unfortunate twist to gender pay inequity—the Motherhood Penalty. In fact, a substantial part of the gender wage gap is due to this penalty. Seventy percent of mothers with children under 18 years of age are in the workforce (DeWolf, 2017). Seventy percent of families rely on this income and in 40 percent of families these women are the sole or main breadwinner (DeWolf, 2017; Jee et al., 2019). Yet, they and their families pay a big penalty. A recent study examining the period from 1986 to 2014 found that "Mothers working full-time earn 71 percent of what fathers earn" (Jee et al., 2019). During the almost 30 years of the study, women's educational attainment and work experience increased, but the Motherhood Penalty did not decrease. In fact, when the investigators controlled for education and experience, the penalty for mothers with one child increased from 8 to 14 percent (Jee et al., 2018). Mothers with more children experienced an even greater penalty. This deserves to be called out and rectified. The occurrence and extent of this Motherhood Penalty across the healthcare professions has not been well-studied but should be.

Nursing Pay

Although there are differing data on the overall disparities between male and female nursing salaries, most studies show male nurses earn more across the nursing disciplines and roles. The differences between studies may reflect the methodology used, the groups surveyed, and the year of the survey.

Although men composed only 11 percent of the registered nurses in 2017, they are more likely to be in the higher paid nursing occupations, with men constituting 41 percent of nurse anesthetists, which is the highest paid of nursing disciplines (Landivar, 2013). In a 2013 survey, the nursing disciplines included in the study showed that male nurses earned more than female nurses. For example, female nurse anesthetists earned 89 cents for each dollar earned by men and female registered nurses earned 93 cents (Landivar, 2013). A 2015 study of registered nurses demonstrated higher salaries for male nurses than female nurses (Muench et al., 2015). A 2018 survey of 4,500 nurses noted that male staff nurses earned $75,833 per year while female staff nurses earned $68,521 per year (90 cents for each dollar that men earn) (Nurse.com, 2018). A gender difference was present across the range of leadership roles from charge nurse to CNO. In contrast, the AONE Salary Study in 2016 did not demonstrate a pay difference by gender in leadership positions across the range of positions from manager to C-suite (AONE survey, 2016). A broad, detailed, well-controlled study would shed light on the issue of gender pay disparity among nurses.

Physician Pay

Women physicians are paid less than male physicians. This is well documented in two recent, large studies—one a survey study, and the other a study of publicly available data from 24 medical schools. *Doximity*, the largest physician social network platform, conducted salary surveys in 2016, 2017, and 2018 with responses from almost 90,000 physicians in the last survey (Doximity, 2019). While the survey revealed a persistent gender gap, with women making less than men, the gap is narrowing slightly over time. On average, female physicians earned 25.2 percent, or $90,490 per year, less than male physicians in 2018. This gap was less than in 2017

(27.7 percent or $105,000). All 50 metropolitan areas surveyed had substantial salary gender gaps. The differences ranged from $28,542 per year in the metropolitan area with the lowest gap to greater than $150,000 in the metropolitan area with the largest gap. Every specialty had a gender wage gap. The largest gap by specialty in absolute dollars was in Urology, $94,000 annually. The gender wage gap exists for physicians both in private practice and employed physicians.

A variety of factors have been suggested to account for the gender salary differences: age, years out of training, choice of specialty, hours worked, family care duties, lack of desire or skill in negotiation, and bias. In an academic environment, track, academic level, publications, and grants are listed as other factors influencing pay. Jena et al. examined these salary factors, including the variables of age, years of experience, specialty, rank, and research and clinical productivity among 10,241 physicians, 3,549 of whom were women, in 24 U.S. public medical schools (Jena et al., 2016). A gender salary gap existed in both in unadjusted salaries ($51,315) and salaries with multivariable adjustments ($19,878). Thus, almost 40 percent of the differences in salaries for women could not be explained by adjustment for faculty rank, age, years out of training, discipline, NIH funding, clinical trial participation, publications, clinical activity, or prestige of their medical school. This is remarkable given that some of these variables, such as research and rank, are themselves influenced by a lack of gender equality. The study found that the differences existed across all faculty ranks. The differences were greater in the surgical subspecialties. Shockingly, adjusted salaries of women Full Professors were comparable to salaries of male Associate Professors and that of women Associate Professors were comparable to that of male Assistant Professors. Based on the average time to promotion from Associate to Full Professor at the University of Colorado (Steven Lowenstein, personal communication, 2019), this suggests women are penalized 7.7 years for their gender.

A 2018 report by the American Association of University Women (AAUW) performed a simple calculation that yielded a mind-boggling result. They multiplied the number of women physicians and surgeons in the United States by the average salary difference between men and women and calculated that the total loss of income to women in these disciplines in one year was over $19 billion (AAUW, 2018). If that doesn't make you gasp nothing will! One can't imagine this number if the gender pay disparities of all the health professions were included.

This difference in salary between men and women has numerous and important implications. A lower salary makes it more difficult to pay off college and medical school debt. This in turn can influence the choice of medical specialty. It puts constraints on women being able to pay for help at home and for childcare, support resources that help create equity.

What does not seem to be discussed in the existing literature is the long-term effect of these large salary gaps on women's retirement benefits and accumulation of wealth, both of which are highly relevant. A salary gap of $20,000/year, which is at the lower end of the reported range over a 35-year career, invested with a low return of 2 percent equals a loss of almost a million dollars in wealth at retirement. If this

$20,000 per year were invested at 4 percent, it would equal almost a $1.5 million loss of wealth. The loss of wealth for those with the biggest salary gaps makes one gasp. The $90,000 per year gap found in the *Doximity* study invested for 35 years at a 4 percent return would generate a staggering loss of accumulated wealth of over $6.6 million. As bad as the yearly wage gaps are, the loss of accumulated wealth is worse. This impact of gender pay gaps on accumulated wealth applies to all health-care professions in which the salary inequality exists.

It is patently obvious that this gender pay inequality is unfair and is a wrong that must be righted through government, institutional, and professional society actions. It affects not only the women directly, but their families as well. As a first step, we need to continue to bring the issue into the open. There are likely a variety of paths to correction. An essential part of addressing this issue requires complete transparency at all levels in all healthcare institutions.

Thought Exercise

Is there a gender pay gap where you work? If there is, have the women raised this lack of equality with leadership? What, if anything, has been done to correct this?

Addressing Gender Pay Inequality

All institutions must commit to eliminating gender and minority pay gaps and to monitoring its achievement. This will require commitment from the top and strong oversight. While there may be some disadvantages to defined, structured pay systems (especially for those who are now benefiting from higher salaries), it worked well at Denver Health. The physician pay system was based on the 50th percentile of base pay by discipline, years since the completion of training, and the position level. For example, a division head was paid differently than a non-division head. There was no discretion for the Directors of Service (or the CEO) to deter-mine salary. An outside firm conducted yearly surveys by discipline. There were no bonuses. A similar structured pay system was used across job categories at Denver Health. Michigan Medicine appears to have adopted a similar structured system (Castellucci, 2018). These physicians are paid based on nationally competitive sala-ries by discipline and position, and uniform raises are given yearly. Defined and structured systems eliminate flexibility and negotiation, but create fairness result-ing in equality across gender and race.

An even tougher nut to crack is how to make corrections to the inequalities that already exist. I would suggest this approach for physicians to bring equality without creating spiraling salaries across the board: all institutions adopt a given reliable sal-ary survey (or surveys) by discipline, rank, and position, and forego salary increases for those already above the 50th percentile while increasing the salaries for those below the 50th percentile. This will create equality for both women and men while placing some restraint on overall increases.

Every organization must create approaches to preventing salary inequities not only for nurses and physicians, but for all employees. These approaches must include preventing inequities on hiring, and at promotion, and a process for rectifying existing inequities. Components of these approaches should include:

- Transparency of process for determining hiring salaries
- Elimination of prior salary questions on hiring
- Transparency of process for determining raises
- Transparency of bonus payments criteria
- Transparency of actual salaries
- Limits on salary and raise negotiations
- Training for women on negotiating skills
- Training on bias for those responsible for hiring
- Reliable salary surveys
- Regular salary audits by gender and ethnicity, and transparent reporting
- Defined and transparent process for contesting and rectifying existing inequities
- Non-retaliation policy for contested salary

Institutions should affirmatively address this issue and report on the progress. Women, especially women leaders, should advocate this for all healthcare professionals and support staff.

Women in Healthcare Leadership

Although women make up 75 to 80 percent of the healthcare workforce, they are significantly under-represented in leadership across the array of healthcare roles. Their under-representation in academic medicine was discussed earlier in this chapter.

An Advisory Board study of 550 healthcare facilities and other studies have shown that the percentage of women in different workgroups decreases as one goes up the organization chart (Diamond, 2014; Stone et al., 2019) (Figure 2.3).

If women were to achieve the 51 percent representation at all levels of the organizations as their representation in the population, the needed increases would range from 8 percent at the Executive level to over 40 percent at the CEO level. On the other side of the coin, the percentage of men would need to increase in the frontlines and at the director level.

Some of the first women healthcare CEOs were nuns, leading major Catholic healthcare institutions. In fact, 9 of the 23 women in the Healthcare Hall of Fame are nuns (Modern Healthcare, 2019 a). In 2017 women were the CEOs of 11 of the 100 largest hospitals (Tecco, 2017). It appears that certain types of healthcare systems may be more open to women as leaders. Thirty percent of the CEOs of

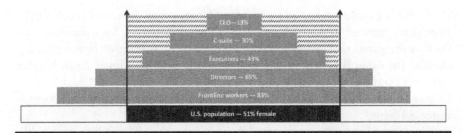

Figure 2.3   Percentage of women in the healthcare workforce in each listed category. There is a steep pyramid with women representing 83 percent of the frontline workforce and only 13 percent of the CEOs in healthcare. The hatch areas represent the percentage of women that would need to be added to achieve equal representation with the percentage of women in the population. (Source: Diamond, 2014; Stone et al., 2019.)

safety net hospitals are women (Annual Characteristic Survey, America's Essential Hospital's, personal communication, 2018) and 24 percent of CEOs of the 50 largest Children's Hospitals are women (Mark Wietecha, personal communication, 2019). Women's ability to be exceptional CEOs is reflected in the fact that women were CEOs of 24 of the 100 Top Hospitals in Truven's 2018 annual hospital ranking (Jean Chenworth, personal communication, 2018). The distribution of CEOs among nurses, physicians, and administrators is not readily available, nor is the data on women in leadership by type of institution. Having such data would create a better understanding of the pathways to this position.

Of the five largest health insurers in 2018, only Anthem had a woman CEO, Gail Boudreaux, whose training is in Business Administration. There were no women CEOs in the top five U.S. pharmaceutical companies in 2018. In 2017 there was not one woman CEO of a Fortune 500 healthcare company (Tecco, 2017). In 2018 no women headed a major federal healthcare agency including HHS, NIH, FDA, CDC, Veterans Administration Health System, or held the position of Surgeon General. However, a critical healthcare component of the federal government, CMS, was led by Seema Verma.

The picture is brighter, but not brilliant, in the other C-suite positions. Overall, women make up about 30 percent of the C-suite positions and constitute 33 percent of the hospitals' Executive teams in the 100 largest hospitals (Stone et al., 2019; Tecco, 2017). When there is a woman CEO, the percentage of women in C-suite positions increases to 40 percent (Tecco, 2017). Over the course of my tenure as CEO of Denver Health, eight of the C-suite positions were held by women (Chapter 1).

There is a paucity of information on the number of women and their professional backgrounds in specific C-suite positions. The relevant healthcare organizations must obtain and publish this data. Given the predominance of women in nursing, it is not surprising that the most common C-suite role for women is the CNO, a position occupied by women 60 percent of the time (Tecco, 2017). Even this otherwise positive number shows how difficult it is for women to enter the C-suite given that women constitute almost 90 percent of nursing professionals. The other Executive positions commonly held by women are in Human Resources and Legal Departments (Tecco, 2017). The position of Chief Medical Officer must be filled by a physician, but the number of women in this position is not available.

Since one of the primary responsibilities of governing Boards is to appoint the CEO, the representation of women on healthcare Boards is relevant. In 2017 22.1 percent of the Board members of Fortune 500 healthcare companies were women (Tecco, 2017). Hospitals were somewhat better with 30 percent of Board members being women and 13 percent being minorities in 2018. This information should be collected and reported by all healthcare industry groups.

A leadership role in a healthcare system is an entry into broader positions of influence. One can get a snapshot of women in the C-suite and their influence in healthcare from Modern Healthcare's "Most Influential" lists (Table 2.2). Their representation in these groups ranges from 22 percent to 36 percent. In 2019, 11 of the 25 of Modern Healthcare's Emerging Leaders were women (Modern Healthcare, 2019b). Among the 2019 "Top 25 Women Leaders," 21 were the top leader in their organization, underscoring that institution leadership roles beget broader influence (Modern Healthcare, 2019c). Six of the 25 were physicians and six were nurses, emphasizing these disciplines as a path to leadership and the role of clinicians as leaders.

Table 2.2   Women on the "Most Influential Lists"

	Number of Women	
List	*2009 List*	*2018 List*
100 Most Influential People in Healthcare	25 (16 CEO/Pres)	22 (18 CEO/Pres)
50 Most Influential Physician Executives	7 (4 CEO/Pres)	13 (6 CEO/Pres)
25 Top COOs	—	9

Source: Moden Healthcare: https://www.modernhealthcare.com/awards/100-most -influential-people-healthcare-2009; https://www.modernhealthcare.com/ awards/100-most-influential-people-healthcare-2018; https:www.modern healthcare.com/article/20090511/NEWS/905079992/the-50-most-powerful- physician-executives-in-healthcare-2009; https:www.modernhealthcare. com/awards/50-most-influential-physician-executives-2018; https://www. modernhealthcare.com/awards/top-25-coos-healthcare-2018.
The numbers in parentheses are those women who were CEO or President of their organization.

Another reflection of the influence of women physicians is their role in professional societies. Given the number of women physicians in training and in practice, one would expect women to have risen to leadership positions, particularly in specialty societies with a very high percentage of women practitioners. This has not been the case. Men have held a majority of leadership positions in most of these societies. In the ten years from 2008 to 2018, only one woman served as President of the American College of Obstetrics and Gynecology; three women served as President of the American Academy of Pediatrics; two women served as President of the American College of Physicians and of the American Academy of Family Practice. Interestingly, despite fewer trainees and women surgeons than in other disciplines, three women have been President of the American College of Surgeons.

Another reflection of influence is the editorship of journals. Women are editors of two of the five highest impact medical journals, serving as Editor-in-Chief of the *Annals of Internal Medicine* and the *British Medical Journal*.

Going Forward

As we reflect on the information in this chapter, we should heed the caution of Stephen Pinker, "It is the nature of progress that it erases its tracks and its champions fixate on the remaining injustices and forget how far we have come" (Pinker, 2018). We should remember that from the early days of healthcare, women pioneers have opened doors that help other women not only enter the healthcare professions but attain leadership positions. Much progress has been made in access to training and research, academic and leadership positions, as well as pay. Yet, for all the progress, the journey to equality is far from over and we, as women, must play our part in paving the road to true, meaningful equality. But the journey will be faster and more lasting if men also support and advance these efforts. Commitment by all the institutions and components of healthcare and government action will be required. Those commitments and the process to fulfill them need to be clearly and transparently articulated and the outcomes must be monitored and readily available. This is not just about fairness for women, it is also about the health and well-being of everyone, by adding our skills to solving the problems in our healthcare system.

Chapter 3

Obstacles and Opportunities

The obstacles and opportunities that exist for women in healthcare are the yin and yang of where we are now. It is common wisdom that timing is everything. We are in a time that can bring us the opportunities to both identify and eliminate the obstacles women face and to enable women to have an equal place at the tables of the healthcare industry.

Dick Lamm, a former Colorado Governor, noted that problems are solved in four phases: "No Talk, No Do" when no one seems to notice the problem; "Talk, No Do" when we become aware of the issue and bring it into the open, but have not yet taken steps to solve it; "Do, No Talk" when we are actively engaged in implementing solutions; and finally, returning to "No Talk, No Do" when the issue is solved and behind us. The range of articles in the scientific literature and the lay press illustrating bias, discrimination, and harassment of women, as well as the #MeToo, TIME'S UP, and TIME'S UP Healthcare movements, make clear that we are now talking about the issues after a long silence. But robust solutions that end the problems await discovery and implementation. So, we appear to be between step 2 and step 3 for a range of the obstacles in the path to healthcare leadership for women. It is our time to clearly identify and articulate the obstacles, to engage in the creation of solutions, and to capture the opportunities.

The obstacles that are strewn on women's path to leadership did not appear mysteriously. They emanate from our culture. Our country's conception gave birth to a novel, great, and noble idea of a country governed not by kings or emperors but by its people. But even this bold vision was of a limited landscape—"All *men* are created equal …," and these men were white. It was not until 1920 that women got the right to vote and then only after a long struggle.

Shortly after that, in 1923 at the first Women's Rights Convention, Alice Paul first proposed the Equal Rights Amendment (ERA) to the Constitution (Equal Rights Amendment). This laid dormant for almost 50 years. In the 1960s, 1970s, and 1980s people (overwhelmingly women) marched and went on hunger strikes to demand equal rights for women under the law. The amendment would guarantee equal legal rights for all American citizens regardless of gender, creating equal rights for "women regarding property, employment, in divorce, and other matters." It was finally approved by Congress in March 1972 and sent to the states for ratification. Fifteen states (Alabama, Arizona, Arkansas, Florida, Georgia, Illinois, Louisiana, Mississippi, Missouri, Nevada, North Carolina, Oklahoma, South Carolina, Utah, and Virginia) failed to ratify the amendment by the 1982 deadline, leaving the amendment three states short of the required 38. The failure to ratify came in large part from the effort mounted by Phyllis Schlafly (Wikipedia d, Schlafly). She argued that passage of the ERA would remove certain privileges that women had in matters such as child custody, alimony, and social security, and would permit women to be drafted in the military. There has been recent activity both for and against the ERA. Illinois recently ratified the amendment, but it is past the deadline, although there is some effort to remove or extend the deadline. On the other side of the issue, five states (Idaho, Kentucky, Tennessee, Nebraska, and South Dakota) have attempted to rescind their previous ratification. If we cannot agree on a legal statement of women's equality, it is hardly surprising that women face obstacles to leadership.

This is only one example of the cultural barriers that women in America experience. A recent study compared the difference in gender equality across countries by examining 11 variables. The United States ranked 19th behind Norway (number 1), Austria (number 6), Canada (number 11), and Spain (number 15) (Conant, 2019).

The obstacles that exist for women at all levels including those for leadership positions are:

■ Institutional and individual conscious and unconscious bias
■ Sexual harassment
■ Penalties for motherhood
■ Workplace-related burnout
■ Imposter syndrome

Many of these issues exist for women across every discipline and workplace. Moreover, there is an intersectionality of gender, race, and social class. Some obstacles, like burnout, may have garnered more attention in healthcare than in other types of work, but they are not specific to healthcare. For those issues that affect all women, our efforts to remove, or at least diminish, the obstacles should be aimed at not just for our professions, but for all working women.

Bias

Bias may be as old as human beings. Perhaps, *Homo sapiens* felt bias against Neanderthals. However, far back it goes, it has been embedded in our societies for a very long time. It is a concern when bias leads to unfairly favoring one group over another. In our society and in our healthcare system this bias has been and continues to be an issue affecting women's journey to leadership.

Institutional bias occurs when procedures and policies lead to discriminatory outcomes. These biases can be conscious or unconscious. These biases influence careers at every step of the way—recruitment, evaluation, promotion to leadership roles, and pay. Policies requiring full-time employment, no paid time off, no parental or family leave, or inability to reset the promotion clock in academic medicine have a disproportionate effect on women and reflect institutional bias.

Conscious and unconscious bias are also behaviors of individuals. Conscious or explicit bias is an attitude or perception that we know we have and often are willing to openly share and put into action. Conscious individual bias aimed at women in health professions has often been quite blatant. During training, I was once told by a surgical attending to not bother coming to the operating room, but rather sit in the front row and wear a short skirt. Clearly, the operating room was not a place for a woman physician. Decades later (after I thought we were past this), one of our very talented female residents with a gender-neutral name went for a job interview in a surgical subspecialty. When she walked into the Department Chair's office his first words were, "I never would have had you come for an interview if I knew you were a woman." Although such blatant conscious bias may be less than in the past, it certainly has not disappeared.

Unconscious or implicit bias is a person's unintentional attitude or action to a group or person (often because that person is in the group) that arises from all the societal input our brain has cataloged. Implicit bias can be favorable or unfavorable. Someone with this type of bias isn't aware of it and curiously it may not even align with his/her conscious beliefs. While we all probably have some conscious biases, we all certainly have unconscious ones. There are readily available tests such as Project Implicit designed by researchers at Harvard University, the University of Virginia, and University of Washington, that can show us these biases. These tests are worth taking, as is implicit-bias training, especially for leaders. Seeing your biases should not make you feel guilty for the simple reason that the biases revealed are unconscious. But knowing them helps us develop approaches to mitigate biases that can influence our decision-making in many areas.

A recent study of 3000 healthcare Executives observed a variant of unconscious bias: affinity (Stone et al., 2019). The authors note that affinity grows out of individuals identifying with people who share life experiences. Since there are currently more men in leadership roles, they have a male network and share more experiences with other men. This affinity reinforces favoring men in hiring. The women in the Denver Health C-suite observed that a benefit of that group was removing the bias against hiring women and leveling that playing field. We may have created female affinity.

Bias in Language

In a twist, something that is positive in one situation can be negative in another. Language usage is an example of this. Gender bias in language is fascinating in both its nature and its consequences. Those who study language state, "Language is one of the most powerful means through which sexism and gender discrimination are perpetuated and reproduced" (Menegatti and Rubini, 2017).

Language bias can be manifest in something we may never have thought of as having the potential for bias, such as a job advertisement. In fact, the wording of job listings can be quite biased and discourage women from applying. Shelly Cornell, a Stanford sociologist, gave an example from a company with whom she works whose job advertisement for a software engineer stated they were "looking for a ninja coder who wrestles problems to the ground" (Bazelon, 2019). Changing the wording of the advertisement increased not only the number of applications from women, but also from men. I guess most men didn't think of themselves as ninjas either! Of course, there can be more subtle use of words with masculine overtones. There are tools such as Gender Decoder that can be used to make certain job advertisements use gender-neutral words.

Thought Exercise

Review the last advertisements that were placed for positions in your area and those you placed. Are they gender-neutral? How does your organization assure gender-neutral job advertisements?

The words used to describe women reflect communal and warmth traits that likely emanate from our roles as caregivers and homemakers through hundreds of generations. These words include warm, caring, generous, kind, helpful and benevolent—traits we should all aspire to have. Unfortunately, these are not traits our society has linked to leadership, and they can carry a negative connotation in the current male-dominated leadership culture (Menegatti and Rubini, 2017). The words linked to men are related to agentic traits and competence and emanate from work that historically required speed and strength. These words include active, independent, forceful, confident, and ambitious (Menegatti and Rubini, 2017). When words associated with one gender are used for the other gender, they can convey negative connotations. Therefore, when women display some of the male gender-associated characteristics, they can be viewed as bossy or overbearing (Chapters 6 and 11). Does this mean that as women we should not display male-related traits? I think not. Similarly, it does not mean that men should not display female-associated gender traits. As more women enter leadership roles, hopefully both men and women can display the traits that most fit the situation. One of the male Directors at Denver Health said that I was both Mother Teresa and General Patton. While I clearly will not be canonized or lead an army, the message is clear—a woman leader can and should be versatile and confident enough to act as the situation requires. Sometimes we need to be empathetic and sometimes we need to take command. Both the current women leaders and the aspiring leaders I interviewed experienced angst about these labels: were they seen as being too soft or too controlling? (Chapter 11). Nonetheless, there was agreement that we all must be authentic and act appropriately for the circumstance.

We need to understand the implication of feminine and masculine-linked words when we write performance reviews and letters of recommendation. We do not want to hold women back from leadership by painting a picture that will be misinterpreted. A study of Deans' letters for medical students applying for residency demonstrated that "women were more likely than men to be described as caring, compassionate, emphatic," organized, and bright (Ross et al., 2017). These are traits we want in physicians, but did these words have a positive, negative or neutral impact on the women getting residencies of their choice? We don't know.

There are differences by gender in letters of recommendation for faculty positions. One study examined 624 letters of recommendation for university Assistant Professor positions looking for "doubt-raising" phrases such as "might be a good colleague"—the old damning with faint praise (Madera et al., 2019). Interestingly, both men and women used such phrases more frequently for women than for men. This difference in language usage held true when number of publications and teaching were considered. These phrases lower evaluation of the application for both genders, but as they were more frequently used in women's letters, their impact was disproportionate on women (Madera et al., 2019). Another study examined letters of recommendation for successful medical school faculty candidates (Trix and Psenka, 2003). Women had a higher percentage of very short letters and men a higher percentage of very long letters. Perhaps because the letters were shorter, women's letters more often lacked inclusion of usual details and had more "doubt-raisers." Letters referred to different skills and talents for men and women candidates. Women's letters referred to teaching and training while men's letters cited research and abilities. If these were the letters for the successful applicants, one wonders what the unsuccessful women applicants' letters contained. Are these issues of language bias that occur with women in academic medicine also present in the advertisements and recommendations for a range of other healthcare positions?

Thought Exercise

Read the last letters of recommendation that you wrote and that you received for female and male applicants. Do they contain these issues?

Motherhood Penalty

Marriage, motherhood and raising children are great joys that enrich many of our lives and can teach us a great deal about leadership. However, as with many things that bring us joy and fulfillment, they can present challenges, not only personally, but also professionally. The collective negative professional effect has been labeled the Motherhood Penalty (Chapter 2). Most of the literature on this subject is drawn from the overall workforce. A study from the Harvard Kennedy School demonstrated a number of these negative impacts on women employees who are mothers (Correll et al., 2016):

■ Among candidates with equivalent characteristics mothers were rated 10 percent lower in competency than non-mothers.
■ Mothers were considered less committed to their jobs than non-mothers. Curiously, fathers were considered more committed to their jobs than non-fathers—what's up with that!
■ Mothers were less likely to be recommended for hiring, received a lower starting salary, and were less likely to be recommended for promotion than childless women.

One study of women physicians from an online community, Physician Moms Group, analyzed the self-reported discrimination from 5782 physicians related to pregnancy, maternity leave and breast-feeding (Adesoye et al., 2017). Thirty-six percent of respondents reported discrimination related to one of these areas. The prevalence of this in the range of healthcare professions requires study.

Addressing Institutional Gender Bias

There is growing attention not only to the occurrence of bias, but also to approaches for eliminating or ameliorating its occurrence. The goals are behavior change related to bias, not necessarily eliminating people's unconscious biases. Carnes et al. demonstrated in a controlled study that well-designed workshops can bring about changes in gender-biased behaviors and departmental culture (Carnes et al., 2015).

However, removing institutional gender bias will require a wide range of interventions:

■ Recognition and acknowledgment of institutional gender bias
■ Training on and measurement of bias
■ Defined processes with clear criteria for recruiting, hiring, evaluation, promotion, and pay
■ Casting a wide net for applicants
■ Adequate representation of women on committees
■ Structured approaches for interviews
■ Clear criteria for assessing candidates
■ Policy changes that facilitate the removal of bias and facilitate equity and equality

■ Measurement of progress and transparent reporting of results of the interventions
■ Increased numbers of women in leadership positions

Clearly, the last one is a powerful remedy against gender bias.

One policy that deserves specific attention is paid parental leave. The United States is the only one of the 35 OECD countries that does not provide paid maternity leave and one of only eight countries the does not provide paternity leave (Donovan, 2019). Estonia has the most generous maternity leave at 85 weeks, and Japan has the most generous paternity leave at 30 weeks. The demonstrated positive impact of such leave on both parents and children led the American Academy of Pediatrics and the Pediatric Policy Council to recommend up to 12 weeks of leave for new parents (American Academy of Pediatrics and Pediatric Policy Council, 2017). There is a paucity of data on how many healthcare institutions have this leave for all their employees. However, overall, large employers and highly paid employees are more likely to have this benefit (Donovan, 2019). One study of 12 top medical schools showed that all offered faculty maternity leave (Riano et al., 2018). But there was considerable variability in length of full salary support (6 to 16 weeks), the mean length of leave (2 to 52 weeks), and in the operational aspects of the policy, such as it being dependent on the Chair of the Department in some cases. Parental leave policies appear more restrictive for graduate medical trainees who are clearly in their childbearing years. A study of the 24 specialty Boards revealed that only 11 specifically mentioned parental leave as an acceptable reason for leave, and no Boards had a specific policy (Varda and Glover, 2018). Another study showed that only 7 of 15 institutions with resident training programs had paid maternity leave for trainees, and it averaged 5.7 weeks (Magudia et al., 2018). Hopefully, there will be changes in these policies that reflect the reality of women being the child-bearers and that they are bearing these children during their training and early in their careers.

Thought Exercise

As you look at the list of interventions that can help eliminate gender bias which of these are your institution adopting? Are you part of any organized effort to pursue their adoption?

Sexual Harassment

The #MeToo, TIME'S UP, and TIME'S UP Healthcare movements have dramatically underscored the widespread sexual harassment that women experience in the workplace. Awareness of the breadth and depth of this issue prompted the National Academies of Sciences, Engineering and Medicine (NASEM) to begin a study in

2016 to define, examine and put forth potential solutions to this issue (National Academies of Sciences, Engineering, and Medicine, 2018). At the outset, the committee agreed sexual harassment "can silence and limit the career opportunities in the short and long term for both the targets of the sexual harassment and the bystanders with at least some leaving their field … [creating] significant and costly loss of talent …" The committee identified three forms of sexual harassment:

1) Gender harassment which is manifested by sexist hostility and crude behavior
2) Unwanted sexual attention in which there is unwelcome verbal or physical advances which can include the criminal activities of assault and rape
3) Sexual coercion in which a person's advancement is conditioned on sexual activity

Of these three types, gender harassment appears to be the most common.

A climate of sexual harassment appears to be present from the initial steps of a woman's training. In one study 20 to over 40 percent of female undergraduate and graduate students in the sciences reported sexual harassment (NASEM, 2018). The severity of the problems that exist at the collegiate and university level for all women has gained national attention in recent years around the issue of date rape and the institutional response, or lack thereof, to its occurrence.

It is shocking that the academic workplace has the second highest reported rate of sexual harassment at 58 percent, just after the military which is at 69 percent (NASEM, 2018).

In a study of female medical students, 50 percent experienced gender harassment and 5 percent unwanted sexual attention (NASEM, 2018). Gender harassment doesn't disappear with increased status. A comprehensive study of over 7000 surgical residents, 2935 of whom were women revealed that 65 percent of the women experienced gender discrimination and 19.9 percent of them experienced sexual harassment (Hu et al., 2019). The harassment came from patients and families (31.2 percent), attending surgeons (30.9 percent), other residents (15.4 percent), and nurses and other staff (11.7 percent). This also remains an issue for faculty women, 70 percent of whom experienced an environment of gender bias. Of this group 30 percent personally experienced harassment and 40 percent of that group experienced the most severe forms of harassment including unwanted sexual attention, threats, or coercion (Jagsi et al., 2016).

Sexual harassment in healthcare occurs across the professions, across types of healthcare workplaces, and from different sources. In a 2018 study of 900 nurses, 40 percent reported bullying or verbal harassment, of which "30 percent … came from other nurses, 25 percent from patients, 23 percent from physicians and 22 percent from administrators" (Cornwall, 2018). Twenty-one percent of nurses reported specific sexual harassment, most of which came from patients.

The National Academies' report identified factors that create an environment in which sexual harassment is more likely to occur (NASEM, 2018). As with all aspects of workplace culture, the example, attitude, and actions from leadership and explicit or implicit acceptance of behaviors are powerful forces. Conditions conducive to sexual harassment are:

■ A perceived tolerance of the behaviors
■ A male-dominated work environment
■ A hierarchical power structure
■ A geographically isolated work area
■ Leadership that does not take measures to deliver change and focuses only on symbolic or legal compliance

In my experience, it is not only male domination in leadership, but a predominance of males within components of the workplace and the macho nature of certain types of work that set up high-risk situations. Also, in my experience, geographically isolated workplaces, particularly those with 24/7 work and night shifts, and the distance of these sites from leadership, create high risk. As clinics and hospitals morph into giant healthcare systems with highly centralized administration and many layers of managers and Executives between the frontlines and central administration, physical and intellectual distance occurs, warning signals and actual problems may never come to the attention of the right people, and the risks of unchecked, bad behavior increases.

Denver Health's General Counsel believed that having many women in Executive roles was a factor that led Denver Health to "take sexual harassment complaints seriously, investigate them all and not shoot the messenger." Thus, as with many gender barriers, one of the most important tactics to eliminate sexual harassment is likely to be an increase in women in leadership roles.

The NASEM committee's understanding of these risk factors and the existing literature on sexual harassment engendered recommendations with numerous subcomponents (Table 3.1) (NASEM, 2018).

Each of these recommendations deserves institutional and personal attention. All leaders, including women, and all women healthcare professionals should know if and how their own institution is implementing and monitoring these recommendations. Several of these recommendations warrant discussion.

The first recommendation to create a diverse, inclusive, and respectful environment, goes beyond standard issues of hiring and promotion. The institution must embrace equality. It seems unlikely that a healthcare institution can genuinely embrace this value for women healthcare professionals without embracing it for minority healthcare professionals, for all the workforce including entry-level employees, and for all patients. Equality, by definition, is inclusive—it is not for the chosen few. If institutions place barriers to the care of the uninsured, the poor, minorities, or immigrants, it is hard to believe that they truly embrace equality.

The recommendation to improve transparency and accountability (Recommendation 4) should encompass not only having clearly defined policies and

Table 3.1 Recommendations from the National Academies of Sciences, Engineering, and Medicine for Institutions Regarding Elimination of Sexual Harassment

1. Create diverse, inclusive and respectful environments
2. Address gender harassment
3. Address culture and climate
4. Improve transparency and accountability
5. Diffuse the hierarchical and dependent relationship between trainees and faculty
6. Provide support for the targeted person
7. Strive for strong and diverse leadership
8. Measure progress
9. Incentivize change
10. Encourage involvement of professional societies and other organizations in efforts to eliminate sexual harassment
11. Initiate legislative actions that facilitate accountability and prevent retaliation
12. Address failures to meaningfully enforce Title VII prohibitions on sexual discrimination
13. Increase federal agency action and collaboration regarding research and accountability
14. Conduct necessary research in a range of relevant areas including incidence, consequences, and prevention
15. Make the entire academic community responsible for reducing and preventing sexual harassment

Source: National Academies of Sciences, Engineering, and Medicine. Sexual harassment of women: climate, culture, and consequences in academic sciences, engineering, and medicine. National Academies Press, 2018.

discipline, but also the demonstration that disciplinary action is taken without regard to the stature or earning capacity of the individual involved in sexual harassment. As the committee points out confidentiality agreements can place barriers to transparency. Efforts should be made to remove or diminish such agreements in cases of sexual harassment. We appear far from this goal. In a recent Modern Healthcare survey only "19 percent said their organization had a formalized process for reporting discrimination and harassment with consequences for offenders" (Castellucci, 2019). Moreover, 35 percent said no action was taken to "address incidents of gender discrimination or harassment they experienced or witnessed." This failure to see action may have contributed to 11 percent of respondents saying they did not report these events.

Thought Exercise

Does your organization have a formalized policy for reporting discrimination and harassment? If not, is there an organized effort to change this?

Transparency should extend to mandatory reporting of disciplinary action for sexual harassment not only to licensing Boards, but also to federal granting agencies (as recommended by the committee), to elite groups such as the National Academies themselves, editorial Boards, and professional societies. Reporting to elite groups does not occur now, but this would not only prevent honoring perpetrators of sexual harassment but would also limit their credibility if they provide negative recommendations, formal or informal, for their targets and other women trainees or colleagues. As we have seen in the #MeToo movement, loss of prestige and influence is a potent punishment for the offender.

As the committee pointed out (Recommendation 6), support for a woman who is the target of harassment is essential. Women believe that objecting to and reporting sexual harassment is a personal and professional liability (Dzau and Johnson, 2018). There are clearly examples to support this fear. Therefore, support needs to not only rectify the verified, harassing situation, but also must address specific consequences such as emotional trauma and barriers to obtaining positions for the harassed individual. The latter is not easily accomplished given the informal network that exists and that influences a range of opportunities. But if it is not focused on, it certainly won't be ameliorated.

The group of younger women I interviewed pointed out a critical role that women leaders can play in altering the culture which accepts sexual harassment, including sexist or crude remarks. When senior women are present in such a circumstance and let it go without comment or action, it sends a message to the perpetrator that this is tolerated, and to the other women that it should be ignored or tolerated. This perpetuates the culture. There is no formula for how to best deal with this. It depends on the circumstance, but there are a range of possible responses from at a minimum the senior women pointing out that the remark would have been better left unsaid, to asking for an apology, leaving the meeting, and reporting the incident. Certainly, the senior women should privately discuss it with the individual who displayed the behavior.

Male mentoring and sponsorship of women represents a particularly challenging issue (Recommendation 5). Mentors and sponsors can have a powerful influence on the professional development of the mentee, from grant funding, to promotion and recommendations for leadership positions both within and outside the institution. This reality makes it difficult for the mentee to report sexual harassment by the mentor and to deal with the potential career consequences of reporting. Institutions need to reflect on how to improve oversight of mentors while encouraging these roles—not an easy problem. Some institutions are developing group mentoring models, but how they will work is unknown. All institutions should develop specific mentor–mentee joint training to establish the rules of the road. Requiring reporting of verified sexual harassment to the array of prestigious organizations listed above could limit the impact of negative evaluation of the mentee by the mentor.

Burnout

Burnout is emerging as a major concern for our healthcare system. Its impact on the healthcare workforce is taking its toll on their well-being and their work. It appears to occur more frequently in women, perhaps in part as a result of the other barriers and challenges they face in the work environment. For these reasons, it deserves the attention of women leaders.

Burnout has been defined by the symptoms of emotional exhaustion, depersonalization or cynicism, and a sense of reduced personal accomplishment or professional efficacy. While we may think of it as a new issue, the first description may be in the Old Testament when Elijah had enough of being a prophet and laid down under a tree and was not going anywhere (Schaufeli, 2017). But since prophets were few and far between, this didn't get much attention. In modern times, it was described in the 1970s by Freudenberger who was working in a free clinic for drug addicts in New York City—almost as tough a job as being a prophet (Freudenberger, 1974). Schaufeli pointed out that "burnout did not develop in a historical vacuum … it is a multi-faceted socio-cultural phenomenon" (Schaufeli, 2017). In fact, Freudenberger concluded that burnout is "a demon, born of the society and times we live in and our ongoing struggle to invest our lives with meaning" (Freudenberger and Richelson, 1980). He also saw it as an outcome of the work environment. These observations of linkage between the lack of meaning of work and the environment to burnout have been underscored by the recent report from the National Academies and seem critical to understanding, preventing, and treating it (National Academies of Sciences, Engineering, and Medicine, 2019).

Since its modern-day description, there have been many articles relating to its occurrence, symptoms, and interventions. However, researchers have pointed out the ambiguity of the concept (Heinemann and Heinemann, 2017; Rotenstein et al., 2018). Rotenstein et al. have demonstrated that we lack clarity about what constitutes burnout, its true incidence, its root cause and appropriate intervention. In reviewing published literature, they found 142 unique definitions and prevalence of burnout from zero to 89.9 percent (Rotenstein et al., 2018). Clearly, burnout needs much better understanding than we now have if we are to prevent, diagnose, and treat it.

When physician burnout first became a subject of frequent discussions, I had some skepticism based on my 40-year experience at Denver Health. As I looked at our patients and even entry-level employees whose lives were filled with so many challenges, and compared that to our lives as physicians, nurses, and administrators, I was puzzled, as we seemed to have so many advantages. More importantly, I did not see the reported institutional markers of burnout at Denver Health (DeChant and Shannon, 2016):

■ Difficulty recruiting
■ High turnover

- Lack of engagement
- Angry complaints
- Demands for compensation for every task

We did not have high turnover in our staff. Everyone from the laundry workers, gardeners, and clerks, to nurses, doctors, and administrators stayed for decades. Often, they recruited family members. One respiratory therapist had eight relatives on staff, and one anesthesiologist's father and grandfather had worked here. Not only did employees make a long-term commitment, all employees, including physicians, were always engaged in initiatives. When Denver Health was in the process of becoming an independent authority, we needed to hire a marketing firm to help us bring the issue to the voters. As a governmental entity we could not use our own money. Many employees at all levels of the organization donated to help us with that.

When we operationalized *Lean* to examine and remove waste from our processes, over 300 mid-managers, and leaders including physicians, trained as skilled *Lean* practitioners (Black Belts) and over 2000 employees participated in week-long Rapid Improvement Events. No one received additional compensation for this. Not only did physicians not ask to be compensated for everything extra they did, they opposed a bonus plan. None of these behaviors fit the pattern of burnout: quite the opposite they showed engagement—maybe even joy. Given the importance of the meaning of the work, value alignment, work environment, and peer support, the Denver Health experience may provide some important insights into this issue (see below).

What has gained both clarity and urgency is the fact that physicians and other healthcare professionals report a high frequency of burnout. Something very negative and important is happening and we know it is not good for the healthcare workforce or for patients.

It is concerning that burnout begins early in training with between 45 and 60 percent of medical students and residents reporting burnout (National Academies of Sciences, Engineering, and Medicine, 2019). One recent survey of residents revealed that 45 percent "reported at least one symptom of burnout at least weekly" (Dyrbye et al., 2018). The relative risk for burnout was higher among female residents and among Urology, Neurology, Emergency Medicine, and General Surgery trainees relative to Internal Medicine residents. Of note, those individuals with a higher level of empathy in medical school had a lower risk of burnout. Perhaps, this is an important clue to addressing the issue. Creating an environment that nourishes and facilitates this inherent empathy may be one institutional approach. Women leaders' skill in building relationships may facilitate creating such an environment (Chapters 1 and 11).

A large 2019 study of surgical residents revealed concerning results. Over 42 percent of the 2935 female residents had symptoms of burnout at least weekly compared to 35.9 percent of the 4438 male residents (Hu et al., 2019). More alarming,

5.2 percent of the female residents and 3.9 percent of the male residents had suicidal thoughts. "The higher prevalence of burnout and suicidal thoughts among women may be explained largely by their more frequent exposure to mistreatment." The authors observed a wide variation of these issues among the surgical training programs which suggests there are environments and interventions that can lessen or eliminate such mistreatment and its consequences.

The 46 percent of physicians reporting burnout appears to be higher than a representative sample of the general population (Shanafelt et al., 2012). But, the incidence among the American population must be highly variable. How could it not be higher among those working two or three jobs and still struggling to pay the rent or put food on the table, or for those living in unsafe neighborhoods? The frequency of physician burnout differs across specialties (Shanafelt et al., 2012; Kane, 2019). In a recent survey, which had different percentages of specialties represented, 44 percent of physicians reported burnout. Those specialties with a percentage at or above 50 percent included Urology, Neurology, and Physical Medicine and Rehabilitation. Internal Medicine, Emergency Medicine, and Family Medicine were close seconds (Kane, 2019).

There is a long list of factors that have been linked to burnout (DeChant and Shannon, 2016). Some of these include electronic medical records, 20-minute visits, and loss of autonomy. When the focus of these initiatives or policies is not on the patient's well-being, but on increasing profit it could undermine the meaning of work. This interpretation would align with the concerns about the impact of the industrialization of healthcare (see below). In the end these approaches may have a greater cost than the revenue that is gained. Recent studies estimate that nationally physician burnout alone costs approximately $4.6 billion dollars a year (Han et al., 2019). That could fund a good many positive changes in the work environment and reduce the human toll on the workforce and patients.

"A growing body of research suggests that the changing landscape of the U.S. healthcare system—how care is provided, documented, and reimbursed—has had profound effects on clinical practice and consequently on the experiences of clinicians, learners, patients, and their families" (National Academies of Sciences, Engineering, and Medicine, 2019). "[T]he shift to the industrialization of healthcare delivery ... [and] the emotional distress experienced by many clinicians between avowed ethical principles and the values and incentives of the work environment further add to burnout" (Carayon et al., 2019; Chapter 4).

One survey study of primary care physicians underscored the relationship of the work environment to burnout. The physicians who reported burnout were statistically more likely to feel time pressure and to rate the work environment as chaotic (Rabatin et al., 2016). This study also found that 36 percent of female physicians vs. 19 percent of male physicians reported burnout (Rabatin et al., 2016).

Although definitive reasons for the reported higher frequency of burnout in women have not been elucidated, recurring, and reasonable hypotheses include that women are more likely to admit to a problem, and that they have greater family responsibilities. One factor said to contribute to burnout is lack of respect. Thus, a climate of sexual harassment and institutional bias could contribute to a higher rate of burnout for women physicians. Whatever the reason, its apparent higher occurrence in women is of concern not only for their own well-being, but also because burnout causes physicians to leave the profession—clearly, we don't want to lose this talent from our physician workforce or lose potential leaders we are trying to develop.

It is important to realize that burnout is not only a physician issue; it occurs among nurses, physician assistants, medical technologists and even administrators. A study of over 95,000 nurses revealed that those working in hospitals (34 percent) or nursing homes (37 percent) had a higher percentage of burnout than did nurses working in other settings (22 percent) (McHugh et al., 2011).

Similarly, burnout does not appear to be only a healthcare problem. It is common among professions that have a high level of interaction with others, particularly when those interactions can be fraught with difficulties. This includes such professions as teachers and police (Schaufeli, 2017). It appears to be a global issue, not just an American or European phenomenon.

There are few controlled studies or data on individualized approaches to ameliorating burnout among health professionals, and the National Academies' study could not endorse any specific approach (National Academies of Sciences, Engineering, and Medicine, 2019). However, the National Academies have endorsed six goals for eliminating burnout and enhancing professional well-being. One recommendation which clearly is important is to reduce the stigma and barriers for individuals to access support and services when needed. Institutions have implemented a range of approaches, the majority of them target treating burnout—addressing the problem after it has occurred. What we really want is a return of satisfaction, joy, and gratitude to healthcare. This is a laudable goal, but how do we get there? I think there may be three important pathways that emanate from existing data and the experience at Denver Health:

■ Empower the workforce to improve their work life by improving the way the work is done. *Lean* is a useful approach to achieving this goal because it respects the entire workforce and trusts their ability to identify and fix problems at a fast pace, taking the chaos out of the day-to-day work (Gabow and Goodman, 2015; DeChant and Shannon, 2016). This addresses not only worker empowerment but also team-based approaches.

■ Make the institution a meaningful community where everyone is important and valued. In this regard, one has to wonder how financially generous bonus plans for physicians and administrators undermine this value at many healthcare institutions. Denver Health had neither during my CEO tenure. Perhaps, having a female-dominated Executive leadership team helped create a sense of family and facilitated the culture that honored the meaning of work (Chapter 1).

■ Be truly committed as individuals and as an institution to noble goals. Most people go into healthcare to do good. One wonders how turning many of our healthcare institutions into business organizations focused on the bottom line has undermined this commitment and has left the workforce without a noble calling. Denver Health's long history of serving everyone, especially the most vulnerable, attracted a mission-driven workforce who were provided with a setting to focus on doing good. This truly embraces returning the meaning to work and aligning professional ethical principles and values with those of the organization (Chapter 4).

The experience at Denver Health has shown me that many find meaning in truly being there for those who need us. This may be the answer for what Freudenberger saw as our struggle to invest meaning in our lives.

Thought Exercise

Do these three descriptions characterize your institution? If not, do you think this would give your work more meaning and decrease burnout?

Imposter Syndrome

One obstacle to the advancement of women may be a lack of belief in our abilities. This in turn may have its roots in some of the other obstacles described above. Experiencing bias, discrimination, and sexual harassment can easily lead a person to question her worth and abilities. This failure to believe in ourselves has been dubbed the "imposter syndrome."

It was first described in 1978 in a study of 150 high-achieving women who, despite their professional successes, thought they were phonies or frauds (Clance and Imes, 1978). They believed their success was luck (which it probably is to some extent for all men and women) and that somehow those around them overestimated their talents. They feared that at any moment the truth of their inadequacy would be revealed. While this original data was obtained from women in academic positions, imposter syndrome appears to be widespread.

While there has been a focus on professional women, studies have shown it occurs in men and in a range of occupations (Sakulku and Alexander, 2011). Up to 70 percent of people have had at least one such experience (Sakulku and Alexander, 2011). This makes one wonder if one episode of anything deserves a label.

Time and success may solve the problem for many. It seems logical that those earlier in their career would be most at risk. Michelle Obama is an example of this. During high school and college years she often questioned if she was good enough, but by the time she was on the presidential campaign trail, she could answer that question with a clear, "Yes, I am" (Obama, 2018).

I probably experienced this issue only once. Of course, at that time it didn't have a name. I attended a small rural high school. When I went to college, even though it was a small, Catholic women's college, I felt I was in over my head. I called home, crying, and asked to transfer to a local college. My Dad's response was, "Don't worry your mother. You will be fine." That was that. Then, he advised me to speak to one of the nuns which I did. I told her that the other women seemed so much better prepared and could always answer the questions. Her response was, "Empty barrels make the most noise. Don't worry." I stayed, gained confidence and excelled. This points out the importance of good advisors and being able to share your concerns with another and receive reassurance. Perhaps, it also suggests learning to compete in women's college was a great way to appreciate one's value.

One of the women I interviewed, Evalina Burger, described a similar experience in medical school. She was not going to attend her medical school graduation because she was certain she had failed and would not graduate. A call from the Dean's office asking where she was, because the newspaper wanted to interview her for being the first women to "ace" surgery, pediatrics and psychiatry, got her to graduation. Now she is one of only two Chairs of Orthopedic Surgery—time and success seems to have cured her!

Two of the 12 senior women I interviewed, Karen DeSalvo and Carrie Byington, reported having experienced the imposter syndrome over a number of years despite their distinguished careers. In fact, Karen DeSalvo said, "I still have it. I have had it all my life. There are some jobs I might want that I think I may not have enough qualifications for. Then I see people in those jobs who don't have as many qualifications as I have. Women think they are not good enough. It's a voice in my head. I have to tell it to shut up." Interestingly, Carrie Byington said, "In some ways it did help me because I was always driven to accomplish more ... There were times that it made my life harder than it needed to be but ... I don't think I would be where I am today if I had not worked on overdrive to manage the imposter syndrome." No one wants to make women's life even harder than it is and Dr. Byington believes we do have to help others avoid this experience. However, it is worth noting my grandfather's reflection on issues like this: "Not everything bad happens to harm you."

Even though the imposter syndrome can occur in senior women, the women on the Denver Health C-suite team stated they did not experience it. They felt that they were competent and had earned their position. Perhaps, having many women in the C-suite contributed to that affirmation and sense of self-assurance and security. It may suggest that as more women are in these positions the occurrence of the syndrome will decrease among women.

If you really do think you are an imposter, what do you do? Many of the suggested approaches are about affirming yourself, such as writing a list of your positive attributes and accomplishments. One of the best solutions I have heard came from a talented young minority physician who felt like an imposter when meeting with leaders. She described a meeting with one of the institution's physician leaders who was interested in her work. In the meeting she could not make eye-contact, and only answered his questions with a yes or no. After the meeting she realized that she would never accomplish her goals without a voice. She called him back that day and asked for a redo. She now has found her voice, speaks, and leads. Her passion for her work was a cure for imposter syndrome. Maybe this could work for others.

Drs. Mullangi and Jagsi have suggested that rather than considering the imposter syndrome an issue for the individual to manage, we should be considering the response to its apparent widespread occurrence at an institutional level in the same ways we are approaching burnout (Mullangi and Jagsi, 2019). They suggest, "imposter syndrome is but a symptom: inequity is the disease. Promoting equitable representation of women and minorities among the leaders of medicine through concerted systems-level intervention is the most appropriate treatment."

It is worth asking the question if feeling intimidated, being afraid, or anxious occasionally or rarely is the same as thinking you are an imposter. Maybe, but I think not. I remember looking around the room my first day in medical school and realizing the class was overwhelmingly male (that was interesting—actually exciting—after a women's college!) and many were from top Ivy League schools. Intimidating, but I did not feel I should not be there. The first time I gave a talk at a national professional meeting, I was sure I would vomit the minute I opened my mouth to speak—I had even prepared what I would say when it happened (which it didn't)! I never had that experience again. Getting over hurdles helps, even if they are low ones like not vomiting at the podium. I have trained enough people to know men are just as afraid in the same circumstance—they just sweat!

Concluding that you are not the smartest person in the room may also not be the same as thinking you are an imposter, neither may be wondering how you got into some position. At the Robert Wood Johnson Foundation Board's new Trustee orientation, as I was seated next to Senator Bill Frist, former Senate Majority Leader, and Peter Orzag, former Director of the Congressional Budget Office, I certainly wondered why I was there (I was CEO of Denver Health). But I believed there was some reason and four years later I haven't been asked to leave. Staying the course and contributing what you can could be a workable plan for others.

Thought Exercise

Do you think that you have the imposter syndrome? If you do, how are you addressing it?

Responses to Obstacles

The first step to finding a solution to any problem is identifying it and bringing it to the table—step 2 in Governor Lamm's problem-solving algorithm. We have ample evidence that women face biases, sexual harassment, burnout, and the imposter syndrome. These problems are now being discussed in many forums—a step in the right direction. Many of the proposed actions in each of these areas are discussed above. However, tackling each separately while important, may overlook that these are likely linked. As noted at the beginning of the chapter they are the result of broader cultural issues at an institutional and societal level. Women leaders and aspiring leaders should consider this reality as we move forward.

At an institutional level we should expect all healthcare institutions to detail the specific actions they are taking to address each obstacle and their intersections. The outcome of these actions must be monitored and reported transparently.

Women leaders must be part of the solution by:

■ Identifying and bringing forward the issues in their institutions
■ Serving on committees and workgroups that are addressing these issues
■ Serving as role models for behaviors and being mentors
■ Reaching out to our male colleagues for their acknowledgment of the obstacles, and their active participation in solutions, and in creating opportunities

We must all be part of the effort because the goal is to have both women and men at the tables of healthcare leadership.

Opportunities

Given the length of discussion of obstacles, one might wonder if they overwhelm the opportunities that exist for women—not so. As we saw, in Chapter 2, many doors are now open for women and some of those doors are open very wide. Within healthcare there is still a glass ceiling, but the ceiling is much higher than it was a decade ago and there are stairways to the top, even if some of them seem hidden or hazardous. Moreover, the identification and open airing of many of the obstacles in themselves create opportunities for cultural change. When Lorraine Hariton, a former Silicon Valley CEO, took the helm of Catalyst in the summer of 2018, she noted that the #MeToo era was a fantastic time to foster gender equality (Olson, 2018).

Changing the Culture

Elections can be a poll of what society embraces. For us it can reflect the ambient culture's view of women's equality. The 2018 local, state, and national elections underscore the opportunities for women and growing equality. A record number of women ran for local, state, and federal offices and many were elected. Twenty-three of the 100 largest cities had a woman mayor in 2018. As a result of the 2018 election 27.6 percent of elected state officers were women; nine women were elected governors; and 28.6 percent of the state legislators were women (Women and Politics, 2019). Nevada is the first state in which women hold a legislative majority and Colorado's House chamber has a majority of women. At the federal level, Congress has a record number of women including the first woman physician and two women nurses. There are now 127 women in Congress—23.7 percent compared to 12.1 percent in 1999. The fact that 102 of these 127 Congressional women are Democrats may suggest that we still have a way to go in achieving a ubiquitous culture of gender equality (Center for American Women and Politics, 2019).

The impact on healthcare and the societal opportunities of having more women in political positions in federal, state, and local government are enormous. At the federal level this is underscored by Congress being responsible for the creation of Medicare, Medicaid, the Children's Health Plan, and the ACA as well as the annual budgets of HHS, NIH, and the CDC. Much of Medicaid policy is created at the state level, and currently states are on the frontline of battles related to reproductive rights. The federal government regulates and operationalizes many other issues that affect gender equity and equality such as equal rights, equal pay, fair housing, paid family leave, all-day kindergarten, and minimum wage. The states are in the front of the parade on a range of these issues as well.

In this country the business community has a substantial impact on both culture and policy. As discussed in Chapter 1, there is an emerging understanding that having women in leadership roles improves a company's financial performance. Other data from a broad range of industries shows that more diverse teams produce better outcomes. When teams are gender and racially diverse, they are more likely to pursue a range of approaches to a problem. This message has been heard by some large and influential companies. In 2016 the Bloomberg Financial Services Gender-Equality Index (BFGEI) was launched. In 2018 this effort was extended to non-financial industries with the Bloomberg Gender-Equality Index (GEI). In starting the group, the Bloomberg team noted that

> Gender inequality is one of the most critical challenges facing both the public and private sectors globally. In today's environment, it's never been more critical for a company to be able to demonstrate how it is advancing women, the value of its products, and its impact on society.

(Bloomberg Gender-Equality Index, 2019)

The GEI measures and reports gender equity through the lens of overall statistics, policies, products, and community support. Over 100 companies across the globe were in the inaugural group. Initially, only one American healthcare company, DaVita, a Fortune 500 company whose primary business is dialysis, was in the group. There are now 230 companies worldwide, with 7 million women employees in the group using and reporting the index. Several American healthcare companies such as Aetna and CVS Health have joined the group, but no major healthcare systems have.

The value of formalized measures, transparent reporting, and sharing best practices is demonstrated in the outcomes of the members regarding the percentage of women in a range of positions:

- 42 percent of the workforce
- 43 percent of new hires

- 43 percent of promotions
- 26 percent of senior leadership
- 19 percent of Executive officers
- 26 percent of Board members (Bloomberg Gender-Equality, 2019)

These do not reflect equality, but certainly a commitment to achieving it.

Many of these companies have policies and activities aimed to concretely advance women, such as:

- Paid family leave
- Evaluation of advertisements for gender bias
- Outreach to women returning to the workforce
- Offering mentoring, sponsorship, and coaching

GEI is an excellent example of how to achieve transparency, deliver results, and create opportunities for women. The entire American healthcare industry should embrace similar goals and transparent reporting of their metrics.

Improving Care

The most important opportunities women leaders have in healthcare are to improve the delivery of care, the health outcomes for the country, and the culture of healthcare organizations. There is an emerging body of literature that suggests a positive effect of women physicians on patient care. Women physicians appear more likely to follow evidence-based medicine guidelines and provide preventive care to patients (Lurie et al., 1993; Henderson and Weisman, 2001; Schmittdiel et al., 2009; Dahrouge et al.,2016).

Women physicians' unique contributions may go beyond this. A Canadian study of over 100,000 patients undergoing 1 of 25 surgical procedures compared outcomes of male and female surgeons (Wallis et al., 2017). Patient and surgeon characteristics were matched for a number of relevant variables. Patients of female surgeons had a small but significant decrease in 30-day mortality. One recent study of a random sample of 1,583,028 hospitalizations for Medicare patients concluded that patients who were cared for by women physicians had lower 30-day mortality and lower 30-day readmission rates for all medical conditions than the patients cared for by male physicians (Tsugawa et al., 2017). The authors speculated that this may reflect different practice approaches between the genders. Both the observations and the interpretation are important, but as others pointed out, both raise questions, including patient attribution within a complex healthcare institution (Maslove, 2017). Another recent study pushed the issue a step further by examining the effect of gender concordance in survival rates for patients with myocardial infarction. That study found higher mortality among female patients treated by male physicians than for female patients treated by female physicians (Greenwood et al., 2018).

There have been some data that suggest there is more patient-centered communication and care by female physicians than by male physicians (Roter et al., 2002; Bertakis and Azari, 2012). A large meta-analysis showed some evidence of greater patient engagement and a small increase in time with the patients by women physicians (Jefferson et al., 2013). Dr. Albert, Denver Health's Director of Medicine, observed a similar difference between female and male hospitalists (Chapter 1). Data on the higher satisfaction of patients with advanced practice nurses, including midwives, the majority of whom are women, than with physicians adds some supports to this (Horrocks et al., 2002; Harvey et al., 2002). However, these studies were not controlled for provider gender.

These studies on care and outcome have important implications for patients and the healthcare systems' primary responsibility for patient care. More study is required to understand how care and outcome are affected by the gender of the provider and by gender concordance. This issue should be examined for other healthcare providers, particularly in nursing given the changing gender ratios in that discipline and also for leadership roles.

We don't know if these differences at the bedside translate to differences in the C-suite. But it is a critical question to answer. It would be logical that these behaviors and perspectives would remain with women as they advance to leadership positions. Certainly, many women healthcare leaders believe that it does (Chapters 1 and 11).

As women leaders, we should encourage studies to elucidate what value and impact women leaders bring to the healthcare system. While healthcare expenditures, profitability, and salaries have increased, the overall health outcomes for Americans have not improved. We do not know if this relates to a focus of male leaders on the business and competitive aspects of healthcare. The reasons given by current and aspiring women leaders to pursue leadership focus on improving the system and lives of patients and suggest a different perspective (Chapters 1 and 11). Just as demonstrating the financial benefit of having women leaders in business has created opportunities there, demonstrating that women leaders improve healthcare and health will create new healthcare opportunities. It is time to test the hypothesis that women leaders within healthcare and government can bring a different perspective to our healthcare system and obtain a better outcome for all Americans.

Chapter 4

First Things First

There are two first steps in a leadership journey:

- A thoughtful reflection on values
- Developing a vision of leadership

Values

Values are the foundation of leadership. Yet writing about them is tricky terrain. Does it imply that I grasped their essences and faultlessly exemplified them in my own life? Since I am neither a philosopher nor a saint, this is certainly not the intent. Would it imply that others who wish to be leaders should faultlessly demonstrate them? Too tall an order for anyone. Perhaps, these difficulties are why courses in leadership seem to omit this subject from the curriculum. On the other hand, ignoring a detailed discussion of values paints over their criticality for both leaders and our health system. This seems unacceptable, so I will boldly venture into the space.

At all levels of healthcare practice, our choices and behaviors are influenced by our values, the values of our organization, and by the values, ethical guidelines, and codes of conduct of our professions. Our values represent who we are, what we believe is important, how we live and conduct ourselves, and what forms our character. They have deep roots in our upbringing, education, friends, community, and often our religion.

The core values of the healthcare professions also have deep roots. For the medical profession, some of these go back to ancient physicians like Hippocrates and Maimonides. In modern times, many professional organizations have articulated both the values they espouse and the code of ethics and conduct they expect from their members. These core values and codes are shown in Table 4.1.

Table 4.1 Healthcare Core Values

Putting the patient's interest above our own
Integrity
Respect for all people
Empathy
Compassion
Altruism
Humility
Competence
Commitment to learning (See Chapter 9)
Advancement of knowledge (See Chapter 9)

Many professional codes include social justice and commitment to universal healthcare. All of these are admirable and important values, and most healthcare professionals would espouse them as their personal values as well.

The list of values is long, and we have seen them so often that it is easy to gloss over their meaning and relevance. Therefore, it is worth examining them and their related behaviors. It is important for an aspiring or even an established leader to define these values in her own terms and understand how they apply in leadership.

Thought Exercise

What are your definitions of these values (Table 4.1)? How do they play out in your leadership?

Putting the patient's interest above our own interests and those of the institutions we work for must be a prime value not only for clinicians, but also for every leader in all healthcare institutions. This is a challenging directive on a number of levels. Clinicians generally realize that understanding what a patient's interest is requires grasping her priorities and circumstances. Leaders need to obtain an understanding of this at a community and population level. Living this value in an era where market share, profits, and quarterly earnings are high priorities is challenging. But, if this value is abandoned, healthcare will have lost its essence.

Integrity is defined as the quality of being honest and having strong moral principles (Oxford American Dictionary). It is demonstrated when there is concordance between what we say and what we do (Diaz, 2012). What is frequently overlooked in discussions of integrity is that it must apply to all our actions. There is no such thing as intermittent or occasional integrity—it is either there or it is not. Does a person have integrity if he/she submits false items or exaggerates expenses on a reimbursement form? Lack of honesty in small things brings integrity into question. Oprah Winfrey hit the nail on the head when she noted, "Real integrity is doing the right thing, knowing that nobody's going to know whether you did or not" (Curtin, 2019). Dr. Barbara Stoll noted in her 2019 opinion piece that great leaders "have integrity and are respected and trusted by the groups they lead" (Stoll,

Integrity ⟶ Trust ⟶ Ability to lead and inspire

Figure 4.1 Integrity is the critical path to trust and inspiration.

2019). This link between integrity and trust is important to grasp. Without integrity, there will be no trust and without trust you cannot inspire or lead (Figure 4.1).

Respect is feeling and showing honor and esteem for others. Its Latin root's meaning, looking back, imparts some insight. Perhaps, we should think of respect as a kind of mirror that lets us look back at ourselves when we look at others. If we respect everyone, we will see the same worth in every person as we see in ourselves.

There is an interesting twist on respect. Demanding it is not the way to get it. I have known physicians and Ph.D.s (by the way all men) who expected to be addressed by their title—the "doctor" part was important to them. Certainly, there are individuals for whom and forums where it is appropriate to address someone with their title. But as a leader should you expect that every employee addresses you by your title? I don't think so. Many employees at all levels of the organization called me Patty. Far from being disrespectful, it underscored our sense of being one family. Titles shouldn't trump relationships. But titles can be a tricky issue for women. If their titles are being dropped but men's titles are not, then it is biased, disrespectful, and can represent microaggression (Lukela, 2019).

Empathy is the ability to understand and share the feelings of others. It is putting oneself in another person's place. As the saying goes, it is walking in their shoes, especially when those shoes are not a natural fit. Those of us who have cared for patients, often in very difficult times in their lives, understand how critical an element this is in providing care and caring. Empathy is easier to experience with a person sitting in front of you, but as leaders we must work to retain empathy when our "patients" are populations.

Altruism is unselfish regard for or devotion to the welfare of others. It fits hand in glove with the responsibility of putting the interests of the patients first. We must be vigilant to retain altruism especially as healthcare systems become less personal and more big business.

Humility is an interesting value because it is often defined by what it is not—pride or egotism. It seems to be frequently misunderstood, perhaps, more often by women than by men. Humility is not putting yourself down or being dismissive of your strengths or talents. As women, our zeal to appropriately acknowledge the contributions of others can lead us to dismiss our own accomplishments and not take credit when it is deserved. This may seem like humility, but it isn't. While the essence of humility seems hard to capture, three definitions seem to do it:

Humility is the balance "between too much and not enough ego" (Brown, 2012), a Goldilocks equation.
"Humility is the ability to be happy with who we are and the realization that we are still incomplete" (Brown, 2012).

"Humility is not thinking less of yourself; it is thinking of yourself less" (credited to C.S. Lewis).

Using power in the service of others is how humility is reflected in a leader's actions (Rockwell, 2012). This interlinks it with altruism and putting the patient's interest first.

It is tempting to think that values march in their own straight lines and never collide, but it is not that simple. When they do collide, you need to know your priorities. The values that most often hit against each other for me were empathy and equality. Equality came out on top. Leaders often are asked to make an exception from a rule for someone they know well, who is well-liked, or who is in a position of authority or important to the organization. A common example I faced was permitting someone who was ill or recovering from an illness and had no more paid time off to work from home. That would have been the compassionate and empathetic thing to do, but not the equitable thing to do—housekeepers couldn't work from home, clerks couldn't work from home, and ICU nurses couldn't work from home. I did not want to give more privileges to the most privileged. Each leader will experience her own value collisions and decide her priorities. Hopefully, that priority has a justification and is consistent.

Thought Exercise

How do you prioritize your values? What is your approach when your values collide?

Looking at the list of professional values, is it possible, in our current health system, to truly live the values of putting the interest of the patient above our own, respect every person, have empathy and altruism if that system excludes access to many people, places such a high value on profit, and works to maintain the status quo despite the system's shortcomings? This is a question that leaders, the healthcare professions, and society should ask.

Our values forge the qualities and behaviors that enable us to be not just successful leaders but great leaders. Four of these deserve specific mention:

- Courage
- Perseverance
- Wisdom
- Humor

When we look at memorable leaders, including the women healthcare pioneers (Chapter 2), and the contemporary women and men who inspire us, such as Malala Yousafzai, Mother Teresa, Mahatma Gandhi, Nelson Mandela, and Martin Luther King—it is their courage and persistence that shine forth. Their lives underscore the importance of courage and sustained effort. Courage enabled them to operationalize their integrity. It enabled them to push for what was right even at great personal cost, to stay the course, and gave them the ability to inspire others to follow. Most of us will not have to endure personal suffering to become great leaders, but we may be asked to muster our courage and be willing to lose our job if that is required to make the right decision. I advised those I mentored, "Only take a leadership position if you don't care if you keep it." Staying in the job should not trump doing what you know is right. A leader who values maintaining her position above doing what she knows is right may disappoint herself and others and will not contribute to forging a better healthcare system.

Perseverance cannot be underestimated. I am not a football fan (the Broncos are an exception, after all I live in Denver), but I understood the message of one of my mentors that the last five yards that are the hardest. If it is important, keep at it. Edison's famous quote captures this: "I have not failed. I've just found 10,000 ways that won't work." Clara Barton had to pester *two* presidents to form the American Red Cross (Chapter 2).

As CEO, I decided that Denver Health could not be successful as Denver General Hospital, embedded in the city's organizational structure. It needed to be an independent entity. Achieving that goal took over four years (Chapter 8). First, the mayor had to be convinced. Imagine the eagerness of a mayor to give up the second largest department of city government, one that had been in the city for almost 150 years. I never let an opportunity go by to plead my case. At one point the Mayor asked me, "Are you ever going to let go of this?" I said, "As soon as you say 'yes'" (Gabow, 2010). Once the mayor gave his approval, there were many other hurdles: the City Council, the state legislature, our employees, the business community, our constituency, and finally, a vote of the people. For years, there were never two people standing together in Denver who did not hear my elevator speech on the need for an independent authority for Denver Health. Ultimately it all came together, culminating in approval by 65 percent of the voters.

Wisdom goes beyond being intelligent or knowledgeable, to being able to discern what is right and true. Solomon was correct in believing that a leader needs this. While we often equate Solomon with wisdom, there is a long tradition of wisdom as a female persona: "what is wisdom and how *she* came to be I will proclaim … and bring to light the knowledge of *her*" (Wisdom 6:22, italics added). To the Greeks wisdom was Sophia and Athena was her goddess. It seems this is a value we women can claim.

Senator Alan Simpson said in his eulogy for President Bush, "Humor is a universal solvent against the abrasive elements of life." Humor can diffuse tense moments, particularly when you can laugh at yourself. There was a great deal of humor in our Executive staff meetings which kept us all from taking ourselves too seriously. I try to bring it into every group of which I am a part. I have never seen it fail to reset a tense conversation or facilitate a difficult discussion.

Leaders need to articulate their values, but in the end, we need to "walk the talk." Those you lead and those you interact with can see what is only talk. Those of us who have raised children have been taught this lesson.

As a leader, your personal values will be conflated with those of the institution. Unfortunately, there is no shortage of examples of an organization's reputation being sullied because of a leader's behavior. Risa Lavizzo-Mourey, CEO emeritus of the Robert Wood Johnson Foundation, pointed out how critical this is for a leader to remember (Chapter 11).

Living the Values

The long list of values is more easily stated than lived. They are guideposts that can help keep us on the right track. But as human beings, even with guideposts, we can veer off the course. The 2018 Price Waterhouse Cooper CEO Success study noted, "For the first time in the study's history, more CEOs were dismissed for ethical lapses than for financial performance or board struggles" (Karlsson et al., 2019).

Nitin Nohria, Dean of Harvard Business School, noted that most of us are not as virtuous as we think, a condition he describes as "moral overconfidence" (Nohria, 2015). While he primarily focused on well-known lapses of values in business, there are numerous examples of lapses in healthcare, from opioid marketing, EpiPen and insulin costs, Medicaid and Medicare fraud, and research misconduct. Nohria pointed out that financial incentives and time pressures are two factors that often push people into straying from their personal and/or professional values. Healthcare leaders' values are stressed by these same forces. The financial incentives in healthcare in the form of bonuses and conflicts of interest can stress our values.

Leaders and physicians must try to avoid organizational policies and practices that bring these factors into play. Bonus plans for clinicians that are based on productivity and billing can represent a value risk. While exceedingly common, these plans may lead physicians to overuse and misuse. Even P4P may not be worthwhile (Khullar et al). Bonus plans for administrators that are based on the organization's bottom line can undermine altruism, patient access, and commitment to community and society.

Another high-risk situation for physicians, researchers, nurses, and institutions relates to conflicts of interest which can lead to behaviors that do not put the patient's interest first and can violate other professional principles. As physicians, many of us thought that low-level financial perks like dinners from industry had little influence on our prescribing practices. But the opioid marketing and the epidemic illustrate that large and even small financial gains influence behavior (Macy, 2018). There are more than a few reports from watchdog groups, such as Pro Publica, of payments in the hundreds of thousands to millions of dollars to individual physicians and organizations from pharmaceutical companies and device manufacturers. These have been linked to behaviors that conflict with espoused personal and organizational values. Coupled with the desire to advance academically and reputationally, these have led to failure to report such conflicts to patients, at lectures, and in articles submitted to scientific journals.

In a survey 33 percent of early and mid-career NIH investigators said they had engaged in some unethical behavior in the previous three years. These behaviors included questionable relationships, plagiarism, data falsification, poor record-keeping, and the most common, "changing the design, methodology or results of a study in response to pressure from a funding source" (Martinson et al., 2005).

Physician ownership of healthcare entities such as surgi-centers, radiology services, and laboratories also raises questions of conflicts of interest. Until recently, nurses appeared to have not been subject to financial conflicts of interest. However, the use of nurse ambassadors by pharmaceutical companies has demonstrated that they also can be pulled into situations in which the patients' interest may be sacrificed, particularly in drug-prescribing (Grundy and Ladd, 2019).

Conflicts of interest can arise for CEOs and other leaders who are paid large amounts of money for serving on the Boards of outside companies, including healthcare vendors (Bannow, 2018). This type of conflict received public attention when a well-established investigator and Chief Medical Officer of a prestigious institution failed to report millions of dollars of such payments in his research publications (Ornstein and Thomas, 2018). These paid relationships are surprisingly common. A study of 442 publicly traded healthcare companies revealed that 41 percent of them had one or more academically affiliated Directors, often from prestigious institutions (Anderson et al., 2015). These Directors included CEOs, Presidents, Deans, Professors, and Trustees. The median individual compensation was $193,000—enough for them to think about it in decision-making. Institutions must have conflict of interest policies that address this circumstance. However, given that enforcing the rules is difficult when the leader is involved, it would be best if leaders avoid these real and potential conflicts of interest. My simple rule of thumb is, "If you can't justify what you are doing in one sentence to the average person, don't do it."

Thought Exercise

What are your challenges in living your values?

Aligning Values

When you are considering joining an organization, especially in a leadership role, it is critical to know if your values align with those of the institution. If they don't, you are likely to be both unhappy and unsuccessful. Conflicts between your values and those of the institution can contribute to burnout (Chapter 3). Kathleen Winsor-Games, an Executive coach, gave a number of other reasons for this alignment, including your reputation, well-being, satisfaction, and personal and professional growth (Winsor-Games, 2019). A commentary on academic medicine noted that "the desire to work in an organization with values synchronous with one's own are important for the success of *all* faculty … these issues are more important for women and have a greater impact on [her] likelihood of success" (italics added, Thibault, 2016).

Many academic faculty perceive a conflict between their values and those of their supervisor or institutional leader (Pololi, 2010). Sadly, this value conflict is often related to dishonesty and lack of integrity, frequently in research, and to lack of commitment to the stated organizational mission. This lack of value alignment, including institutional disregard of social mission and administrative tolerance for breaches of academic integrity, was felt more commonly by female leaders than by male leaders (Pololi, 2010). One reason women gave for not pursuing leadership roles was that they believed they would have to compromise their values and their integrity (Pololi, 2010). This high importance that women place on values and value concordance is actually a reason they should lead, not a reason to reject leadership.

Of course, the first step in knowing about alignment is to have clarity on your own values. But the question with the more elusive answer is, "What are the values of the institution?" It is not as simple as the tag line or mission statement. As the saying goes, "Actions speak louder than words." Once you know what is most important to you in how you live, think about what institutional behaviors reflect those values, and gather information relating to those behaviors. This is part of your homework in considering a leadership position. You can assess institutional values by examining:

■ The legal structure
■ Board composition
■ The institutional policies
■ Interviews

An entity's legal structure conveys priorities or obligations. For example, a for-profit entity has a primary fiduciary duty to stockholders. Similarly, an entity backed by venture capital has an obligation to create significant return on investment, often over a short period of time.

The institution's Board composition reflects its priorities. A Board without gender and racial diversity makes a statement, as does a Board composed solely of wealthy businessmen or women.

For hospitals and health systems, policies regarding hiring, salary structure, patient admission, conflict of interest, and their competitive vs. co-operative behaviors with other healthcare entities and the community, all shed light on the institutional values. Given the obstacles that women face regarding discrimination, bias, and sexual harassment, the policies, actions, and commitment to transparency for ameliorating these obstacles are relevant to women as they assess their value alignment with an organization.

Interviews are part of any hiring process and you should view them as a two-way street. They offer the institution insights into who you are and provide you with insights into the organization. The material provided, what is included and what is not, reflect priorities, as do the interviewers selected. Ask your interviewers about institutional values and the actions that reflect those values. Some applicants may be reluctant to do this, but it is a missed opportunity. The questions can be as straightforward as asking what the organization's key priorities are, and what are the key leadership values and qualities they seek. The deep-seated values, what really drives an organization, can be garnered from the frontline employees. Go to the cafeteria and talk to physicians, nurses, clerks, housekeeping staff, and assistants. If it is a hospital, go on rounds. If it is a teaching facility, talk to the trainees—they have no hesitancy sharing their perspective.

Thought Exercise

How would you assess an institution's values as part of a job interview process?

If you are looking at a position in a new geographic area, doing a search of the local paper, blogs, and other social meeting posts can reveal the organization's values. I have found cab drivers (not so much Uber and Lyft drivers) are an amazing source of the community's perspective.

On rare occasions people take on leadership roles with their own or other's expectations that they will change the values and culture, but this is a very tough, long-term endeavor even for the CEO. For other levels of leadership, differing values present even more challenges than for the CEO, since lower-level positions have less ability to change the culture. This is not a task for the faint-hearted or novice leader. My grandfather had a saying, "You can always tell a day by the morning," which he explained was about dating and marriage—don't think you will make the man into someone different after you marry him. Good advice for both marriage and leadership.

In my own career, Denver Health's values of serving everyone willingly and its commitment to equality and educating the next generation all aligned with my own. It was easy to see these values in action by the open-door admission and clinic policy, the amount of uninsured care, the clinic's sliding fee scale, the racial and ethnic distribution of the patients and the workforce, the pay structure, and the commitment to training programs for students and residents. Denver Health's pay policy and lack of a bonus plan or contracts for physicians and administrators served as a highly effective filter for those whose values did not align with the organization.

Value alignment is so important that as leaders we should use employee orientation as an opportunity to state clearly the organization's values. At new employee orientations I shared these core Denver Health values and said, "If the Denver Health values are your values, you will have a great career here, but if they are not your values you are probably sitting in the wrong chair" (Gabow, 2010). This may seem startling, but it made very clear that value alignment is foundational for success.

A Vision of Leadership

As you consider a leadership position, it is important to ask two questions:

- Why do I want to be a leader?
- Why do I want this specific position?

Many people launch on an established trajectory. You go to college, enter professional training, get an entry-level job, and try to move up the ladder. If you are an academic physician, you get on the Instructor, Assistant Professor, Associate Professor, and Professor march. You may look ahead to being Section-Head, Division Chief, Departmental Chair, CMO, and CEO. As a nurse you may seek specialization, a master's degree, or a Ph.D. You may look ahead to be a head nurse, nurse manager, director, CNO, or CEO. Administrators have much the same educational and responsibility advancement in their sights. At the other end of the spectrum, many other people get in a role and never consider any other one. When I was a junior faculty member, Dr. Kassirer (subsequently Editor of the NEJM) was a Visiting Professor. He asked me what I wanted to be doing in 7 to 10 years. My quick answer was, "Exactly what I am doing now." He expressed doubt about that. I loved what I was doing but loving your current role doesn't mean you wouldn't love another role with more responsibility. Why and how your healthcare career moves should be the result of a conscious decision, not an assumed trajectory or a failure to consider options.

Physicians have told me they wanted to "get into administration" to stop being on call, have fewer work demands, or reduce the pressure of their current job. I have also been told by physicians that they want to get out of the day-to-day hassles and deal with strategy. First, you should never pursue a job simply to run away from something else. The grass is rarely greener somewhere else. You should be running toward some desirable role. Moreover, leadership roles are very demanding. While strategy and innovation are critically important parts of leadership, much of the job is building relationships (read "meetings"), mentoring, making the trains run on time, holding people accountable, making many big and small decisions, and managing conflicts (Chapter 8). If these roles and activities don't appeal to you, leadership will not be fun.

Women seem to view the leadership role through a different lens than men. It is rare for a woman to say, "I want to be a leader" (Pololi, 2010). But men often have this motivation. Studies reveal that women's desire for leadership is to make meaningful improvements or advance ideas (Pololi, 2010; Korn Ferry Institute, 2017). This was validated in my interviews with established and aspiring women leaders (Chapters 1 and 11). The best reason to pursue leadership is to contribute to improving patient care, the institution or healthcare broadly—certainly there is no shortage of opportunities to make things better.

Sometimes our zeal to lead can make us jump at whatever comes along. Over the years one such reason I have heard more than a few times is, "If I don't take this, it may never come along again." Victoria Moran had an insightful response to that: "That old saying about opportunity knocking only once is as archaic as the flat earth theory and as patently untrue. Opportunity knocks all the time—and it rings your doorbell, calls you up, and sends you emails" (Moran, 2018).

The first time I was asked to put my hat in the ring for Director of Medicine, I was told by my mentor, "If you don't apply now, the position may not be open again for years." I didn't believe I was ready, and the same opportunity came my way again quite soon. Of course, this is not a guarantee. My belief that I was not ready may have reflected the thinking that appears to be common with women. We often undersell our abilities, skill set, and readiness. An often-quoted observation is if a certain role has ten job criteria, women tend to focus on the one they don't have, while men will focus on the five or six they do have (Sandberg, 2013). Carrie Byington's experience in academic medicine echoes this, believing that women wait excessively long to apply for leadership roles (Chapter 5).

As you examine your fit for a specific role, consider where the sweet spot is (Figure 4.2). You need to consider:

- What are the duties and roles of the position
- What you really like to do
- What you are good at doing
- What provides meaning
- Will you mesh with your colleagues, boss, and the organization

As Linda Burnes Bolton observed, "You need to know your What." What are you passionate about? If the position's central role revolves around what you like to do, what you are good at doing, and what you find meaningful not only to you, but

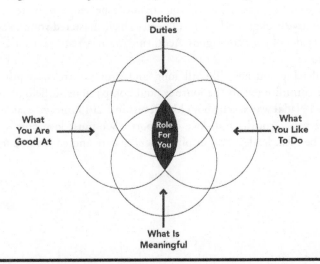

Figure 4.2   Identifying the ideal leadership fit.

also to the organization and society, you have found a position fit. This combination will give you satisfaction and maybe even joy. It is hard to say which one you should be willing to sacrifice if you can't have them all. I never really had to choose, but if I did, I would say if you are curious, smart, willing to learn, and have a track record of success, you can become good at the skills required.

Who you work with and for also matters. They don't have to be your best friends, but you should be comfortable interacting with them. Just as value alignment is important between you and the institution, there should also be value alignment between you and your boss and hopefully you and your peers. You need to assess this in the interview process and in your information gathering. If the institution conducts employee satisfaction assessments, ask to see them for the area in which you will be working. Look at the turnover in the position you are considering and in the work group. Of course, your boss can change and that can present a challenge.

Once, I took a leadership position knowing that I did not respect or trust the person to whom I would report. It was the most difficult professional decision I ever made. I made it because I felt I needed to take the position to defend the values of the organization. However, it was a very trying experience. You should only make such a decision after very careful consideration, being cognizant of the burden you will be taking on.

Thought Exercise

What do you really enjoy doing at work? How do you think those activities fit with leadership?

If you are coming from a clinical role, it is important to be a committed and capable clinician. If you are a physician, nurse, or other healthcare provider, it will be hard to lead other practitioners if you are not respected. If you are coming from an administrative background, you will need to have mastered your discipline to be an effective leader of your colleagues. Acquiring mastery requires time and preparation (Chapter 5).

The leadership journey, like all long and arduous treks, requires personal strengths, a commitment to the journey, and companions to help along the way. When Rafael Nadal was asked about his success in a 2019 interview at Wimbledon, his response was, "You have to love our sport." We must love our "sport" too if we want to be great leaders and inspire others to care and contribute to American healthcare.

Chapter 5

You Can't Parachute into Leadership

You cannot and should not parachute into leadership for two reasons. Parachuting depends on there being a place to land and leadership is not simply a piece of geography like the corner office. Nor is it just a title. Rather it is a way of seeing, thinking, acting, and contributing, wherever you are and whatever your title. Leadership emanates from what motivates us, what is important to us, what we will speak up for, and what will move us to act.

This view of leadership is wrapped in the concepts of leading from where you stand and in thought leadership, in contrast to positional leadership. Not every woman needs to become a positional leader to bring her perspective to the table, improve healthcare, or be an influencer. This is well exemplified by America's First Ladies. They were not elected leaders; they didn't even have a defined job, but many had great influence. Michelle Obama's focus on good nutrition and physical activity for children resulted in 45 million school children eating healthier breakfasts and lunches and 11 million students participating in an hour of physical activity every day—impressive impact for someone with no defined job (Obama, 2018).

Karen DeSalvo noted that government service taught her about different types of leadership. When she reported to a mayor, she enjoyed seeing him articulate ideas she had given him. "You can lead by generating good ideas that other people adopt and carry forward." I have said if you have a good idea keep talking about it until someone in power picks it up and runs with it. Women may be more willing to participate in this type of leadership that is not linked to getting credit (Chapter 11).

In leading from where you stand, you can become an influencer, a thought leader, and make important contributions. It can prepare you for and create the path toward positional leadership (Figure 5.1).

Figure 5.1 Leading from where you stand is the path to influence and change.

The second reason you can't parachute into leadership is that you should prepare for the role by maturing the characteristics and philosophy of leadership, and by acquiring the necessary knowledge and the skills to be not only a successful, but an outstanding leader. This maturation and learning develop as does all other maturation and learning: by observation, experience, formal training, and the guidance and support of others. This chapter discusses each of these reasons.

Leading from Where You Stand

Leading from where you stand is critically important on a leadership journey. This involves your being engaged in many ways (Table 5.1).

As simple as it seems, the first step in leading from where you stand is to show up. Showing up is not only about being present physically, but also about being emotionally and intellectually engaged. You need to care about what you are doing, think about what your work means to you and others, and act to make improvements now. You need to fix what is under your control. Don't kick problems "upstairs" or kick them down the road. Sometimes you should even step out and fix something that is not actually under your control. Given the dysfunction and waste in every nook and cranny of healthcare, there is no shortage of things in

Table 5.1 Leading from Where You Stand

Show up
Learn an approach to seeing problems and fixing them
Identify your passion
Become an expert
Be where the action is
Do your homework
Raise your hand

your work that need to be fixed. If you see a problem and have a solution, and the solution doesn't create a problem for someone else, go for it. You don't have to start with world peace—take on an easy win.

Lean offers everyone the tools to see and solve problems (Gabow and Goodman, 2015). In fact, if you want to lead from where you stand, learn about *Lean*. One of the easiest *Lean* tools creates structure and order, literally where you stand. It is called 5S, with the S's standing for Sort (getting rid of the junk); Set In Order (arranging materials for efficient workflow); Shine (getting out the bucket, mop, and cleaning cloths); Standardize, and Sustain, which are linked processes to keep everything in order once you have completed the first three steps (remember what happened after the last time you cleaned your garage) (Gabow and Goodman, 2015). You might think of it as the work-variant of *Tidying Up with Marie Kondo*. You can start with your office and your computer. If your office is in disarray, your computer is worse! After your office and computer pass the Marie Kondo inspection, you could put a team together and 5S the common space. The assistants in the C-suite at Denver Health 5S'ed the work area that contained the copier, paper, etc.—what a difference for them and for us to have an organized space. This may not seem like leadership, but it is the first step in learning a set of tools that teach you to see problems and execute solutions. Moreover, it fulfills an essential component of leadership—being a good example. If the entire organization were 5S'd, the work would flow more efficiently, and employees would be freed from some of the chaos.

Thought Exercise

Take a real look at your office. If Marie Kondo would gasp, begin 5S.

Here are four examples of leading from where you stand:

At Denver Health, a clerk organized all the doctors' paper forms on the unit in an orderly, visible way with labels, making it easier for everyone to find what they need (Gabow and Goodman, 2015). Who wants to spend precious time hunting and gathering? Soon other unit clerks followed. This clerk was leading (Figure 5.2).

The nurses on one hospital unit realized that critical information about the care was being communicated in nonstandard ways by pieces of paper taped to the patient's door. When communication is not standardized, critical items of patient care can be overlooked or misinterpreted. These nurses developed a color-coded flip chart and it spread to all the units (Gabow and Goodman, 2015). These frontline nurses were leaders (Figure 5.3).

A respiratory therapist who had *Lean* Black Belt training observed that inhalers designed for a month's supply of doses were routinely underused and wasted. Working with a pharmacist who was also a Black Belt, they designed a program for inhalers to be given to the units rather than to individual patients (unless the patient was in isolation or on a ventilator). This saved over $300,000 acquisition costs in one year (Gabow and Goodman, 2015). They were taking initiative and demonstrating leadership.

Figure 5.2 Organization of physician's forms by a clerk. (Source: P. Gabow and P. Goodman. *The Lean Prescription: Powerful Medicine for Our Ailing Healthcare System.* CRC Press. 2015.)

You can lead from where you stand in academic medicine as well. I was the only renal faculty member at Denver Health for a number of years. I had the opportunity to interact with every fourth-year student taking the renal elective. There was no organized curriculum throughout the university system for this elective. I created a set of lectures on key concepts and collected patient cases that elucidated each didactic lecture. I taught this every month to the students, residents, and fellows. This became one of the most popular rotations at the School of Medicine and resulted in a published book, *Fluid and Electrolytes: Clinical Problems and Their Solutions.* This was leading from where you stand and was a path to thought leadership.

Nancy Agee believes her positional leadership career began by leading from where she stood. She felt that "we were missing the boat, and not doing what we needed to do for the [oncology] patients. I wrote a paper about where I thought the gaps [were] and gave it to the administration with a suggestion to create a position [akin to a] clinical nurse specialist (not called that at the time). After a short time … I got a call saying … will you take the role. This was my initiation into a leadership role."

Major government policy changes can result when you lead from where you stand. Dr. Lillia Cervantes, a frontline physician at Denver Health, cared for a woman who was an undocumented immigrant with end-stage renal disease, requiring hemodialysis to sustain her life. However, ongoing maintenance hemodialysis

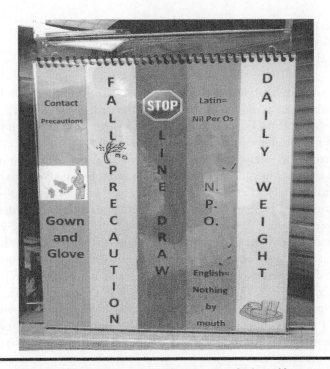

Figure 5.3 Flipchart for the door of a patient's room designed by nurses. (Source: P. Gabow and P. Goodman. *The Lean Prescription: Powerful Medicine for Our Ailing Healthcare System.* **CRC Press. 2015.)**

was not available to undocumented immigrants. As a result, this patient, and many like her, would come to the Denver Health Emergency Department every six to ten days when they were in a life-threatening condition and be admitted for emergency hemodialysis. The stress of this for the patient and her family led her to discontinue emergency hemodialysis and she died. This began Dr. Cervantes' campaign including learning research skills and publishing a paper which was instrumental in changing Colorado's Medicaid policy on end-stage renal disease enabling undocumented immigrants to receive maintenance hemodialysis—an impressive example of values and passion driving leading from where you stand (Cervantes et al., 2018).

Thought Exercise

What in your workday is frustrating or could be improved? Start a process to fix or improve it.

These examples underscore key aspects of leading from where you stand:

■ Learn approaches for critical observation and problem-solving.
■ Start fixing what is in front of you.

- Focus on things you care about.
- Don't wait for someone else to tell you what to do.
- Spread your solutions.

Not every problem that you see is one you can fix. This brings up another way to lead from where you stand: be willing to raise the issues you see but can't fix with those who should know the problems and can fix them. You can take it to the next step by sharing possible solutions you think might work.

The directive to "show up" goes beyond your own worksite. You need to be at relevant meetings in your organization, at local professional organizations, and even national ones. Not being at such meetings has two consequences—you don't know what is going on, and you can't contribute to decisions. As at the worksite, there is more to it than showing up—contribute. At organization and local meetings, you need to read and understand what will be discussed. Do your homework. Think about what you want to say. If you are hesitant about spontaneous remarks, write them down. You may even want to practice saying it. If you prepare in this way, you may find you're the most prepared person in the meeting. Then raise your hand and speak. Lilly Marks noted, "I might not be the smartest person in the room, but I was the most prepared [she probably was also the smartest!]. People started to notice this." Asking questions at national meetings may be intimidating at first, but the same rules apply.

Although women have been accused of talking too much, others have observed that women don't speak up. An unusual study of 155,000 corporate earning calls (an important event in the business world) found that men were speaking 92 percent of the time (Maranz and Greenfield, 2018). This may have been because there were many fewer women on the calls, but their percentage of speaking time was less than their percentage of people on the call. Moreover, a substantial part of their time was in the introductions! It may reflect women's hesitancy to speak at all and men's speaking too much. In fact, the study's author noted, "Male Executives provide significantly more verbose answers to analyst questions than their female counterparts." Apparently, this phenomenon of men speaking more than women occurs in other group settings including school Board meetings and other public forums (Karpowitz and Mendelberg, 2014).

I have not silenced my voice nor did the women on the Denver Health leadership team. I would say I always spoke up—perhaps too often—balancing the overall ledger!

Examining why I am willing to speak may be useful. I attended a small rural high school in Pennsylvania. My father taught my history classes. He had three rules for me:

- Do your homework.
- Sit in the front row.
- Be the first to raise your hand.

He could have written the guidelines for how women should engage! Since my father was an ex-Marine Lieutenant, I obeyed. We can't time travel back to our teens to learn to follow these rules, but we can encourage these behaviors in our female children, students, trainees, and colleagues.

A second lesson in speaking up came during my internship where, by the way, I was the only woman. It was advice about duty to patients from a mentor, Dr. Arnold Relman: "When you know you're right, don't give up." A patient with kidney stones was on my service. Being compulsive about "doing my homework," I examined her urine under the microscope and saw many distinctive cystine crystals—an unusual cause of kidney stones. I ordered a urine test for cystine which came back negative. This had to be wrong. I called the laboratory, escalating my concern to the physician director. He responded to me by saying, "How many cases of cystinuria have you seen?" My response was, "None, but I can tell a cystine crystal when I see one." He "invited" me to come to the laboratory to watch him do the test—it was positive! This changed the patient's diagnosis and treatment.

There is another lesson to be learned from this example—one positive outcome from speaking up gives you the courage to do it again. This was by no means the only time in my training or career that I followed Dr. Relman's advice. This advice is not just for physicians, nurses, and other clinicians who can and should speak for patients—administrators must do this too. If we all followed this directive, our healthcare system would improve, and patients would get better care.

There seem to be many times, in many different forums, when women do speak and are ignored, or when their comment is of value, it is credited to a man in the room (Sandberg, 2013). The group of aspiring women leaders I interviewed all have had these experiences, and not only once. Just as you have the power to solve the first problem of women not speaking up by raising your hand, you can help with these problems as well. Women can play a supporting role in meetings by underscoring the comments of other women. It can be as simple as pointing out that you agree with her point. You can use another woman's comment to add your own perspective by saying you are building on her comment. Don't be passive and let someone else take your colleague's credit—other women will return the favor. As there are more women at the leadership tables, it will be easier to have someone there to reinforce your comments. Kim Bimestefer gave such an example. "When [a woman] says something in a room and the group moves on, I interrupt the group ... and say I just heard Lisa make a very important comment. I think we need to spend a little time on it because ... it might be the difference between a successful strategy and a missed opportunity." We may eventually reach a point where such reinforcement is no longer needed.

None of us can engage on every issue in front of us. We need to focus on those that we really care about and for which we have a passion or an obligation.

■ Become an expert.
■ Go to where these issues are discussed.

- ■ Raise your hand.
- ■ Persist.

You will become a thought leader and perhaps a positional leader.

Another aspect of leading from where you are is to volunteer for committees and assignments. Denver Health's General Counsel, Darlene Ebert's advice was, "Accept every challenge. Stretch yourself. Make yourself valuable to the organization." Nancy Agee recommends taking advantage of leadership outside of work. "I got involved in a couple of voluntary organizations—the American Cancer Society and a local theater group. I ended up being on their Boards. The opportunities you have in those smaller organizations … can be very influential in your career building." These need focus, too. Go where you want to plant a flag.

This brings up the converse of volunteering and saying "Yes." When do you say "No"? How can you say no without limiting future opportunities or advancement? The group of aspiring women leaders I interviewed found this difficult terrain. As women, they felt they were often asked to do tasks that helped men in leadership but had little benefit to them. Some of these can be small tasks such as "Can you take notes in this meeting?" (When was the last time this question was directed to a man?) These can be irritating and may reflect microaggression, but they are not time-consuming. However, some requests are nontrivial like helping on a project that has little or no relationship to your own work. One woman described a clever approach which her mentor gave her. He told her to respond to such requests, "My mentor wants to discuss any additional activities with him, before I accept them." This wasn't a decoy. Her mentor did advise her on which activities she should accept and which she should decline.

Another young woman offered sage advice. "It is important to be clear about your values early in your career. That is hard because in the beginning your value is to succeed, and you say yes to everything … When you have a clear picture of your values and where you want to go, it is easier to be more resolute about saying no."

Sometimes we all need to be a team player and do tasks that don't benefit us. Like everything in life, we need balance—you can't always say yes, and you can't always say no. Where that line is depends on your own circumstances and judgment.

Thought Exercise

What are your guideposts for saying "Yes"? How do you say "No"?

The rules for serving on committees are the same as for attending meetings. Do your homework. Read the materials that are sent out. If no materials are sent out, or they are incomplete (not an infrequent occurrence) ask for what you need to be prepared. If you have questions about the material, contact the Chair in advance—it shows you are prepared, and it doesn't catch the Chair off guard at the meeting. You can and often should still ask the questions in the meeting. If you don't understand something, odds are that others don't either—they just may not know it yet.

The majority of assignments that you accept should be in your areas of focus and offer you learning or an opportunity. They could be a range of activities from speaking at a meeting to writing a book chapter. Often, they will come from your sponsor. It seems obvious, but if you take on an assignment deliver it on time, complete, and of high quality. Lilly Marks has an important insight about assignments. If you are on a committee or task force that is required to deliver a report, volunteer to write the first draft. This is how you take the lead in the future discussions and solutions—your ideas are the starting point. This is another technique for women to make certain their perspectives and ideas are neither ignored nor credited to a man.

By leading from where you stand you can make contributions, and you will gain leadership experience. It will give you an opportunity to see your strengths, areas where you have the potential to excel, and areas where your skills need shoring up. While many of us focus on the areas for shoring up, it is equally important, if not more so, to know your strengths, as most successful leaders lead from their strengths.

Using Clinical Training

As Nancy Agee pointed out, clinicians may feel intimidated when they consider leadership positions. The financial reports that those with administrative training read with ease can give them pause. They question if they have the right skills to assume a leadership role. However, clinicians should realize that many components of their training are very helpful in leadership (Gabow, 1999):

■ Commitment to patients
■ Ability to discern the critical information
■ Ability to be professional and clear-headed in a crisis
■ Willingness to consult others for advice
■ Comfort in making decisions with incomplete data
■ The structured approach to patient problem-solving

When we become leaders, we should not minimize these valuable skills from our clinical training. We should adapt and apply them to our new role.

Commitment to patients should be the Holy Grail for any healthcare leader. This is something of great value that clinicians can bring to healthcare. Many of the women with a clinical background who I interviewed embraced this as their reason for becoming leaders (Chapters 1 and 11).

As clinicians, we have experienced the need to separate the important details in the history, physical, and laboratory data from the irrelevant ones. Our years of training helped us see the difference efficiently and effectively. As a leader you will receive enormous amounts of information, some important and some not (Chapter

8). You can apply that same sorting skill now to non-clinical data. You don't want to waste your limited time on what is not helpful.

Every clinician has been called to many emergency situations. We have learned to stay calm, muster our powers of observation, quickly pull up the relevant knowledge in our minds, and act expeditiously. This is how you need to approach administrative emergencies such as opposing gang members brought to the Emergency Department after a shooting, a suspected diagnosis of Ebola in a hospitalized patient, a water main break in the basement, or the HIT system crash.

We learned early in our training that we had important gaps in our knowledge. Even as experienced clinicians, there have been patients whose illness puzzled us. We didn't hesitate to ask for a consultation, another set of eyes, a different perspective. Our core values of putting the patient first, and humility, let us admit we didn't always have the answers (Chapter 4). Remember to do the same for administrative problems. Use your team members as your first-line consultants. Pick up the phone or send an email to those who have become your peer group (Chapter 11).

Think of how many times you cared for a patient without all the data that you would have liked. This applies to leadership decisions. As with patients, the more complex the issue, the less likely you are to have every piece of helpful data. But you must move forward, decide on a path, and act (Chapter 8). As with patient care, if you get more data, you can modify your approach.

The structured approach we were trained to use in patient care is a helpful template for administrative decisions (Gabow, 1999):

- Gather the data.
- Make a diagnosis.
- Develop a treatment plan.
- Monitor the treatment plan.
- Be willing to change the diagnosis or the treatment.

You can follow the same steps in an administrative problem. There are examples of clinicians and leaders failing to make a diagnosis of the root cause of a problem, instead treating the symptoms—treating the headache and missing the brain tumor or expanding the number of operating rooms rather than addressing the poor flow in the operating room. Once a leader launches an approach to solve a problem or a new initiative, she should monitor the outcome. If it is not what she expected, she must either rethink the problem or change the approach to its solution.

As valuable as clinical training is for a leader, it is incomplete for the task of leadership. Both a perspective change and new skills are required (see below). Whether our clinical background is in medicine, nursing, or other disciplines, we have been trained to focus on the patient in front of us. As a leader, especially one with a large span of control, you must broaden your focus from one patient to groups of patients, the population for which you have responsibility, and the community (Chapters 7 and 8).

Formal Leadership Preparation

Leading from where you stand and your clinical skills teach you much about leadership, but it is not the only training you can obtain. Clearly, there are specific management and leadership skills and a variety of formal paths to learn them. I did not pursue formal leadership training. I did not find that a barrier. But times have changed. Training is more available than it was when I started my career, and healthcare has become more complex. A formal degree may not be necessary even in today's environment, but leadership training, seems worthwhile if you can accommodate the time and cost demands. The type of training to pursue depends upon your path to leadership. For those with a clinical background there are important skills areas that are not part of our training that need to be acquired:

- Finances
- Legal issues
- Personnel management
- System thinking
- Strategic planning
- Communication

If your path comes from the administrative side, you will need to understand the clinical side including:

- Responsibilities of direct care
- Obstacles that caregivers and patients face

Training for the Clinician

One approach to this "two path problem" is combined degrees. The number of offerings for combined MBA and M.D. degrees has increased from six in 1993 to 65 in 2018 (Johnson, 2018). The University of Pennsylvania was one of the first to offer this. Since its inception, 31 percent of the 175 individuals who received the combined degree were women (Joanne Levy, personal communication, 2018). A number of schools offer a master's degree in nursing combined with an MBA or a master's degree in healthcare administration.

While these combined programs have the benefit of convenience and a shorter time than pursuing separate degrees, the timing may not be ideal. Will those who pursue dual degrees obtain the experience and expertise in either discipline to jump into leadership immediately? Even more to the point, will anyone be offered a leadership position immediately after training? Will a person remember these skills when she finally does obtain a leadership role? Having data on the paths that dual degree graduates followed would be useful to students and advisers.

There has been a proliferation of business schools offering degrees in healthcare administration and healthcare-focused MBA's for clinicians interested in Executive positions. While formal degree training can provide some additional stature and currency in the job market, it requires a substantial financial and time commitment, and often includes traveling to another city. This may be more difficult for women, particularly those with a family.

Almost every professional society offers leadership training, and some organizations like the AMA, the AAMC, and Drexel's Executive Leadership in Academic Medicine (ELAM) offer specific leadership training for women. While this requires a time commitment and some travel, it appears more manageable than a formal degree program. These types of programs not only provide skill training, but they help develop a network of colleagues. Evalina Burger and Carrie Byington found the learning communities that were a core part of ELAM were one of the most helpful aspects of the training (Chapter 11). Leah Devlin has used members of her public health training groups for advice and insights for decades (Chapter 11).

Many academic medical centers offer leadership training for their faculty and some, including the University of Colorado, offer the training specifically for women. This training can be niche training, such as for grant applications, or broader leadership training. The course at the University of Colorado for faculty women designed by Dr. Judith Regenstein focuses on topics such as women's ways of leading, Executive presence for women leaders, resilience, and promotion criteria, as well as financial and management issues. The training provided at your institution, while still a time commitment, may be more manageable. It has the advantage of creating an internal network where you work and raising your visibility by offering you a chance to interact with the institutional leaders who are course teachers.

Some have suggested that women aren't equally represented in leadership because they do not wish to pursue those positions. However, the interest of women in these roles is reflected by the number of applicants for the University of Colorado training, which exceeds the 50 open slots every year.

The ELAM course, which is focused on women in academic medicine has characteristics that seem desirable for all courses (Morahan et al., 2010; Magrane and Morahan, 2016):

■ Nomination for the fellowship by the top leader (in this case the Dean)
■ Commitment by that leader to mentoring the woman
■ Interviews with senior leaders at the institution
■ Specific skills training
■ A learning community approach
■ An institution-based project chosen with the Dean
■ Continued engagement of the graduate with the group

These components raise the visibility of the participant at her institution and create an ongoing peer network.

ELAM has evaluated the benefit of this type of training for women on a career path of academic leadership. Compared to a matched control group, the ELAM participants were significantly more likely to hold a major leadership position (Morahan et al., 2010). Program participants (approximately 1000) hold Executive leadership positions at 259 academic healthcare organizations (ELAM, 2019):

- 206 Center Directors
- 220 Departmental Chairs
- 191 Associate/Senior/Vice Dean
- 22 Deans

Formal training differs substantially in content, approach, cost, and time commitment. If you are going to pursue additional training, you need to evaluate what you most need and want to acquire from the training. Unfortunately, there are no studies that point to the best path for clinicians on the leadership trajectory.

The issue of time commitment is of great relevance for women who are already balancing work and home responsibilities. Institutions that address this by providing time off to pursue training are not only facilitating the development of future women leaders, but they are also demonstrating a commitment to equity.

Thought Exercise

As a clinician, what skills do you think are important for you to acquire? What is the best way for you to acquire those skills?

Training for the Administrator

Given the availability of training in administrative skills for clinicians aspiring to healthcare leadership, it is surprising that there is no comparable training for individuals with MBAs or degrees in healthcare administration to gain an understanding of clinical skills and perspectives. Since the primary role of healthcare is caring for the needs of patients, this is disturbing. Is this a message about what we think is the core of healthcare—business, not care, not health?

Anyone entering healthcare leadership from the administrative side should gain an understanding of the clinical side. It is as critical, maybe more so, as it is for a clinician to understand the business side. In the absence of formal programs, a solution is to spend time with clinicians and patients. There are myriad ways to do this. Some suggestions are:

- Participate in shifts with a paramedic service.
- Spend some weekend nights in a safety net hospital Emergency Department.
- Shadow bedside nurses.
- Make hospital rounds with physicians.

- Spend time with physicians, nurse practitioners, or physician assistants seeing patients in the clinic.
- Attend a hospital ethics consultation meeting or a tumor conference.
- Attend a session with a social worker trying to help a patient get insurance coverage or a long-term care bed.
- Have a clinician mentor.

You will need to verify that your participation is compatible with HIPAA. Unfortunately, these experiences do not provide formal training, so you will need to abstract what you learn in these settings. One suggestion is to write down what you see, and what you learn in each experience that reflects the essence of the care and caring. Consider the dilemmas the clinicians and patients face. See what the barriers are to the delivery of patient-centered care, and what societal obligations are not being met. A clinician mentor can both help you interpret the experiences and provide guidance. Hopefully, some innovative institutions will formalize this training in the future.

Unlike formal administrative training for clinicians, these activities don't have a financial cost, but they do have a time cost. As with women clinicians, this can tax an already difficult schedule. Unfortunately, since there are no formal training programs, it is unlikely that there will be time off for these activities.

Thought Exercise

If you are on the administrative track, how are you going to pursue clinical preparation?

Not only have training opportunities proliferated, but so have leadership books (here is one!) and articles. The number of leadership books available on Amazon has reached almost 58,000; some of these are focused primarily on healthcare and some are pitched to a broad group of women, as was the best seller, *Lean In* (Sandberg, 2013). The number of articles dwarf the number of books.

The number of training programs on leadership and the mountain of books and articles suggest several things. Perhaps, there is a great deal of valuable knowledge about leadership and a burning desire of aspiring and current leaders to grasp that knowledge. On the other hand, perhaps there is a crisis in leadership in this country, and we are searching for answers. Probably, both are true to some extent.

Documenting Your Accomplishments

Leading from where you stand and acquiring necessary skills are both important for aspiring leaders, but if no one knows about them, you will not leverage your opportunities. Many aspiring leaders only begin to think about documenting what they have done when they have a mid-career evaluation or must submit a promotion

Table 5.2 Components of a Curriculum Vitae

Education
Licensure
Positions
Committees—organizational, regional and national; memberships and chairperson positions
Institutional projects and special assignments
Teaching and mentoring activities
Professional society memberships and activities such as program committees and leadership roles
Board appointments
Presentations—professional and community
Publications including Letters to the Editor and newspaper op-eds
Grants
Awards and honors
Languages spoken
Volunteer activities

packet (academic faculty) or when they are applying for a position. If you use the "wait until I need it" approach, you will overlook valuable items. Start developing your curriculum vitae (CV) the minute you start your training. There are many books, articles and websites on how to write a CV. They delineate the technical details. Look at the categories and maintain an ongoing CV file which includes all the categories that will eventually be important (Table 5.2)

Thought Exercise

Examine your CV. If it needs updating, now is the time to do it.

Applying for Leadership

Remember the joke about the person who is complaining to the higher power about not winning the lottery. A voice from the clouds says, "Buy a ticket." If you want a leadership position, buy a ticket.

Carrie Byington who has chaired and been on many search committees thinks women wait too long to apply for leadership roles. She gave an example of a national search for a leadership position that had about 90 applications, only three from women. These women were very senior and accomplished. "[They] could have been … [in the position] a decade ago." In contrast about half of the male applicants were Assistant Professors. She sees this hesitancy in buying a ticket as a fear of failure. To address this fear, she asks women to articulate what is the worst thing that could happen if you apply. If it is "being told no, then why not take the risk."

Use your networks, your sponsor, and the many available online sites to see what "tickets" are available. Review the steps in Chapter 4 regarding value alignment and fit and apply. Remember you don't have to check off every box listed as a desirable or even every "necessary" requirement. Sometimes a mentor or sponsor will give you a push—take that as an endorsement of your readiness.

Often advancement requires a move. This is both a cultural and actual challenge for women. There is a cultural norm that women will move for their spouse's job, but it is less of a societal norm for men to move for their wife's job. As the percentage of two-career families has increased, finding acceptable jobs for both spouses in a move is challenging. Some institutions have focused on this issue. While both male and female parents have concerns about disrupting their children's lives and schooling, this may be more of an issue for women.

Battlefield Promotions

While most people who aspire to positional leadership plan and consciously prepare for it with the experiences and training detailed above and "buy the ticket," this is not always the case. There are circumstances where you may suddenly be asked to assume a new leadership role. What should your response be? You should ask the questions which were delineated in Chapter 4, including whether the position is a fit for you. The good news is that in this circumstance you are usually moving up from one position of leadership into a new, higher one. You are not being pulled from the frontlines. You already know whether your values align with those of the institution. Most likely you were being prepared in your current role for a larger role—presumably you have taken some practice jumps. You have demonstrated leading from where you stand and are considered a thought leader. This is why you are being tapped. Still, this can be a challenge as there will quickly be new demands and required skills.

I had a "battlefield promotion" from Medical Director to co-CEO when the serving CEO was dismissed. Replacing a dismissed leader has the additional challenge of dealing with the circumstances and consequences that resulted in the dismissal. Usually in a "normal" unexpected promotion, you can rely on the leadership team that is in place to help with the transition. In the circumstance of a leader's removal, it is possible that others on the team will also be removed. This occurred in my situation. In this case, you need to rely heavily on your previous team members and others in the institution to help you achieve a successful transition. Don't hesitate to ask for help. It will benefit both you and the institution.

A variant of battlefield promotion deserves comment. That is being asked to serve in an acting capacity. Should you do that? You should go through the same thinking as for any battlefield promotion with a few additions. You need to realize that you may not get a permanent position. How will you feel about that and deal with it? If you can chalk this up to a worthwhile experience and a contribution to the institution, it is worth accepting. If you will be very disappointed and it will change how you feel about yourself, your leadership potential, and the institution, then it is not a good choice. However, you may be chosen for the permanent position. One determinant of whether that is the outcome depends upon how you interpret "acting." If you remember that this is a dynamic verb and you assume the responsibilities of a leader, address issues, and solve problems, you will increase the likelihood of being chosen. If you think of "acting" as a passive word and you become a place holder, it is likely that someone else will fill the place.

Role Models, Mentors, Sponsors, and Coaches

Few people can rise to leadership solely by their own devices. Most of us need others to help us see the road and walk the path. These individuals can be role models, mentors, sponsors, and coaches. These four roles have many similarities, but they are not generally seen as the same (Travis et al., 2013; Table 5.3).

A role model may not even know she is functioning in that capacity. You may not know her personally. You simply admire her and try to emulate her. The marvelous aspects of role models are that you can have as many as you want, they don't have to agree to serve that role, they don't have to be on the same continent, or even still be alive! I had many role models throughout my life beginning with family members and including Mayors, Presidents, and even Saints and patients whose courage and grace in the face of illness and difficult life circumstances were inspiring.

Table 5.3 Guides on the Leadership Journey

Characteristic	Role Model	Mentor	Sponsor	Coach
Provides inspiration	++	++	+	–
Senior leader	–	+	++	–
Builds on personal relationship	–	++	++	–
Provides career guidance	–	++	+	–
Provides feedback	–	++	+	++
Facilitates networking	–	+	++	–
Has "skin in the game"	–	+	++	–
Opens doors	–	+	++	–
Trained for role	–	+/–	–	++
Contractual relationship	–	–	–	++
Mature leadership skills	–	+	+	++

Mentors and sponsors are both important on your leadership journey. The difference between them is not a hard line. The same person can fill both roles at the same time or different roles at different points in their career and yours. What unites a mentor and a sponsor is a genuine interest in you as a person, facilitating your making contributions, and in advancing your career. One young woman leader noted that "A mentor can help you find your voice." Mentoring and sponsorship are personal. They require effort and commitment from both people in the relationship, and both people benefit.

Mentorship has been defined as a reciprocal relationship between an advanced career individual and a more junior person in which the mentor advises the mentee on their career (Mylona et al., 2016). In many institutions, this has become formalized. In that case, there is a structure for identifying the mentor, providing training for both the mentor and the mentee, and having clear expectations about engagement and outcome. A study of these formal programs for 12,779 faculty members at 26 medical schools demonstrated that only 30 percent of the clinical faculty had mentors, but half of those without one believed that having a mentor was important for their career (Mylona et al., 2016). This lack of available mentors is an existing gap in leadership development. Those individuals with a formal mentor had higher job and career satisfaction than those without a formal mentor. Having someone caring about our success makes a difference.

There is a variant of the classic mentor–mentee role which many established and aspiring women have found helpful. That is peer mentorship. Peer mentorship can be one-on-one or in a group. The groups can be independent or facilitated by a more senior person (Fleming et al., 2015). An example of one-on-one is when a new leader is linked with an experienced leader in a similar role at the organization. This person can help a newly promoted person learn the ropes. A group of peer mentors can come from a training cohort, as discussed above, or it can be specifically formed. Ellen Daniell's book, *Every Other Thursday*, provides helpful guidelines for establishing and maturing such a group, as well as the personal and professional benefits that women experience in that setting (Daniell, 2006).

Thought Exercise

Do you have a mentor or a peer mentoring group? If you have a mentor, have you developed a career plan? If you don't have a mentor, how do you plan to get one?

Interestingly, women and minority faculty were more likely to have a formal mentor than were men and majority member faculty (Mylona et al., 2016). But, as we saw in Chapter 2, they do not obtain leadership positions as often as men do. This suggests that while having a mentor is important, it may not be sufficient to facilitate women and minorities in achieving leadership roles.

This leads to the importance of sponsorship (Gottlieb and Travis, 2018). As with a mentor, a sponsor has a relationship with their sponsored person. In fact, a mentor can evolve into a sponsor. Sponsors do offer advice, but they do more—they advocate, and they open doors. Sometimes, given women's reluctance to believe in their readiness for a role, they might have to be pushed through the door. Sponsors can give that push. The doors can lead to a small stage—being on a panel at a national meeting, a big stage—CEO or anything in between. Sponsors have more "skin in the game" than mentors because their own reputation can either be enhanced or tarnished (great talent scout or a poor one) depending on whether the person for whom they opened the door trips and falls or shines.

Although some corporations have formalized sponsorship programs, this appears to be uncommon in healthcare (Gottlieb and Travis, 2018). A survey of 1066 individuals who had received NIH K08 or K23 awards examined the impact of sponsorship on academic success (Patton et al., 2017). Both men and women faculty members with sponsors had a higher occurrence of success than those without sponsors. However, men were more likely to have had sponsors than women. This may result from the predominance of men in leadership and their existing affinity and networking with other men that enabled the sponsorship to occur via informal pathways (Chapter 3).

Thought Exercise

Do you have a sponsor? If yes, have you suggested some opportunities you would like him to help you get? If you don't have a sponsor how do you plan to identify one? (I used "him" deliberately).

A woman's mentor and her sponsor can be a man or a woman. Some women may prefer a woman who has walked the path. However, since most individuals in influential leadership positions in the current environment are still men, it may be more feasible and/or helpful to have a male sponsor. Hopefully, this will change as more women attain major leadership roles.

Unfortunately, a potential consequence of male mentors and sponsors is now being pointed out in the power imbalance and sexual harassment that can occur. This has led some organizations to consider team mentoring (Chapter 3).

Executive coaches differ in important ways from both mentors and sponsors. Unlike mentors and sponsors, Executive coaches are usually professionally trained for their role: it is their primary job, and they are paid to perform the function. Mentors and sponsors can help you achieve a leadership role, Executive coaches come into play when you are in a leadership role. Executive coaches have a one-on-one relationship with you and use a variety of methods and approaches to improve your effectiveness as a leader. Generally, they will not tell you what to do, but they can help you think through what you should do in a situation and help you analyze what you did and the outcome. They can help you build your strengths and address areas for improvement. They have become popular among healthcare leaders. I did not use an Executive coach, but I have used them to facilitate the development of others. We both found that it was helpful to them.

It is important for women on a leadership journey to realize that mentors, sponsors, and coaches rarely appear at your office door. This is particularly true in the institutions that don't have formalized programs for these roles. So, you need to actively seek them out and/or ask for them. Although there may be some advantages in having them down the hall, they don't have to be in your institution. With video conferencing, they can be virtually down the hall.

My own career illustrates the importance of role models, mentors, and sponsors, although none of them had those formal titles. My first role model outside of my family was Sister Florence Marie Scott who headed the biology department at Seton Hill College (now Seton Hill University) (Gabow, 2012). She was unique in many ways, including being the first woman (and a nun to boot) on the Board of the Marine Biologic Laboratories at Woods Hole. She was a role model, mentor, and sponsor all in one—a woman to be taken seriously. Acting as a sponsor, during two summers of my college years she took me with her to Woods Hole as a student researcher. Watching her hitch up her habit (yes, they wore them then) and wade into the water with the men to collect specimens showed me in a dramatic way, that you didn't have to change who you are to be successful—even as a nun in a man's world. As a teacher at a Catholic school she began every class with a prayer, but hers was different from everyone else's: "Lord, help me to understand the truth, and when I grasp the truth fire me with the courage to use it ..." (Gabow, 2012). This indelibly put into my mind the link between truth and courage.

In medical school, the only woman faculty member I ever interacted with was Dr. Donna McCurdy. She was an amazing teacher in the renal division. It was my dream to emulate her teaching. She undoubtedly contributed a great deal to my becoming an academic nephrologist.

When I began my career at Denver Health, two male physicians served as both mentors and sponsors. Dr. Robert Schrier, an influential leader at the University of Colorado School of Medicine, guided my academic career, reviewing my talks and drafts of papers. The first paper I gave him came back with many comments on the first page, and an attached note, "You need to start over." I had never received that kind of message before. If you want a mentor, be prepared for some tough messages. He opened doors, inviting me to write book chapters and arranging for lectures. This facilitated my becoming an Associate Professor of Medicine in six years and a Professor of Medicine eight years later and being Principal Investigator on a large NIH Program Project grant.

Another leader, Dr. John Sbarbaro, at Denver Health, guided my administrative growth, teaching me the skills of administering discipline, not giving in to bullies, and interacting with political leaders. He gave me a memorable lesson on what to do when someone threatens to leave when they don't get something they want: Bring out a glass of water, have him put his finger in the water and pull it out, then ask "Where is the hole?" While I never used that approach, I took the message to heart—don't be bullied. This lesson came in handy in my early months as Medical Director. Previously, there had been no real evaluation of physicians in the city system. Every doctor received an "Outstanding" and the accompanying pay increase. I introduced guidelines for evaluation. A Director came into my office with a physician on his staff who had received his first "Meets Expectations" rating (both males). They sat on either side of me at my round table and began to raise their voices, informing me I couldn't do that. I stood up, went to the door, and asked them to come back when they were prepared for a civil conversation. (I am glad my EKG was not being displayed on a monitor!) In addition to his guidance, Dr. Sbarbaro supported my leadership positions at Denver Health, culminating in CEO.

Your commitment to lead from where you stand, to acquire leadership training and skills, and utilize the guidance and advocacy of others, will enable you to become a leader who can facilitate the development of a more equitable, effective, and efficient healthcare system.

Chapter 6

Now You Are a Leader

Leadership provides a twist to the old saw, "The good news is … the bad news is …." The good news is now you are a leader. There is no bad news! But leadership at every level can be scary and overwhelming to even know where to begin. As in everything, you need to begin with the basics—what may seem like small things can define your future.

Part of the challenge of being a new leader is that you are learning while you are expected to do the job. Therefore, a new leadership position requires a great deal of time and energy. Plan for this commitment when you apply for a leadership role. Sometimes you were specifically being groomed for the new position and/or have had a period of transition. This certainly is useful, but in the end, once you sit in the chair, the buck stops with you. You now view the landscape from another perspective, and you are viewed in a new way.

Undoubtedly, you have heard leaders say that people are the institution's most important resource. You need to not only say it but believe it and act on it right out of the shoot. Therefore, much of what you should do at the start and as you continue in a leadership role revolves around people. This chapter focuses on key aspects of people leadership:

- Introducing yourself
- Building your team
- Evaluating, mentoring, sponsoring, and supporting the workforce
- Accountability
- Communication

Introducing Yourself

It is an obvious truth that a first impression happens only once, and first impressions matter. When, how, and what you communicate out of the gate is important. Employees are anxious about a new leader and your first task is to let them see they don't need to worry.

- Send out a communication.
- Have face-to-face meetings.

On day one send out a communication or email introducing yourself to the relevant group of employees. But if that is all you do, it doesn't make you seem approachable. Those you lead need to see your face. If you are leading a relatively small group, it is easy. You likely spoke to all or most of them in the interview process, but you should still meet with the group now that you are appointed. Even in a very large, geographically dispersed organization, technology allows you to be "present."

There is no script for the introductory meeting but there are important components:

- Be authentic.
- Paint a picture of who you are and what is important to you.
- Convey genuine gratitude for being chosen.
- Commit to honoring the culture.
- Start inspiring.
- Don't lay out a 10-year plan.

You want people to walk out of the room glad that you have the role and not scratching their heads or yawning.

Thought Exercise

What was the best introduction from a leader you ever experienced? What made it the best?

Don't end your introduction with one meeting. If you have a large span of control, have employee meetings with various divisions, departments, and locations. This lets employees see the person behind the name, helps you see what is going on, and lets you know what people expect from you.

Be prepared for some surprises in those employee meetings. After I became CEO, I visited Denver Health's neighborhood health centers. In one question period I was asked, "Who did away with Dress Down Fridays"? I said it was me. I explained it didn't seem respectful to patients. I should have stopped there but added that perhaps it reflected my age. The young woman then asked how old I was. When I told her, she agreed that it was my age. And I was young then!

Leadership positions have a written job description, but all of them also have unwritten expectations from those to whom you report and those you lead. Often these are more critical to your success than the written description. You learn these expectations by meeting with your boss, colleagues, team members, and employees. These expectations are embedded in the past, and reflect organizational culture, as well as the style, performance, and perception of the previous leader. If you were promoted to the new position, you know the culture and previous leader's style. If you are new to the organization, hopefully you were diligent in assessing the culture and expectations, and now you are simply adding to that understanding.

Building Your Team

Establishing Relationships

The Kellogg Foundation had a saying, "Relationships are primary and everything else is derivative." In my experience this holds true. Building relationships is a strength that women bring to the table and it can be an important trait in making them not only successful leaders, but great leaders (Chapters 1 and 11).

Most of the time, you will start a new leadership role with some or all your team members in place. You may well have been a member of that team and now you are the leader. This can be tricky particularly if one of them was also vying for the position. However, you cannot continue to function as another team member; you have responsibility, the buck is stopping with you. On the other hand, you need to be sensitive to the situation. As women, we are good at managing situations such as these that require emotional intelligence.

Whether you were promoted or are new to the organization, schedule individual meetings with every member of your team promptly. Send out an agenda to each team member indicating what you would like to hear from her, and what you would like to share.

Information from her:

- What does she want you to know about her?
- What are her strengths, and the areas she is working to improve?
- What were her biggest successes and disappointments in the last year?
- What were the goals for the year from her last evaluation?
- Are there any issues you should know about immediately?
- What are the biggest issues her area is facing now?
- What would she most like to discuss?

Information from you:

- How often you want to meet
- How future agendas will be developed

- When you want a "heads up"
- How you do evaluations
- Some of your short-term goals

This is too long a list for one or even a few meetings, but it serves as a road map for the future.

While many leadership books espouse fewer and shorter meetings, time with your team creates a common vision. As CEO, I met twice a week with the entire C-suite team and once a week with the physician Directors of Service as a group. I met weekly with the individuals in the C-suite with the greatest breadth of responsibilities, and either every two weeks or once a month with my other direct reports.

Geography is important. Most of the Denver Health Executive team was on the same floor, providing for coffee pot and other informal conversations. Don't underestimate the value of these.

Recruiting

One of my mentors. Dr. Schrier, made two important observations about recruiting and hiring. First, every vacancy is an opportunity to add new talent, upping the game. Second, often you hire a person for what they bring to the position, but sometimes you should hire a person for what the position will bring to her. Some people will seize an opportunity and flower even if they are not quite ready. While this approach may have some risk, it is important especially in hiring women and minority candidates who may not have been given all the antecedent opportunities.

There are two sides of the coin for women leaders hiring female team members. There are women who are not eager, or even willing, to bring other women into leadership. This has been labeled the Queen Bee Syndrome—only one female in this hive! These women may evaluate female candidates more critically than they do male candidates. Having succeeded in climbing the ladder of success they seem disinclined to help other women up the ladder. On the other side of the coin, there are women who may be overzealous in hiring women in leadership. They can make gender a primary criterion. As women leaders we must be fair and without bias. We don't want to do what hindered us. However, part of being without bias is being open to women's potential even if they have not checked all the boxes. In this regard, Carrie Byington pointed out that women and minority candidates may have had different experiences that give them the capacities those boxes represent without having formally checked the box.

Several times I ignored red flags in women candidates that I would not have ignored in a male candidate. These women were not successful in their roles, benefiting neither them nor facilitating the pathway for other women in the future. Fortunately, overwhelmingly the women I hired were of the highest quality and very successful in their roles.

Thought Exercise

How would you describe your own approach to hiring other women?

If there are key vacancies on your team when you assume the leadership role, they need to be filled. Unfilled critical positions create areas of vulnerability. But, the timing of hiring for these positions can be tricky. Leaving critical positions empty too long can lead to unidentified or unsolved problems that will eventually be on your plate—likely uncooked and unappetizing. Filling a position too quickly before you know the lay of the land can lead to a poor fit. While a critical position is unfilled, there must be a competent person acting in that role. Even if a person is in an acting role, it is important to get to know her, listen carefully to their concerns, and assess them for the permanent position.

The values of your team members are important. They should align with those of the organization (Chapter 4). The four most important characteristics that I looked for in a candidate reflected those values:

■ Integrity—otherwise there could be no relationship
■ Commitment to learning—new challenges require new knowledge
■ Committed work ethic—they can't view the position as just a job, because no leadership role is 9–5, Monday through Friday
■ Belief in and commitment to the mission of the organization

Obviously, a person also needs the training and skills required for the position.

Thought Exercise

What are your top criteria for team members?

Every leader has gaps in her skill set and knowledge. Knowing what yours are can guide you in identifying which skill sets and knowledge must be strong in other team members. This not only helps you; it also helps the team meet its challenges. Surround yourself with the A-team. Don't be intimidated by the excellence of your team members. The better your team, the better your own performance will be, as well as that of the entire team. These values and skills are ones that other senior women leaders also consider in hiring their teams (Chapter 11).

If you come from a clinical background, you will likely need support in administrative areas. If you are leading a unit, section, division, or department your best friend will be your administrator and budget analyst. If you are the CEO, the CFO will become your new best friend. Likewise, if you come from an administrative background, the clinical leaders of the area are those whom you will need to rely on for that perspective and voice. If you are the CEO, your CMO and CNO will be critical in addressing the real focus of healthcare, the patient. Both clinicians and administrators will quickly learn to value the legal and human resources leaders and teams. Be open to learning from your team members who have something to teach you

One team member you should not overlook is your assistant. She will be one of your most trusted colleagues. She can make your professional life easier and more successful. Pick a person who shares your values and those of the organization and who has the skills you most need in that role. For example, if you have trouble saying "no" make sure she can and will do it for you. My assistant did that. When requests came in that were impossible to fulfill, she would say, "Don't say yes. I will just have to call them back and tell them you can't do it."

Recruiting always raises the question of internal vs. external candidates. Each has advantages and disadvantages. Healthcare organizations seem to have a bias for internal hiring. In one study, 63 percent of healthcare CEOs were promoted from within the organization (Stone et al., 2019). Internal hiring shows employees there is a pathway to leadership within the organization. However, if the individuals are being pulled from a group that lacks gender and racial diversity, this lack will be perpetuated. If there is a conscious effort to identify and groom women and minority candidates for leadership, this will help alleviate that problem. Internal candidates certainly will know the culture and the "ropes," but they may not bring new ideas and "new eyes" which is the advantage of external candidates. For organizations overall, "external hires are 61 percent more likely to be fired or laid off and 21 percent more likely to voluntarily resign than internal hires" (Beard and Weiss, 2017). Apparently, neither the organization nor the candidate had clarity about cultural and positional fit.

For all C-suite and physician leadership positions Denver Health did a national search. Many times, we chose the internal candidate, but the search process gave endorsement to the internal candidate and affirmed the choice to others.

When you are recruiting, reach out to the leaders you know, your colleagues and networks. But this is unlikely to cast a wide enough net. You should also reach out to specific professional and affinity groups that can provide a diverse group of candidates. Social networks facilitate casting a broad net.

Thought Exercise

How do you approach casting a wide net when you are recruiting?

Search firms are often used for leadership positions. There are pros and cons to this. Since it is their business, they have developed a network and a standard approach. They can find and interest a candidate in the job who you might not have identified or convinced to apply. However, these firms may not capture the culture of the organization. They are expensive, and they may have a bent to advance external candidates. When you do use a search firm, it is still important to talk to the references yourself and speak to their colleagues even if they are not listed references. The best way to assess an external candidate is to go to her organization, and see her in action. Unfortunately, this is rarely feasible.

In any recruiting effort we rely heavily on interviews (Chapter 3). Therefore, it is important to think carefully about who will interview a candidate. Don't forget to get input from your assistant. She provides a valuable perspective from her interactions. When I was on the intern selection committee for the Department of Medicine, I found it very helpful to hear the secretary's opinion of the candidate. Someone who is rude, demanding, and condescending to an assistant is not someone you want on the team. Some people focus on relating up the chain and think little of relating down the chain.

Given the unconscious biases that we all have, Carrie Byington points out the value of implicit-bias training for interviewers and search committees. This facilitates enabling committees to discuss bias, and it also helps to limit its impact on the process.

In many, if not most healthcare organizations, the final steps in a leadership recruitment come down to negotiating the salary and a package. Unfortunately, there are many problems with this process that have probably not served women or healthcare well (Chapter 3). The outcomes of these negotiations depend on the skill of the negotiator and the bias of the leader, and hence there will never be an even playing field across the organization. Women may be those left with the short straw. This variability undermines fairness, equality, and trust. Moreover, what gets negotiated often is what the candidate believes is in her (more often his) best interest, not necessarily what is in the best interest of the organization. Candidates tend to start with a "wish list," rather than a "need for success" list.

There are two different perspectives at the negotiating table—the candidate's and the organization's. There is different advice for each of these people, particularly for women. The senior women I interviewed, as well as others, pointed out that women often fail to negotiate for what is fair and equitable and what they need in salary and in the recruitment package (Chapter 11). Women, particularly married women, even in today's environment, have been told they should not worry about salary. Those with physician spouses have heard, "Why do you care about your salary? Your husband is a surgeon." I have never heard of a male physician asked this question when his wife was a physician or other highly paid professional. Halle Wright-Fisher points out that in an organization your salary reflects what the company thinks you are worth. Lilly Marks has observed that many women do not ask for the resources they need to do the job they have accepted. This makes the hill they need to climb steeper. Several aspiring female leaders felt that even when they asked for the needed resources, they had more difficulty getting them than their male colleagues. These consequences of negotiation have resulted in the gender gap in salaries and smaller recruitment packages for women (Chapter 2). These outcomes have led to the suggestion that aspiring women leaders acquire specific negotiating skills.

If you are the woman leader of the organization, your perspective must be what is best for the organization and for healthcare more broadly. It can be very tempting to give the chosen candidate what they are asking for so the search has a successful end. The ideal situation is a clear organizational process that narrows the boundaries of negotiation. Therefore, if you can, try to set some organizational parameters and guidelines that are transparent and limit the "loudest voice getting the most." At Denver Health we had a fixed salary structure and limited resources, so negotiations were nonexistent or minimal (Chapter 2).

Evaluating, Mentoring, Sponsoring, and Supporting

Chapter 5 details how important these activities are for you on your quest for leadership. You must "pay it forward." An important role for any leader is helping your colleagues and other employees to be successful.

Evaluating

Meaningful and regular evaluations are a key part of developing any individual. After I had been CEO for a year, I asked the Mayor's health liaison if I would have an evaluation. The response was, "You're here, aren't you?" While that may work for government cabinet positions, it is not the best overall approach for mentoring and development. Surprisingly, "30 percent of firms don't have clear and specific criteria set before performance reviews begin" (Nunes and Stevenson, 2019).

You can only evaluate an individual fairly and meaningfully if they have clarity about what is expected. This should be a joint effort. The individual should provide a self-evaluation. Input should be gathered from the individual's colleagues and direct reports. No input should be anonymous to you. That input from the individual's colleagues and subordinates should not be shared directly with the person evaluated and certainly not with others. Gathering this input gives you insight into both the evaluator and the person being evaluated. Is the evaluator taking that responsibility seriously and providing meaningful input? A fascinating observation from years of gathering input is that evaluators often project their own areas for improvement onto others. When an evaluator notes that the person is a poor communicator, more often than not, so are they—projection is a real phenomenon. As Carl Jung observed, "Everything that irritates us about others can lead us to an understanding of ourselves" (Jaffe, 1989).

A written evaluation should be discussed in person. As a leader, you need to provide both the positive input and be clear about the areas that have not been strong, are problematic, and need improvement. All of us (well, almost all of us) know we aren't perfect, but none of us relish having it pointed out. Therefore, constructive criticism should always, in fact, be constructive and given in a true spirit of helping. That does not mean sugarcoating the facts. Lack of clarity and innuendos are not useful.

Women seem more able to be direct without offending. Those of us with children have had practice with this type of feedback. While women may be better at giving feedback, studies suggest that they are less likely to get specific feedback than men.

> Men are offered a clearer picture of what they are doing well and more specific guidance of what is needed to get to the next level. Stereotypes about women's caregiving may cause reviewers to more frequently attribute women's accomplishments to teamwork rather than team leadership.
>
> **(Correll and Simard, 2016)**

This stereotyping may also relate to the fact that when specifics are actually given, it is most often in the area of communication and they are often negative. In reviews "76 percent of the references to being 'too aggressive' happened in women's reviews vs. 24 percent in men's" (Correll and Simard, 2016). No wonder women are concerned about this—they are reflecting reality (Chapters 1 and 11).

While formal evaluations can be yearly, you should never save either praise or significant concerns for that one time of year. There is one critical caveat to real-time praise and concern. Praise can always be given publicly, and it will be appreciated. Criticism should almost never be done in front of a group. A leader who "dresses down" an employee in front of others will lose the respect and loyalty not only of that employee but of all those who are present. The one exception in which criticism is acceptable if done professionally is when microaggression or sexual harassment occurs. In that circumstance, the leader should call it out. Letting it pass perpetuates this behavior (Chapter 3).

As a leader, you must also be evaluated at least yearly with the same process. However, since women often don't receive specific feedback, it is important that you do a self-evaluation and that the evaluation includes your accomplishments, clear goals for the upcoming year, and what help you may need to accomplish those goals. Self-evaluation offers each of us an opportunity for self-reflection. In that process, it is worth remembering that sometimes our greatest strengths are also our greatest weakness. This has been true for me.

As with those that report to you, this can be yearly, but your boss and especially your team should be encouraged to give you real-time feedback when they perceive a problem. You can be killed with kindness, and despite the kindness you will still be dead. Any leader surrounded by "yes-people" will not grow personally, will be an average or even a poor leader, and will limit what they can do for the organization.

Thought Exercise

How would you assess your process of evaluating your employees? How would you assess the process by which you are evaluated?

Mentoring, Sponsoring, and Supporting

The number of employees that you can directly mentor is obviously limited. However, unlike mentoring, you can serve as a role model for every employee and be a sponsor for multiple people—opening doors, recommending people to write book chapters, for grant teams, for Boards, and other opportunities. Recommending your best and up-and-coming stars for positions at other institutions is a bit of a dilemma. There is a natural tension between keeping your best and helping them achieve their goals. One factor that influenced me in choosing which side I was on was the position the person was considering. If it was a step up at an institution that aligned with the person's values, and we had no such opportunity, then sending our best to another institution to spread our culture seemed a worthy goal. It is more difficult to be positive about someone leaving, if they seem to be making a poor choice. But it is their choice.

Along with mentoring and sponsoring remember the other development tool of coaching. Providing coaches for those in leadership can help them develop their strengths and address areas of improvement (Chapter 5). This support shows the person you are committed to their leadership development.

While it is important to focus our mentoring, sponsorship, and coaching on those who report directly to us, as leaders, particularly those with a large span of control, we need to have a sense of responsibility for the broader workforce. This often is reflected in organizational policies and formal programs. Therefore, the timeline for this is substantially longer than evaluating, mentoring, and sponsoring.

Supporting the Workforce

One lens through which to view and direct your efforts for the support and development of the workforce is an understanding of the social determinants of health. Health and well-being are critical components of employees' engagement, creativity, and productivity. There is a large body of data regarding the influence of social determinants on health and well-being. Income, education, and housing are powerful drivers of well-being. Some healthcare organizations are investing in these areas for their patient population. As leaders we must invest in these for our own employees as well (Besser and Gabow, 2018).

Despite the limitations of healthcare in assuring health, we know that affordable, quality health coverage is important. In 2009, more than 13 million Americans, or one in eight workers, were currently employed in the healthcare sector, yet one-quarter of them were not offered employer-based health coverage (Bureau of Labor Statistics, 2009; Besser and Gabow, 2018). Now there are 18 million people in all aspects of healthcare. Nearly 6 million individuals work in hospitals, and almost 10 percent of them do not receive medical benefits. Overall, part-time workers are less likely to be offered coverage than are full-time workers (Bureau of Labor Statistics, 2018). Healthcare systems should be the least likely entities to have their workforce go without healthcare coverage.

As women we are concerned about gender pay equity. As women leaders we must also be concerned that our organization pays a living wage to all employees. In Colorado in 2017, many of the lower-paying healthcare jobs such as medical assistant, occupational and physical therapy assistants, and phlebotomists, had an average entry-level annual salary of $24,661 (Colorado Department of Labor, 2018; Besser and Gabow, 2018). This was below the living wage of $26,936 for a single adult in Denver, and far below the $58,260 living wage for a family of four (Colorado Department of Labor, 2018; Besser and Gabow, 2018). It is likely that similarly low salaries occur in entry-level non-healthcare specific jobs such as housekeepers, food service workers, and contract employees.

Many of our institutions offer tuition reimbursement for employees to pursue advanced training. This is appropriate. We should also consider how to facilitate educational opportunities for other employees, particularly for entry-level workers who are not fluent in English, and/or have not completed high school or earned a post-secondary degree. Although Denver Health had limited resources, an employee could apply for tuition reimbursement for GED courses, associate degrees, and other professional training such as EMT certification (Besser and Gabow, 2018).

Stable affordable housing is an important determinant of health. Housing assistance in the form of loan programs and housing allowances are incentives used to recruit and retain high-level Executives and physicians. There is evidence that housing stability positively affects workplace retention and job performance (Desmond, 2016). Therefore, health systems should explore how to facilitate homeownership for employees at the lower end of the income scale. At Denver Health we learned that many employees could afford monthly mortgage payments but had difficulty with down payments. Therefore, we permitted employees to borrow from their 401A for down payments on homes, paying it back with appropriate interest (Besser and Gabow, 2018).

Paid time off, parental leave, and childcare facilities on or offsite are valuable benefits, especially for women employees who often have primary childcare responsibility (Chapter 3).

Many of these policies occur at the institutional level. But even those who are not in the C-suite can advocate for them and institute them in their area. Dr. David Schwartz, Chair of the Department of Medicine at the University of Colorado, did that with parental leave. It was not available to employees, so he used departmental resources to provide two weeks of paid leave for all new parents, faculty and non-faculty. This in turn encouraged institutional change. One aspiring woman leader I interviewed was leading an effort for parental leave for fellows in her specialty. These are examples of a broad commitment to the healthcare workforce and leading from where you stand.

Thought Exercise

Given your current position are there ways you could support not just your direct team but the broader workforce?

Accountability: What Are the Rules and What Do They Mean?

As a leader of an area or an organization, you will be viewed as a rule-maker and enforcer. When Denver Health transitioned from a department of the city to an independent governmental entity, we had a unique opportunity to go from a rule-intensive governmental organization to something different. We had a large personnel committee composed of employees at all levels of the organization and outside experts. My initial thought was to have no rules, only guiding principles. Employees soundly rejected that. They had a strong belief that rules prevented arbitrary decisions. Rules may do this, but too many and too detailed rules also can lead to "hair-splitting" and an adversarial approach.

Once when I was standing in line at the pharmacy, I saw an employee bringing a large dog into the area. Since I didn't think the dog was there to pick up medication, I went into the pharmacy. There was the dog and his water bowl. When I asked what was happening, I was told the dog was sick and had to come to work with the employee. Imagine what an accrediting body's response would be. When minor discipline was pursued, I was informed that there was no city personnel rule against this! While we didn't get a guiding principle-based system, we did move the needle, decrease and simplify the rules and the disciplinary processes.

Most of us don't have an opportunity to construct our personnel system and its rules. We enter an organization with rules. However, as a leader you do have to answer the question, "Do these rules apply to everyone: frontline people, high profile physicians, Executives, and you?" Hopefully, you answer "Yes" to that question, both in principle and in action. You also need to work to change rules that create barriers to equity and equality.

In many states and organizations, physicians are governed by organized medical staff rules. This can require careful thought and guidance when pursuing disciplinary action or termination for employed physicians. However, what you should never do is excuse behavior in a physician that you would not excuse in another employee. The same can be said for an Executive. In fact, one could justifiably argue that physicians and Executives are called to a higher standard of behavior.

Changing Roles, Disciplinary Actions, and Terminations

The issues of changing roles, disciplinary actions, and terminations are stressful, especially for a new leader. But avoiding these obligations will have a negative impact on the culture, undermine your other efforts, and limit the success of the area you lead. Always be clear, both to yourself and to the employee, that any of these actions are driven by the person's performance and behaviors, not by some other issue you may have with them.

If you have a team already in place when you assume a leadership role, they may not be the people you would have chosen. However, you must give them a fair chance to perform. They may well exceed your expectations.

There will be the circumstances when a team member, even one you hired, is not performing as expected. Their performance can range from being mediocre to unsatisfactory. You have two choices in the first circumstance:

- An improvement plan
- A position change

You can jointly develop a performance improvement plan and a timeline for progress. This can include specific training or a coach. A mediocre performance may reflect that the person is in the wrong position for their talents. This can be because they were promoted into a position with a poor fit, or the person was overly eager for a position, taking one that was not a good fit. It could also be that over time their skills no longer mesh with the position's current requirements. A mediocre performer in one role could be a superstar in another. As Carrie Byington points out we are lucky to have a talented workforce who can do many things. When it seems likely they could succeed in another position and they are willing, make the change. I have done this, as have other women leaders, and it benefited both the individual and the organization.

The difficult question is what to do if mediocre performance continues? We know that human beings and their performance represent a bell-shaped curve. Clearly, everyone is not in the top 10 percent—unless you are in Lake Wobegon. Lilly Marks has pointed out the organizational risk of keeping mediocre performers in leadership roles. Their underperformance is "frequently multiplied by many of the people they hire who are also mediocre and under-managed. With time they can pull down the performance of an entire unit."

For unsatisfactory performance you have two choices:

- An improvement plan
- Termination

As above, the improvement plan can include training or coaching. If performance does not improve on the timeline outlined and performance issues remain, you need to move expeditiously to the second option. You can consider a different position if there is reason to believe that it is a viable solution but moving an unsatisfactory performer just to remove them from their current role is a bad solution. You should never move someone whose actions deserve termination simply to avoid confrontation, legal action, or negative publicity. You are simply delaying the pain and may, in fact, produce more negative consequences. It tells others that you lack the courage to do what must be done. This undermines credibility and trust.

Terminations are never something anyone wants to do, but not doing them when they should be done is a leadership failure. Keeping people who are not doing the job or have behaved badly is demoralizing to others and undermines the organization. Terminations should be done in the most respectful manner possible. Surprisingly, this can be done amicably. In fact, I have remained friends with employees who I had to let go. But life is not always so easy.

If you are terminating someone for malfeasance, patient harm, violation of professional standards, or criminal activity, the situation is rarely amicable. In these circumstances, every leader should rely on the advice of human resource professionals and legal counsel. What you should not do is hesitate because of the person's position, reputation, earning power, or downstream impact on the reputation of the organization. It is surprising what people will do—even people you thought you knew. My jaw has dropped more than a few times. This means that you cannot accept someone's word that an allegation against them is untrue because of their status or your opinion of them. We now understand this has been a recurrent issue in perpetuating sexual harassment of women.

In my experience, individuals who did not follow the rules or have acted inappropriately or wrongly in one area, often did so in other areas as well. Therefore, pursuing allegations or concerns requires a thorough, careful, and often broad investigation. All investigations should be done in a timely manner. Using an investigation to drag your feet or pass the buck to a committee is unacceptable unless your rules require a committee. There were a few times when I had to use private investigators. Once I even had to employ an undercover agent in a drug-related case to arrive at the truth. These are clearly unusual approaches, but sometimes the situation is unusual. Don't be squeamish and rule these approaches out if you need them.

This leads to another important point. Not only must you act on what you know, you are legally and ethically responsible for *what you should have known*. Think about the recent scandals involving the USA Gymnastic Association, and the USC Medical School Dean and obstetrician and the people who should have known.

Some terminations involve financial arrangements. Tread carefully here. On the one hand, some payment may be justified and may avoid lengthy legal procedures. On the other hand, large payments may be seen by others in and outside of the organization as accepting or even rewarding bad or inexcusable behavior. In 2018, Google's reported $90 million payout offer for an Executive accused of sexual harassment elicited unfavorable responses from employees and the public.

While personnel actions are generally protected information and may be accompanied by a confidentiality agreement, there are circumstances when the offense and the response become public. In that situation, if you are in the C-suite, hiding behind your public relations person does not help the organization either internally or externally. If there has been a performance failure, you need to say it, provide a meaningful apology and outline the corrective actions you have or will take. Don't beat around the bush—say what should be said. I once called a press conference around issues involving paramedics that had resulted in negative press coverage. It was not a high point of my year, but it settled the issue and ended the discussion of that issue in the press.

Given the country's opioid epidemic and the high occurrence of abuse among health professionals, the issue of substance abuse deserves specific comment. Your organization should have, and regulatory agencies do have, guidelines and/or rules about how issues in this area are to be handled. Drug diversion or actions that endanger or harm patients require termination. However, there are other circumstances that require disciplinary action but not termination. My philosophy in those circumstances is that people deserve a second chance. However, this second chance should be accompanied by a detailed, multi-year stipulation agreement that requires specific treatment and regular, random testing. Be clear on the action to be taken if the agreement is violated. This has often had a positive outcome. Any requirements for reporting to the government, police, licensing agents, or other bodies should be done promptly.

Communication

Communicating is a critical obligation of every leader. The first steps of leadership are detailed earlier in the chapter. We all know you have to "walk the talk," but you also have to "talk the walk." Your team needs clarity on your priorities, initiatives, and the processes to operationalize and evaluate them. Often leaders, particularly CEOs, think that their communication is primarily external. While that is important, communication, like charity, begins at home. Organizational communication serves four functions:

- Transmitting information
- Developing relationships
- Solving problems
- Inspiring

We communicate in words and actions; by what we say and what we don't say; by what we do and what we don't do; by where we go and where we don't go (Chapter 10).

Your communication should be frequent, regular, straightforward, and transmitted in a variety of ways. Many leaders choose to send out emails—daily, weekly, monthly, or quarterly. I doubt if there is anything important to say to everyone every day. Moreover, this can be an example of my grandfather's saying, "Too much is like not enough." You don't want your emails filling the spam folder.

However, daily quick, structured huddles with your direct reports is a component of *Lean* management and should be strongly considered (Gabow and Goodman, 2015). These huddles get everyone on the same page and let the team know what issues need to be addressed today. Other managers will model that behavior, increasing organizational communication at all levels.

Email has become our primary mode of organizational communication. Many leaders choose to have their assistants screen and/or answer emails. This is appropriate and can be a great time saver. I preferred to answer all my emails every day. If you read it, answer it. Doing this comes from the guidance Dr. Sbarbaro gave me, "Never touch the same piece of paper twice" (Gabow 2012). If an email is so complex that it can't be responded to quickly, it is likely that email is not the best mode of communication. Frequently, my response to emails cc'ing everyone or those with a long back and forth chain was, "Stop the emails and talk to each other."

Any employee could send an email to me and many did. These covered a range of concerns from childcare needs to policy issues. This offers employees access to leadership that was unavailable before email. The scope of your responsibility will determine whether this is doable. It was for me with about 5000 employees. Of course, only a few would email on any day.

While they are amazing tools, we have a growing awareness of the downsides of email, text messages, and other electronic communications. As with many things in life, their positive qualities of speed, group communication, and constant availability are also their negative qualities. One unbending rule is to never respond in anger or frustration. President Lincoln often wrote letters which he never sent (Goodwin, 2009). His writing a letter took much more thought and time than a text or email, yet some of those were best not sent. How many emails or tweets should have never seen the light of day?

Since our communication is mainly electronic, a handwritten note takes on great meaning. I tried to send such notes to employees for an important occasion, award, or accomplishment. Sometimes they were as small as a hand-drawn star! To my surprise, I often saw these posted in people's offices. The University Chair of Medicine, Dr. Schrier, was a great example of how meaningful written communication can be. When I was promoted to Associate Professor, he wrote a letter, not just to me (which would have been great) but also to my parents (Gabow, 2012). My mother became his biggest fan. Few of us would even think of this, let alone do it. Such notes are meaningful not only to those who report to us, but also to our colleagues and bosses. Often leaders only receive missives about problems, so it is a pleasant surprise for any leader to receive one of gratitude or praise.

Thought Exercise

When was the last time you sent a handwritten note to an employee? Would you do it in the future?

While electronic and written communication can transmit information, develop relationships, and facilitate problem-solving, they are no match for the spoken word or actions for inspiration and leaders must inspire. Individuals and organizations will only do the hard work to achieve greatness if they are inspired to do so.

Words are critically important; however, actions often speak louder than words. One rule is to do what you expect others to do or what others must do. When I was Chief of Medicine, one attending rotation was on the detoxification unit—not a particularly desirable rotation. So, I did it. When I was CEO, if I had a prescription at our pharmacy, I stood in line with the patients. What a great way to see patient service. The Director of the Emergency Department at Denver Health worked his share of night and weekend shifts, and often worked holidays. The Director of Surgery took regular entire weekend shifts. These actions sent a message about privilege. The Chief of Pulmonary picked up an elderly woman who had no means of transportation in the middle of the night to be at the bedside of her dying husband. Leaders, physicians, nurses, and other employees often attended employees' and patients' funerals. These actions underscore that leaders at every level can support their teams. They also sent a message about empathy and community. A thousand emails or letters could not communicate and inspire as did these actions.

As part of Denver Health's *Lean* work, every Executive staff member participated in two Rapid Improvement Events per year. These were week-long events with a team of 8 to 10 people that focused on solving a problem in a structured way with a facilitator and team leader (Gabow and Goodman, 2015). My last event before retiring was on surgical scheduling. The two people sitting next to me were surgical clerks. No money can buy what this meant to employees.

Leaders should create opportunities for their team to interact informally to build camaraderie. Here are some examples. We had a quarterly book club on a leadership book at my house for the physician Directors of Service and the Executive staff members. These books focused on healthcare and/or leadership such as *The Spirit Catches You and You Fall Down*, *Checklist Manifesto*, *Good to Great*, and *Shackleton's Way*. These gatherings educated us, provided an opportunity for administrators and clinicians to interact, and gave us the opportunity to see dimensions of people that you don't see at meetings.

I had a New Year's Day brunch at my house for this group, the Board members, and their spouses. Every holiday season all the Executives took our assistants to lunch as a group. None of these activities were paid for by Denver Health. This sends a message about inclusion and entitlement. Others modeled these behaviors. The mid-managers read the books we read, had events at their homes, and took their teams to lunch. Each small act builds relationships and a sense of family. How you choose to accomplish this goal of informal gathering is not important, doing it is what matters.

Thought Exercise

What are you doing to build team camaraderie in your area?

Celebrations communicate who and what is seen as important. They create and sustain a culture. Denver Health held a monthly employee award ceremony that was both meaningful and inspiring. Employees were recognized for their years of service and retirees were honored. Employees' supervisors commented and family members attended. Learning about the many often unrecognized contributions of employees inspired us all. Many of the C-suite and managers attended these ceremonies regularly. I should have attended more than I did.

Three traditional events were about serving—literally. Each year there was a summer picnic with Executive staff flipping burgers, and holiday meals around Thanksgiving and Christmas in the cafeteria with Executive staff serving. We all learned first-hand how hard that work was—I always decided to stick to my day job!

Each year there was a "Day of Celebration" to showcase our successes with events and awards. Employees submitted poster presentations (much like a scientific meeting) on a variety of categories including quality and *Lean* projects. This provided an opportunity for employees who would not have access to similar formal forums. The posters were on display for everyone to see the breadth and depth of our activity. Each category had a Best Poster Award. There were annual CEO awards that had no specific criteria and could be awarded to anyone from a Department Chair to a frontline employee. One of my favorite CEO awards was given to a long-term groundskeeper who took great pride in our landscaping. He received a standing ovation. None of these had a financial component, but they were valuable and valued. In fact, not having monetary awards underscored that the organization did not see money as a measure of success—a valuable message in our profit-driven healthcare system.

For me and for the employees, a high point of the annual celebration was my State of Denver Health presentation, which included acknowledging awards that individuals and groups had received, presenting the healthcare landscape, the accomplishments of the organization, and future directions. Our Board and city and state leaders were invited to view the posters and attend the State of Denver Health, and many came.

Like other organizations, Denver Health had an annual gala, but for a number of years during my tenure it had a feature that distinguished it from most fundraisers. It was held at a place where inexpensive tickets could be sold to employees for the entertainment part of the event—Garth Brooks; Earth, Wind and Fire; Lionel Richie; Train; and Michael Franti. The celebration was not just for the wealthy in the community but for our employees as well.

How you choose to celebrate will depend on the size and geography of your area of responsibility. The important thing is to acknowledge people and their good work and nourish the culture of a family.

Many of these events speak to the respect for everyone. Many of the things that were not done also spoke to that cultural value. There was no doctor or Executive dining room. There was no special doctor parking. Everyone had the same benefits package. There were no Executive bonuses. Another small example of limiting privilege was Denver Health recruiting dinners. Those of you who have been recruited know these can be expensive events. At Denver Health, any recruiting dinner had to be at one of several pre-selected, modestly priced restaurants. One investigative reporter examining our expenses, wanted to know if we didn't know about the great Denver restaurants. All of our retreats, including Board retreats, were held at Denver Health or locally at a free venue. These also reflect frugality. This is important if you are going to say no (which you will) to requests for equipment, space, or personnel.

As you step into leadership try to be the best role model you can be.

- Believe your employees are the most important resource.
- Recruit a diverse A-team.
- Communicate with your employees.
- Support, develop and treat them fairly.
- Hold everyone accountable.
- Make your organization a family.

These may seem like small things in the grand scope of American healthcare and the issues we face. But people are what can make and change the system. They must be every leader's focus right from the start. Gaining employees' respect and trust, will enable the group you lead to deliver amazing accomplishments.

Chapter 7

Even Leaders Have a Boss

Every healthcare leader has many "bosses"—the people and groups to whom she owes accountability as well as those who assume that she has accountability to them. Who those bosses are depends on the leadership position and the type of organization in which you work. Healthcare organizations are complex and their responsibilities broad, which results in many internal vertical and horizontal relationships and many external relationships. We are all familiar with the standard organizational chart with its solid and dotted lines. We remember the solid lines, but we should not forget the dotted lines or those written in invisible ink.

Ultimately everyone in healthcare leadership should consider themselves accountable to the patients and the community they serve. This obligation is the core healthcare value of putting the patients' interests above our own and above those of the institution (Chapter 4).

Thought Exercise

Who are your bosses?

The Boss on the Chart

As we discussed in Chapter 6, it is important to develop a meaningful relationship with the person to whom you directly report. If this person appointed you, you have a head start. If you were in your role before your boss and she "inherited" you, establishing a relationship becomes even more important. There are critical aspects to developing a mutually positive relationship:

- Help your boss know your area.
- Avoid surprises.

■ Be honest and transparent.
■ Accept constructive criticism and advice.
■ Be respectful but don't "butter up."
■ Be willing to challenge.
■ Provide relevant information in a timely manner and an understandable format.
■ Understand your boss's priorities.
■ Let your boss know your personal goals.
■ Understand your boundaries.

The meetings with your boss will often happen in her office. But it is important to have her come to your frontlines (not your office) some of the time. This presents an opportunity for your boss to meet members of your team, which is a benefit to both the boss and the team. At least once a year invite your boss to your team meetings.

Thought Exercise

When was the last time you met with your boss outside her office? Do you see that it could be helpful? How did/would you structure that meeting?

We all know that negative news is unwelcome, but it is disturbing when it is a surprise. You must be honest and transparent and not hide problems or bad news. But you do need judgment about what rises to her need to know. This threshold differs for different people; it takes time to learn where that line is for your boss. You need to consciously develop an understanding of that line. But there are certain items that are a "must share":

■ A serious quality-of-care failure
■ An actual or potential ethical violation
■ A matter of organizational integrity
■ A matter with the potential for regulatory or legal action
■ A matter of press interest
■ A matter that should go to the Board

Too many surprises in these areas, and you will be dusting off your resume.

Even good surprises should be reserved for your family and friends, not for your boss. You don't want your boss to get a call from someone congratulating her on a large grant you were awarded and her not knowing about it. No boss wants to appear uninformed about what is happening in her area. But as with bad news, you need to understand where the threshold for her knowing is.

There is one surprise that deserves specific comment: leaving the organization. Hopefully, you have discussed this possibility with your boss in advance. Perhaps, your boss functioned as a sponsor, and steered you to the opportunity. When you have decided to accept an offer, your boss should always be told face-to-face. This is not an email notification, especially if you are leaving because of dissatisfaction with your current position. This is about more than not burning your bridges. It is about your values, about being respectful to your colleagues, your boss, and the institution. The more senior your leadership position is, the more lead time you should provide. How long it took to recruit you can provide a yardstick for the period of notice.

Kim Bimestefer pointed out that if you are dissatisfied with your current position, discuss it with your boss before deciding to leave. Working together you may be able to find another position in the organization which is a good fit, and will be rewarding to you, and of benefit to the organization.

Just as how you enter a leadership role is important (Chapter 6), how you leave is also important. How engaged you stay during the end of your time reflects your values. You should work the same on the last day as you did on the first.

One of the roles of a good boss is to help you develop as a person and leader. Sometimes that entails her giving constructive criticism. Most of us know we can be better and do better, but that doesn't mean we have learned how to accept advice or constructive criticism. You need to accept it willingly and act on it, just as you must be able to give it willingly and expect action. Your boss can't be your mentor or sponsor if she has no idea of your goals or the opportunities you are interested in pursuing. Carrie Byington pointed out that women must be clear and specific about this.

Feedback is a two-way street. You don't want to be killed by kindness, nor do you want your boss to experience death by over protection. Be willing to voice your concerns or disagreement in a respectful manner in the appropriate forum. Many leaders even hesitate to give constructive criticism to those they lead. How much more hesitant are they to provide this to their boss? Giving this feedback to your boss can be scary, especially for a new leader.

In a cabinet meeting shortly after my appointment as CEO, I disagreed with the Mayor. One of the other cabinet members said, "We should do what the Mayor asks us to do and not question him." My next question to the Mayor was, "I understand that you don't want us to disagree with you in a public forum but isn't it our role to tell you what we think in these meetings?" Of course, he agreed. We developed a highly effective working relationship (the other cabinet member didn't last too long). Good leaders appreciate honest input, they realize it is important, helpful, and in their best interest.

Thought Exercise

What is your comfort level with receiving and giving constructive criticism from and to your boss? Have you changed as a result of her guidance? What was your boss's reaction to constructive input from you?

Understanding your boss's priorities helps you align your priorities with hers. Boundaries are worth some thought. For example, would your boss approve of you approaching a potential donor for one of your projects without her knowing and agreeing? Maybe, yes; maybe, no. What would your boss's reaction be to your meeting with a Board member or the press without telling her?

My first lesson in boundaries came the hard way when I was a new Director of Medicine. At the time we were part of the Denver city government. Every purchase above $500 had to be approved by City Council (yes, it was $500). Moreover, if there was unspent money in your budget, it reverted to the city's coffers. I had a dilemma. I was trying to recruit a Chief of Cardiology who needed a $50,000 piece of equipment. I had squirreled away $25,000 and had convinced the Chair of Medicine at the University to contribute $25,000, but there was no way this expenditure would be approved via the usual process. So, I had a "creative" solution, asking the company to provide multiple invoices of $495 for the equipment. When it arrived as one machine with 101 pages of $495 invoices attached, questions arose. The response of my boss, Dr. Sbarbaro, and the dressing down I got are best left unwritten. He had to go to City Council to explain this. This is clearly not the ideal way to learn your boss's boundaries. Nor is it advisable to try and outmaneuver the boss. Fortunately, we developed a great working relationship and he became both a mentor and sponsor. (Not to encourage this behavior, but I did get the equipment and the cardiologist.)

Thought Exercise

What are your boss's guidelines for need to know? Where are your boundaries?

If you understand your boss's threshold for "need to know," and your boundary lines, your boss will trust you and give you more autonomy.

Your Peers

You need to understand the meaning of those dotted lines on the organization chart. These lines can be to other senior leaders or your peers. What do those individuals expect from you, and what do you expect from them? Don't assume you know the answer—ask them. The invisible lines are tricky. Often these lines are to your colleagues who are at the same leadership level. You may have previously reported to one of them. They may have helped you get promoted into this role (or not). Expect some scrutiny from your peers. You are on their team. They have a major investment in how you play the game. Build relationships with them and keep them in the loop regarding your work, especially if some of that work overlaps with theirs (Chapter 6).

Thought Exercise

To whom do you have a dotted line relationship? What are your mutual expectations?

The Board

In most non-governmental organizations, the Board is the final boss. For the CEO and to some extent the Executives, the Board is the functional boss. In these leadership roles, relationship with the Board is critical. Boards should offer healthcare leaders a different perspective, an independent set of eyes, and another guardian of the organization's mission and values. This is highly valuable. There are many books, articles, and consultants that provide guidance on working effectively with Boards. Learning these skills is important for you and the organization as you achieve senior leadership roles.

The necessary components of Board interactions mirror those of successful relationships with any boss, with a few additions:

- Get to know each Board member personally.
- Understand what's most important to them about the organization.
- Avoid surprises, especially in the media.
- Be honest and transparent.
- Never hide your mistakes or the organization's mistakes.
- Provide relevant information in a timely and organized manner.
- Encourage dialogue and discussion.
- Provide relevant education.
- Create opportunities for the Board to interact with the Executives, other leaders, and frontline staff.
- Hold each other accountable for the organization's performance.

For Executives there is no substitute for spending time with Board members. Risa Lavizzo-Mourey, the Robert Wood Johnson Foundation CEO Emerita, called every Board member before each meeting to discuss the upcoming agenda, any concerns, and any ideas they wanted to share. This is an excellent practice and is especially prudent if there are important votes on the agenda. Knowing what your Board members are thinking in advance of a Board meeting prevents surprises for you and the other members. As a Mayor told me, "Always count your votes."

The CEO should develop a trusting and meaningful relationship with the Board Chair. Executives should develop a relationship with the Chairs of their relevant Board committees: for example, the CFO with the Finance Committee; the CMO and CNO with the Quality and Patient Safety Committee; the Director of Human Resources with the Personnel Committee. You can serve as Executive coaches to each other.

No leader should withhold negative or concerning information from their Board, including any concerns that may have been raised about her. Those items which must be shared with the Board are the same as the "must share list" for any boss (see above). If you are not the CEO, these concerns must first be shared with the CEO. A CEO's or Executive's nightmare should be the Board Chair or a committee Chair getting an early morning call from a friend, reporter, community leader, or politician about a major problem of which they were unaware.

The Board has a fiduciary and ethical responsibility to ask the hard questions and to address critical issues, problems, mistakes, and shortcomings. In recent years we have seen the consequences of Boards' failures to do this in industry and healthcare.

Information for Board meetings should be provided in an organized, well-formatted, and timely manner. You cannot expect busy Board members to digest all the information that emerges from our complex health systems without adequate lead time. The CEO and Executives should decide with the Board and committees what lead time is best for them and meet it. It is not respectful to be late. Boards and their committees differ on the format they find the most useful. Most organizations have a performance dashboard that minimally includes quality/safety, finances, access, patient satisfaction, and population health. Any presentation should include clarity on what you want from the Board or the committee. Decisions regarding laying new tracks require a longer period of discussion and more information than those about operations. Richard Besser, the CEO of the Robert Wood Johnson Foundation, informs Board members not only of items requiring a vote at the next Board meeting, but he also provides information on future Board agendas. This is an excellent practice.

The CEO and the Executives should recognize the difference between positive votes that result from having a Board or committees that were prepared for a decision with timely, accurate, and relevant information vs. positive votes from a Board or committees which reflect perfunctory approval of everything. The former is good; the latter is bad. This does not mean that you want disagreement within the Board or its committees, especially on major decisions. You want meaningful discussion and data-driven consensus. Follow the standing rule—you don't want them to kill you or the organization with kindness.

Healthcare is challenging to understand even for those who do it every day. Imagine how hard it is for those to whom even the terminology is a challenge. There should be regular Board education. Board education must start with informative and effective orientation. That orientation must include:

- The history and mission
- The legal duties and obligations
- The legal and functional structure
- The finances
- The patient population
- The quality of care
- The needs of the community
- The current and looming issues

They should see what the organization looks like on the ground with a meaningful interaction with the day-to-day activities. This can be accomplished by having them accompany a nurse, doctor, or social worker, by participating in a Rapid Improvement Event (RIE) (Chapter 8), attending an ethics consultation meeting, or myriad other activities. Touring beautiful buildings is not sufficient. The ideal way for the Board, or any other leader, or employee to connect with the institution is to be a patient (hopefully, not for something serious). I asked every mayoral candidate publicly during his campaign whether he and his family would get their care at Denver Health. They all did. Some, but not all, of our Board members did as well.

One important aspect of Board education is the opportunity to interact with the members of the Executive team, the Directors, the physician and nurse leaders and even frontline employees. Executive team members and their teams should be regular presenters at Board meetings. Not only does this let the Board know them, but it also prepares them for future leadership positions. Any leader or aspiring leader should seize any such opportunity.

Thought Exercise

Have you presented at your Board? How would you rate your performance?

While not a routine agenda item for most Boards, there should be structured interaction with the frontline staff. An effective approach we used was to have RIE teams present their work. The impact of a group of frontline nurses, therapists, clerks, and others presenting a problem they tackled and solved in a week was incredible, both for the teams and for the Board. Rarely in healthcare do frontline staff come to the Board saying, "This was a big problem, and this is how we fixed it in a week." This met the goals of transparency, accountability, and education all at once. While the staff was nervous, the pride was palpable.

The Board and the Executive staff are a team. They should hold each other accountable not only for their performances, but also for the organization's performance. One aspect of accountability is appointments by and to the Board. Clearly, the Board appoints, evaluates, and determines the salary of the CEO. The Board should also have an orderly process for filling vacancies and evaluating itself. The Board Chair and the CEO should discuss what role the CEO has in Board appointments. It seems appropriate for the CEO and relevant members of the Executive team (e.g., CFO for finance committee) to have some input. A Board should bring needed talent and perspective to the table. I told the Mayors that the city could never give us all the money we needed, but they could give us Board members who would challenge us to improve. Just like picking your team, try for an A-team Board.

Thought Exercise

What would your assessment be of your Board?

The Community

The community, the political leaders, and the press are also the "bosses" of every leader in all healthcare organizations—even for organizations that are not a public entity. Every healthcare entity receives taxpayer dollars, directly or indirectly, and this makes them responsible to governmental entities, the larger community, and to public oversight.

In many ways, albeit less structured, the same obligations of building relationships, transparency, honesty, and education apply to these relationships as they do to any boss. These relationships require genuine interest, time, and effort. In building them it is important to spend time in their terrain, positionally and geographically. Invite them to spend time in your organization seeing what you do that intersects with their efforts. In many situations, including crises, these entities will be important in an effective response. Planning for the potential interaction in such events helps both build relationships and facilitates an effective response in a crisis. Remember the rule: You never want to meet someone for the first time when you need their help.

Just as written notes have meaning to your boss and team, they also do to other leaders and groups. If they have received a large grant, won an election, or were lauded for a major accomplishment, send them a congratulatory note. Little things mean a lot to everyone.

Thought Exercise

Which community groups have you met with? Have you built enough of a relationship so that you could ask them for help in a crisis?

Leaders must remember that these entities have different goals, duties and responsibilities than those of your other bosses and your Board who have a fiduciary obligation to the organization. The community, political leaders, and the press do not. These different obligations can produce conflicts. Hopefully, if strong relationships have been established, these will be minor and infrequent. But you should not be surprised if they can be contentious.

Given the critical role that government plays in healthcare, leaders must develop relationships with political and governmental leaders and entities. Most healthcare CEOs will bring members of the Board and Executive team to Washington, D.C. on a regular basis to meet with their Congressional delegation. It is also important to establish relationships with state and local government officials as much health policy occurs at this level. While these meetings often involve some request, that is not all they should be. They should provide information. Even after we became an independent entity, I met with the Mayor regularly and each City Council member yearly. We also met with state legislators, cabinet members, and the newspapers' editorial Boards.

Frequently, leaders will be part of professional organizations that visit federal and state legislators. In these meetings remember you wear two hats—that of your professional society and your organization.

It is important to reach out to the broader community. During my CEO tenure, we had a monthly meeting in which we invited 15 to 20 leaders from a wide range of groups, including the business community, to a morning breakfast presentation on Denver Health. Even though most of them had been in the community for years, and Denver Health had been around for 150 years, the most frequent response after the meeting was, "I had no idea what Denver Health did." We should not assume that the community knows what our organization does.

Stories that tie what you do to what others identify with are a powerful way to engage the community (Chapter 8). As a safety net institution, the larger community might not identify with our mission, but there were several aspects of our care that touched people's hearts. One of those was delivering babies. About 50 percent of all U.S. births are covered by Medicaid. Denver Health, as the major Medicaid provider, delivered many babies. Often these babies were born into poor families that could not afford baby clothes, let alone a car seat or a stroller. We started a series of baby showers hosted, and attended by prominent women—the Governor's wife, the Bronco coach's wife. Hearing the story of a mother who washed and dried disposable diapers and a father who said he couldn't believe that people who didn't know him would give his baby a gift, connected them to our mission.

Leaders also have robust data on the health of their community with information such as the Commonwealth Fund's State Health Rankings, the Robert Wood Johnson Foundation's County Health Rankings, and the CDC's Small Area Life Expectancy Estimates. Not only do leaders need to use these data to achieve health for the population, but they also need to share it with community leaders, political leaders, and the press. Sharing this helps to bust the myth that American healthcare is the best in the world, allows them to see them where we fall short, and starts to create societal will for change.

Thought Exercise

Have you used any national Community Health data to help you improve your area? Have you shared that data with any internal or external group?

Even if you have planned meetings with these groups, there are fewer opportunities to present information. As a result, a single anecdote, positive or negative, can take on great significance. All leaders (ideally everyone) in an organization must understand that they should never do anything that could become a negative story on the front page of the local newspaper that questions the organization's values or commitment to the health of the community.

Even though we all must support a free press and investigative journalism, the press can present challenges at times. One challenge is how to respond to something that is both false and negative. Judging when it is useful and important to respond and when responding will turn a one-day story into a multiple-day story takes guidance, experience, and thought. Discuss the issue with others, especially your boss and your communications group before you respond.

One frustration for leaders is when you have little or no option to present your side of the story. This occurs when the negative news involves a personnel matter or a matter in litigation. You simply must wait for the outcome.

On rare occasions, an investigative reporter will add humor to your day. One reporter examining Denver Health expenses, triumphantly announced that he found Denver Health purchased thousands of condoms in a year. We pointed out that we ran the public health department and the sexually transmitted disease clinic, both of which dispensed condoms. I often wondered what he thought the punch line of that story was.

Thought Exercise

Have you had interactions with the press? Would you do anything differently in the future?

Affiliated Organizations

Many healthcare entities, especially hospitals, clinics, physician groups, and insurers have affiliations with other healthcare entities. Often these relationships are with medical, nursing, and other professional schools. These entail mutual responsibilities for faculty and students which should be clear to both parties. Denver Health has an important relationship with the University of Colorado School of Medicine. For many years these relationships were conducted by handshake. While this can reflect mutual trust, such unwritten relationships can be left open to a different interpretation of roles and responsibilities. When I was CEO, we formalized the relationships with the School of Medicine. It was also critical that there be a personal relationship. The Dean and I met every month for the 20 years we were in our roles. The Directors of Service at Denver Health met regularly with their respective Chairs at the School of Medicine and the Denver Health faculty were active members of the university departments.

Healthcare leaders are gaining an understanding of the critical importance of the social determinants of health. Many entities that affect these factors are outside the boundaries of the healthcare institutions. This requires that healthcare leaders develop meaningful and operationally functional relationships with housing groups, food suppliers, social service groups, educational institutions, and criminal justice departments. This creates other external relationships and other bosses. It is ideal if these relationships are codified so that everyone is on the same page regarding issues of governance, employment, patient responsibilities, information ownership and use, flow of funds, and conflict resolution. Formal agreements are important because leaders change, and institutional memory can be short-lived. This is demonstrated by the contract between Denver Health and the city including its many departments from the police and fire departments to social service.

Without this detailed document there would have been many different views of the relationship and accountability over the years.

While many of us might see an ideal world without any boss, or even just one boss, having a broad accountability helps us and our organizations improve, meet the goal of providing for the health and well-being of everyone we serve, and educate the public about healthcare.

Chapter 8

Making the Trains Run on Time and Laying New Tracks

Two key functions of leadership are making the trains run on time and laying new tracks. Every leader, regardless of her span of control, needs to be engaged in both activities to ensure her area performs well today and is ready for tomorrow. The mix of these two functions depends on the role. For example, if you lead a frontline, patient-facing area, you will focus more on the first effort. If you lead an entire organization, you will focus equally, if not more, on the second. The activities in the first area focus primarily on access, stability, reliability, efficiency, quality, equity, and safety. Gaining an understanding of these problems, their solutions, and operationalizing those solutions are hard work, but it is relatively familiar terrain. Activities in the second area are more challenging and require seeing and understanding where healthcare is today, where it is heading, and, more importantly where it should be tomorrow. Preparing for and creating the future for your area of responsibility requires risk-taking because none of us have that special crystal ball.

Achieving success in both areas requires:

- Observation
- Team approach
- Communication
- Timeline and roadmap
- Data/evaluation
- Decision-making and problem-solving

These are all discussed in this chapter, including the difference between the two domains.

Observation is an important starting point. We often think that the trains in our own area run smoothly, and efficiently, and have the best destination. But the patients' experience of our systems of care, our outcomes, and observations of our processes would say otherwise. We need to receive this information on the shortcomings in our care delivery with humility and without bias and use all these sources to improve our current system and establish new directions. You need to know what is happening in your areas. Leaders need to trust and rely on their teams to assist them in these efforts. This requires having built high-functioning teams and knowing their capabilities (Chapter 6).

Making the trains run on time and laying new tracks are both team activities. A leader functioning independently can't deliver outcomes in either domain. You will need your core leadership team and teams that are formed to address a specific issue. The latter teams like committees (see below) require structure, clear charges, deliverables, and timelines. These will differ depending on the issue the team is addressing. A team addressing appointment access or antibiotic stewardship will not be the same as the project team for an IT installment or construction of a new building. At Denver Health, the teams for the issues in the first bin were often our Rapid Improvement (RIE) teams (see below).

In a real sense, all the employees in your area need to be part of the team in order to achieve both improvement and innovation. A critical part of engaging them is communication (Chapter 6). The bigger and broader the initiative, the more important communication is. But even in small changes, it is needed. We learned this in our first *Lean* efforts. Having 6 to 10 people define and solve a problem and implement the change in one week is valuable (even miraculous), but if employees in the affected area are surprised on Monday morning, it will take more than coffee to make them smile. Effective communication requires a clear message and process for getting the message from the right person, to the right people, at the right time, and at the right frequency.

Thought Exercise

How did you communicate the last change you instituted? Was it effective?

There are different time frames for achieving success in the two areas. It is possible, desirable, and sometimes necessary to deal with fires and operational crises in hours or days. There is a caution for leaders. Remember the first version of the actual event is rarely accurate, let alone establishes its root cause. So, while you may need to jump to action, don't jump into conclusions.

You can manage and improve how well the trains are running in a time frame of weeks or months. However, innovations and system transformations take months to years. The bigger the ship you are trying to turn, the longer it takes. If you are creating major change, you may also be steering against the current. You need a roadmap with a timeline for a change you are initiating, whether the change is improving operations or system transformation. As Yogi Berra said, "If you don't know where you are going, you might wind up someplace else." The timeline and the roadmap not only guide the process, but they also enable you to communicate the process and progress to everyone affected by the change.

Focusing beyond today's operations to see tomorrow's reality is not only about the organization's well-being. It is also about your well-being. There will always be some fire or crisis that demands your attention. But even if you are successful in putting out fires, if crisis management is all you engage in, it will not feel like progress, and you may succumb to frustration or burnout. You need goals to march toward in both leadership domains that let you see your progress month by month or year by year.

The metaphor of putting out fires relates to creating change in response to the proverbial "burning platform." The Deepwater Horizon catastrophe points out that the only valid response to a burning platform is to get off it. Ideally, you improve operations and pursue innovation without the urgency of a crisis but rather as part of a thoughtful process.

Data and decision-making require in-depth discussion. After that the chapter will turn to making the trains run on time and laying new tracks.

Data Is Your Friend

An abundance of data is available to every leader. This is both a blessing and a curse. The challenges are to know what data are important, what analyses and formats are useful, and the frequency of data monitoring. It is critical to identify the data that will define the success or failure of your area of responsibility. You need both internal and external data. Internal data lets you manage and evaluate your area in real time. External data enables you to see what others consider important and to compare your performance to theirs.

Lean methodology posits that a leader needs data in the following domains: quality, service/access, cost/productivity, growth, and employee development (Gabow and Goodman, 2015). For healthcare leaders, quality encompasses safety, and service/access should include equity and population health. The financial components at a minimum include revenue, expenditures, operating margin, cash flow, debt, liabilities, assets, and reserves.

There are many available measurements in each of these areas. However, there is often a lack of clarity about which measurements are the most valuable, particularly in quality, access, and employee development. There will be times when the data you want is not readily available. Then you need to weigh the benefit of having that data against the resource cost of acquiring and analyzing it. Often you must pick from what is available, understand it, and act on it.

Denver Health's Executive team, like all leadership teams, developed a limited number of measures to provide a picture of our performance and present actionable targets for improvement. The actionable part is important. If a measure has critical components outside your control, it may be interesting, but it is unlikely to drive improvement. A few meaningful, high-level measures are useful in providing an overall picture, but they give a panoramic view. You need granular data both to make the trains run and to lay new tracks. For example, you may know that the overall organization is profitable, but you need to know which components are generating a positive margin and which are losing money. You may know that your hospital's overall mortality rate is better than expected, but that doesn't tell you if all areas are performing well. In fact, there is almost always variability in financial and quality measures across an organization. Similarly, you may understand that your system should have innovative ways to deal with population health, but you need to know the needs of specific population segments.

Thought Exercise

What data are you using to assess performance in your area?

Not all data are equal—even the data from your own organization, and certainly not the data from external sources. It is critical to know how the data were gathered, how they were analyzed and their reliability. The complexity of our healthcare systems and the lack of transparency across most components, make these important points. Any data that you are using has been formatted and/or analyzed, often using a variety of statistical methods. Unfortunately, few of us are facile, or even competent in this realm. There are numerous examples of the pitfalls that can occur even in what seems like straightforward data (Levitin, 2016). The following examples underscore the importance of scrutinizing the data.

Looking at healthcare systems' advertising, one would get the impression that existing ranking systems accurately reflect quality. For example, a study demonstrated that U.S. News and World Report's Best Hospital Guide is more heavily influenced by reputation than objective data (Cua et al., 2017).

Common measures of productivity include clinical revenue and RVUs. Given that as much as 30 percent of the healthcare delivered in the United States is either low value, no value or even harmful, you should ask if the revenue generated reflects overuse or misuse, and whether it has contributed to patients' health or only contributed to the organization's bottom line. One example of this variance between the patient benefit and profit is Executive physicals offered by a number of prestigious healthcare systems (Korenstein et al., 2019).

Healthcare systems generally do not have the granular cost accounting systems seen in manufacturing. Cost is often equated with charges and the hospital's uncompensated care is reported as charges. Thus, the system with the highest charges may incorrectly appear to have provided the largest amount of uncompensated care in a group of hospitals with a similar or larger commitment to the uninsured.

A common quality measure is readmission. In a national data base of academic institutions, Denver Health's readmission rate was high. Dissecting the data revealed the rate was driven by frequent readmissions for urgent dialysis for undocumented immigrants who could not receive routine outpatient dialysis. The rate could only be improved by governmental action which would expand dialysis eligibility to this group.

These examples underscore the importance for a leader to understand the data she uses to make decisions. If she does not, she may find herself heading in a wrong direction.

Thought Exercise

How do you determine which data to use in your decision-making? How do you scrutinize that data for accuracy and relevance?

If you are in a major leadership role, most likely one or more individuals will be reporting to you. They will be a source of data. This leads to the tension of trying to know everything vs. having too much data filtering. I believe it is better to know more than less. Knowing is not micromanaging; it is seeing and understanding the whole picture for what you are responsible. Nancy Agee said what keeps her up at night is what she doesn't know (Chapter 11). That should be a concern for every leader.

A decision that leaders need to make regarding data is its distribution. Because data is power, some leaders limit its access. This is a mistake for data that do not demand confidentiality. Early in my tenure as Director of Medicine, I wanted to gain an understanding of the Department's finances. This seems an obvious need, but at that time as part of city government, Denver Health was not routinely billing for the services it provided. I started with something simple and straightforward: how did the number of billed EKG's compare to the number the cardiology service performed. When I found out that we weren't billing any, I went to the CFO. He apparently shared my findings with the CEO whose response was to end my access to the data. This clearly did not help improve the organization. A good leader welcomes many eyes on the data.

Part of sharing data is presenting it in a meaningful way to others. Both clinicians and scientists have been accused more than once of failing to do this. How you present the data depends on the audience. A presentation at a scientific meeting is not the same as one to your Board, a legislative committee, or a community group. You are not changing the data, just the presentation. In general, a more visual format such as a pie chart is easier to understand than a table. Giving the data personal meaning is useful for non-healthcare groups. For example, we did not present Denver Health's observed-to-expected mortality data to community groups as a bar graph with a p value. We showed a slide with people's faces for the number of people who would have left the hospital alive at Denver Health compared to the prediction. The audience could see themselves or their loved ones in such a picture. Being able to make data into a story—a true one—is important.

This is what Mayor Webb meant when he told me, "Patty, most decisions aren't made from data" (Gabow, 1999). People need to be able to see what it means to them. The more we do this as leaders, the more likely it will be that we can change our healthcare system.

Thought Exercise

What is your approach to sharing data within your team and with others in the organization?

Research is a Teacher

A research background is excellent preparation for healthcare leadership. As academic medicine illustrates, this is not to say that every researcher can be a good leader. But research teaches an array of skills for assessing the situation and understanding and utilizing data that serve any leader well in the two leadership domains:

- Thoroughly understanding what is known in the area
- Functioning in a team
- Identifying both a problem and an opportunity for improvement, discovery, and/or innovation
- Designing approaches to examine and test solutions
- Gathering and understanding data
- Understanding basic statistical methods
- Transforming data into a useful format
- Selling your ideas to others
- Learning from failures and successes
- Persevering through ups and downs

Understanding what is already known requires digging. Early in my research career, I learned that what is accepted as dogma can have little data behind it. The literature emphatically stated that the acid-base disturbance of aspirin intoxication was respiratory alkalosis. Digging into the data demonstrated that this was based on a physician's pronouncement years ago, and it was wrong. This lesson is true not only in the clinical realm, but also in the management and leadership realm. A classic example, dubbed Brooks' Law for its creator, came from the IT world. Brooks showed that the common response of adding more people to a late project, makes it finish even later, not earlier (Brooks, 1995).

Research is frequently a team effort. It teaches you both to lead a group and to work effectively with others. It often involves the participation of individuals early in their career, teaching you mentorship.

Both good research and clinical care require moving beyond the symptom to the cause of the problem. We can expend a great deal of effort on treating symptoms, rather than the core problem (Chapter 5). One *Lean* technique for getting to the core issue is "The Five Whys," asking why five times. For example, if there are long wait times for appointments, the answer to the first why may be that there are not enough appointment slots. The answer to the second why might be because clinicians have too few scheduled clinics. The whys keep peeling the onion until you move beyond the symptom of the problem to the root cause.

We should institute solutions that have been tested and evaluated. Much of the overuse and misuse in clinical practice reflects a failure in this area for new therapies and technology. There may be even less evaluation for many management and operational approaches. Think about the assertations on the benefits of open-office design which are now questioned (Westfall, 2018). Similarly, think about the construct that horizontal and vertical consolidation of healthcare providers lowers costs which it has not (Boozary et al., 2019; Scheffler et al., 2018). As leaders, the data we rely on should include not only the work of others, but also our careful evaluation of our own interventions.

As a fellow, I was told if one-third of my studies supported the hypothesis I advanced, I would be doing well. Another part of that insight is that we should learn from our failures and persist until we find the answer.

One intangible benefit of research is the satisfaction that comes from discovery—a potent vaccine against frustration, cynicism, and burnout. To quote Kurt Vonnegut, "You will get an enormous reward. You will have created something."

For all these reasons, I encouraged those I mentored, as well as those who reported to me, to engage in research at some level. This doesn't have to be worthy of a Nobel Prize. It can simply be examining the work you are doing, how you have improved it, and sharing it in some formal way. As discussed in Chapter 9, sharing your learnings is an obligation of every leader.

Thought Exercise

Have you engaged in research? What has it taught you that you apply in your leadership role?

Making Decisions

While gathering and discussing data are important, don't succumb to data and discussion paralysis. A leader needs some level of comfort with ambiguity. You will not always have every piece of data you would like for a decision. In fact, you rarely do. There are times to act like a trauma surgeon in the operating room and proceed based on what you have in front of you. There are also times to act like a psychiatrist conducting psychoanalysis, slowly gathering insights. Depending on the urgency of the situation, the gravity of the issue, and the likelihood of obtaining other relevant data in a timely fashion, you can arrive at the appropriate approach. When something is obvious, just do it. One of my mentors, Dr. Sbarbaro, said, "Don't be afraid to make decisions. If you never make a decision you will never be right" (Gabow, 1995; Gabow, 2012). Leaders should relish decision-making. It is how you operationalize leadership. It shows your values and priorities.

To avoid the opposing pitfalls of acting precipitously or being paralyzed, a leader should:

- Be willing to be a decision-maker.
- Accept that not every decision will be correct.
- Learn from mistakes but don't agonize over them.
- Adopt a decision-making approach.

If you are not comfortable making decisions, leadership is not for you. Kicking tough decisions to a committee or down the road is not useful. I told medical trainees, you will make some mistakes, and some will be very bad, but you must learn from every mistake, and never make the same one twice. Over your career, there should be many fewer mistakes than right decisions. This clinical lesson applies in leadership.

The best decision-making requires a leader's willingness to say no, results from clear priorities, and has defined approaches to solving problems. Inherent in making decisions is that sometimes you say, "Yes," and sometimes, "No." It is critical that both the leader and those being led know the values, priorities and metrics used in deciding between yes or no. The reason for a yes should:

- Fit with the organization's mission and values.
- Be supported by data.
- Be beneficial to patients and/or the population served.
- Improve quality.
- Improve efficiency.
- Align with strategic goals.
- Have a higher priority than other requests.

All of these will not come into play in every decision, but they should be used when relevant.

A yes should not be about the loudness of the voice or the stature of the asker. Conversely, the reasons for no reflect the other side of the coin but are worth listing:

- Not a fit with the organization's mission
- Not backed by data
- Having no or little patient or population benefit
- No improved quality or efficiency

- Not a fit with strategic goals
- Not a priority above the other needs

A no should not be about the softest voice asking.

Thought Exercise

What are your criteria for saying yes? Do those you say no to understand the reasons for your answer?

Being comfortable with "no" is a critical leadership skill. I said no often. The Director of Medicine gave me a box of yellow Post-It-Notes stamped with "Yes," and asked me to use them. I returned the box to him unused when I retired! When I first became CEO, Dr. Sbarbaro told me that soon no one would like me because I would have told so many people no. Most of us prefer to be liked—no surprise there. Although I have observed that men were not particularly willing to be the person saying no, women are vulnerable to the likability trap. Over time I said no to virtually everyone. It became clear that it was not personal.

One of the most difficult situations in which to say no is when the request is legitimate, even needed, but the resources are not available for it. While this may not occur often in healthcare organizations with an abundance of resources, it will likely arise at some point. This is when it is most important to have a process that everyone knows and is fair and transparent.

When I became CEO, we held a meeting with the physicians and an ethicist to discuss which ethical principle would guide our decision-making: the most care for the most people or the most care for the sickest. We decided that as a safety net institution, the first was most appropriate. Discussing the ethics of decision-making and resource allocation would be useful for healthcare leaders at all levels in every healthcare institution.

Decision-making and resource allocation processes are particularly relevant to women as they may not always be the loudest voice, the best negotiator, or as likely to get what they need to be successful. Therefore, women leaders should be especially committed to set an example of fair, transparent, and process-based decision-making.

It seems that frequently in healthcare the highest priority is profit or market share. We should expect that the priority would be what is best for the patients and the population. As discussed in Chapter 1, women leaders tend to produce better use of resources. Hopefully, having more women in leadership roles can help to move priorities from profit to patient.

Not surprisingly, there can be conflict between profit and the patients' needs and the population's needs. There can also be conflicts between individual patient and population needs. Here are two illustrative examples. The first illustrates the tension between patient needs and profit. During my time as CEO, Denver area hospitals were closing their inpatient psychiatric units as mental health payments were low, particularly from Medicaid. Denver Health remained the only adult inpatient psychiatric unit. It was losing money since Denver Health accepted not only Medicaid patients but uninsured patients as well. So, what to do—a great need coupled with significant losses. The answer came from an unexpected source, the CFO. She said, "If we don't provide this care, where will the patients get care?" Subsequently, as the only remaining provider, and a high-quality one to boot, Denver Health was able to attract commercially insured patients and turn the psychiatric service into a revenue-generating department. As is often the case, when you choose to do good rather than do well, you achieve both.

The second example illustrates the tension between individual patients' needs and population needs. It is illustrative of the recurring decisions regarding new (and always more expensive) technology. Often new technology may only benefit a few patients (perhaps, we don't even know if it is beneficial), but it consumes resources that could have great impact on a larger population. Years ago, when other hospitals began acquiring MRIs, Denver Health was the only major institution without one (Gabow, 1999). The physicians saw the benefit of this technology for patient care. But a competing need was for school-based clinics in a poor area of the city, which would facilitate the well-being of many children. Given limited resources, there was a choice to be made. We chose the school-based clinics, following our guiding ethical principle of the most good for the most people. Of course, we eventually did acquire an MRI.

Thought Exercise

What decision have you made where there was tension between critical priorities? How did you resolve the tension?

Not only must a leader be willing to decide between conflicting priorities, but also conflicts between individuals. Hopefully, these are very few, but if they occur you cannot ignore them. A leader cannot tolerate interpersonal conflicts on the team. There must be a prompt and sustained resolution. Begin by asking the individuals to resolve their differences. If you need to mediate, listen to both sides, gather the data, and help them come to a resolution. If the differences cannot be resolved, one or both team members may need new roles or new jobs.

Disagreements can occur in the team about processes or decisions. While you must encourage dialogue and discussion to arrive at the best solution, once a decision is reached the team must be on the same page. There can be no loyal opposition.

A common issue in decision-making is the role of voting. We voted on one issue during the eight years that I was Chief of Medicine. Many of the division heads voted against the proposal on the table. It passed as I exercised the Lincoln prerogative of having one more vote! I don't think we ever voted in Executive staff when I was CEO. I am all for democracy. But it seems there is only a need to vote when there is no agreement on an issue and the leader doesn't want to make the decision. We spent so much time together as an Executive team that we were always on the same page. In fact, when we had outside visitors, guests, or regulatory bodies, a universal comment was how everyone in the organization was on the same page. Having said this, you must respect the organizational culture on the issue of why and when to vote.

Although *Lean* was not in the toolbox at the beginning of my career, it became our principal problem-solving and decision-making approach. It offers an amazingly versatile and robust set of tools for making decisions to both keep the trains running and laying new tracks (Gabow and Goodman, 2015). Two tools illustrate this, the A3, defined below, and later in the chapter, the Rapid Improvement Event. The nine components of an A3 enable structured problem-solving and concise, clear communication of the problem and the solution—all on a single 11 × 17 piece of paper (Table 8.1) (Gabow and Goodman, 2015).

The A3 resembles a scientific abstract. It first lays out the problem (Reason for Action); the observations that support that it is a problem (Current State); where you want to be and the gap between that and the current state (Target State and Gap); the proposed solution; the experiments that verified the solution rectifies the problem; the plan for completing any components not yet done; the confirmation that the new process is totally or mostly in place and works as planned; and any insights. This became our standard method of presenting problems and solutions for everything from improving pediatric asthma care to capital equipment requests. Having such a tool creates a common language for problem-solving across the organization—speaking the same language is a major asset in creating a common vision, enabling transparency, and trust. Think about the barrier to problem-solving that can come from different languages between the finance team and the clinical team.

Committees or "working groups" are a standard approach to problem-solving. They can be a valuable and functional approach to complex problems with many perspectives and components. Precisely because of these aspects, the process requires structure:

- A clear, definitive, and achievable charge
- The right number and mix of participants
- A leader who can keep the focus
- A defined timeline
- A defined deliverable

A committee should not be formed to offload the decision from the leader, delay a solution, or commit a problem to indefinite limbo.

One type of committee, the standing committee, deserves comment. A new leader should assess the number, function, and output of all these committees in her purview. Although some are required by regulation, many that were established in the past linger on with little purpose. As the saying goes, "They waste hours and save minutes." Decommissioning committees that provide little or no value is an important component of deciding what not to do. The

Table 8.1 Components of A3

Reason for action
Current state
Target state
Gap analysis
Solution approach
Rapid experiments
Completion plan
Confirmed state
Insights

need to stop doing things that have little or no benefit goes beyond decommissioning committees. Many of the activities within our healthcare system add little value. Therefore, we must adopt a process to identify those activities and stop doing them.

Another robust, rapid, and democratized approach to problem-solving is a *Lean* tool, the Rapid Improvement Event (RIE) (Gabow and Goodman, 2015). These events differ from committees in the members, their time frame, and the focus of power. Most committees are composed of leaders; often they have every possible stakeholder at the table. In contrast, RIEs have 6 to 10 members, a mix of frontline people, managers, and leaders. Not every stakeholder is at the table. Some of the participants are not even from the area in which the problem lies. These are new eyes—a plus in problem-solving. While committees and RIEs both have a start date, committees often have a long duration (some never end). RIEs last five days and follow a standardized structure. A committee's proposed solution is often not tested, and it usually requires approval before implementation. RIEs test the proposed solutions during the week. There is no approval process and ideally, the solution is implemented by the end of the RIE week. We had only two RIE rules: no new resources and the solution must comply with all legal and regulatory requirements.

Not infrequently a proposed solution to a problem is more people, more space, or more technology. Most often the real need is a better process. Given the $1 trillion of waste in our system, a better process that eliminates waste will provide the resource. Given the regulatory environment, when a group looks at a process, they may conclude that some regulation adds waste and should be eliminated—not an option. It doesn't work to tell a regulatory body that their rule is wasteful and hence, you decided not to follow it!

Another benefit of the RIE problem-solving approach is that each event is part of a much larger process, creating broad solutions. For example, a series of RIEs were in Supply Chain and another series were in a patient-facing area, Perioperative Services (Gabow and Goodman, 2015).

As a leader you may not choose *Lean* as one component of your problem-solving toolset, but it is advisable to have defined approaches to problem-solving that are timely and robust, have a common language, and that everyone knows and understands. It is difficult to have trust if no one knows how decisions are made.

Making the Trains Run on Time

The first order of business is to know how many trains you have, where they are going, who's driving them, who's using them, and myriad other operational issues. In other words, a leader needs to start by understanding what her areas of responsibility are and what her span of control is.

- What components of healthcare are your areas responsible for delivering to the organization and the population?
- How does your area interface with other areas in delivering those components?
- What data will enable you to assess the performance of your area and see the gaps (see above)?

A leader needs to know her team, what they do now, and what they can do (Chapter 6). She needs to go to where the work is being done, see it, and see the people doing it (Chapter 6). This takes time and effort. Even if you have been promoted from within the organization, do not assume you have obtained this understanding by osmosis. Without a broad and deep understanding of the scope of your responsibility, you will not be able to provide guidance and direction, anticipate problems, and sustain and improve operational processes. In fact, when leaders fail it is often because they don't grasp the scope and scale of their responsibility (Beard and Weiss, 2017).

It is not sufficient for this view of your responsibility to be at a 30,000-foot level. As Stephanie Thomas, Denver Health's COO said, "You can swallow the camels, and choke on the gnats." So, you better know about those gnats. Lily Marks and Peg Burnette pointed out that this is something women seem to be better at doing. "Men leaders like to function at the 100,000-foot level where the birds fly, but the people are on the ground. Many male leaders live on the top floor of the organization. Sometimes [you need to take the elevator] to the ground floor or the basement—that is where many problems are" (Lilly Marks). Kim Bimestefer actually operationalized this. When she was at Cigna, she did not put her office on the top floor with the Executives, but in the middle with the sales force. "Women are more attentive to details than men ... these details can be important and ignoring them can have serious consequences" (Peg Burnette). Your understanding needs to be granular or you will not see the problems or the opportunities to improve. This means you need granular data. You need real-time, high quality, relevant operational information (see above).

If clinician leaders stay involved in frontline care, they can glean an important and unique perspective on day-to-day operations. I have seen this continued clinical involvement more often in physician leaders than in leaders from other clinical disciplines. At Denver Health every physician leader, except me, continued to be clinically active on a regular basis. When I became CEO, I continued seeing patients initially, but could not sustain it. However, I think some level of clinical activity would have been desirable. Many of the physician leaders were not only clinically active, they were also active researchers. Clinical leaders in all disciplines should continue to be engaged to some meaningful degree in frontline care. There is no better way to identify operational issues in the care we provide.

A critical group for both identifying and fixing the day-to-day operational issues is the mid-managers. If you are at that leadership level, don't hesitate to lead from where you stand (Chapter 5). If middle managers report to you, you should understand the value and needs of this group. They are a vital link between the frontlines and upper management. This is one reason why we trained all Denver Health mid-managers as Black Belts. Every organization should train and develop this level of leaders not only because they can facilitate making the trains run on time, but also because they are the future leadership pool.

There are times when you need outside help to maximize the performance of your area. We came to this point a number of times. This help can come in the form of consultants who can provide insights or contractors who can assume the direction of certain functions. Be certain you need them, because bringing in outsiders sends a message to the organization. If you decide to go this route, you need a clear understanding of why you need them, and what they can and must bring to the table. The contracting for certain services has become common in healthcare. In the few instances in which we did this, we only contracted for a few leaders and the contractors' support services. The majority of employees remained Denver Health employees, keeping the family together.

There are a few helpful rules about hiring consultants and contractors. Unless it is something circumscribed and focused such as an Executive coach for one or two people, use an RFP process. When you are interviewing the finalists insist that the people who present the proposal will be the ones with whom you will be working. If they send the sales team or other people, they are not for you. Always deal with the highest-level person in the organization that your position permits and meet with that person regularly throughout the engagement to review performance. Don't be afraid to escalate important issues up the chain of command (of course, with your boss's knowledge). I once escalated an issue up to a meeting at the level of the corporate Board.

Thought Exercise

How are you assessing the scope and span of your area of responsibility? What needs to be improved in your area to make your trains run on time?

Laying New Tracks

Making the trains run on time clearly deserves a leader's attention. It is difficult to lay new tracks if the current operation is dysfunctional. But attending to operational issues should not be all-consuming. A leader, particularly a new one, may let precious time elapse before she thinks about new tracks. This is an error to avoid. On the other side of the coin, a new leader must avoid the temptation to start new directions simply to separate herself from the previous leader. It takes wisdom and humility to recognize when you are doing this.

Laying new tracks is about new directions, pushing boundaries, exploring the frontiers, innovation, and transformation. The goal cannot be the status quo, staying in the same place, tweaking old approaches. To push the analogy, there is no point in laying new tracks if you keep a steam engine and go to the same railway station.

How do you know which direction to go, which boundaries to push and which frontiers to explore? No one can provide you with a formula, but the first step is asking two key questions:

- Do I want real change and transformation?
- Where can my organization be the most transformational?

Do you want the organization to be a bigger caterpillar, crawling along, gobbling up everything it can, or do you want it to emerge as a butterfly and soar to a different place? Looking at much of healthcare, it seems we often choose the first. Getting bigger may grow the bottom line for your area or organization. It will likely please your boss, but it is not transformation.

You cannot and should not push every boundary. An organization has (or at least it should have) a true North Star—what is most important, what it does better than anyone else. Let the organization's North Star and your own guide the focus and direction.

If you are leading one component of the organization rather than the entire enterprise you must ask one other question, "Do the new tracks I want to lay align with where my boss and the organization are laying new tracks?" Laying spurs off the main track isn't usually a useful destination.

Thought Exercise

Do you have the right balance for your role between making the trains run on time and laying new tracks?

You can identify new frontiers and new approaches to your core work by:

- Looking both inside and outside of your organization
- Looking at other fields of innovation
- Looking at the rest of the world

Looking inside your organization lets you see where you excel and where you have the potential to offer innovative solutions to system problems. Given all the problems within American healthcare, looking to other healthcare organizations may not seem a likely place to see the future, but there are bright spots that offer new perspectives and creative solutions to old problems. Some of these bright spots include the medical–legal partnership that links legal and clinical intervention (Regenstein et al., 2018); the identification of and intervention approaches for "hot spotters," as was done in Camden, New Jersey, and replicated by others (Kaufman et al., 2014), the concept of food as a prescription (Goddu et al., 2015), and gun violence intervention in the Emergency Department on the initial visit of a victim of this violence (Carter et al., 2015). It is noteworthy that among these examples, many bright spots were looking outside their walls to the needs of the community in achieving health.

There are many industries in America's and the world's history that have been and remain innovators. If we can move past the view that "healthcare is different," we can see some new directions that are applicable in the work of caring. For example, the aviation industry helped healthcare in the quest to improve safety. Dr. Atul Gawande's Checklist Manifesto illustrates this well (Gawande, 2010). The adoption of Toyota Production Systems, *Lean*, is another example of an industry method transplanted into healthcare (Gabow and Goodman, 2015).

As a nation, we tend to believe that other countries do and should look to us for solutions, but there is much to learn from others, especially those nations that are solving healthcare problems using many fewer resources and at lower costs.

In looking inside and outside of healthcare and at other innovators, you must beware of falling into the "bandwagon" trap, the silver bullet approach, or the pursuit of solutions that lack solid data on success. Hiring strategy consultants is a frequently used way to identify new directions. Think carefully about this approach. Before you take that step ask, "Do the consultants have a broad and innovative vision that aligns with my organization's core mission?" Frequently, these groups can be in the "follow the bandwagon" mode with a cookie-cutter approach. Of course, there are groups that do offer valuable insights. If you opt to use a consultant in laying new tracks, identify one that understands your True North, and has the right goals and methods.

Denver Health could not answer that question for a strategy consultant group with a yes. Nor did we see a vision of transformation in the groups. Therefore, we did not use a strategy consultant, but we believed that new thinking and new eyes were needed. We established an advisory group that included healthcare and non-healthcare members, such as the head of Global Health for Microsoft, the Associate Director of the Fed-Ex Center for Supply Chain Management, an author, and an astronaut (Gabow et al., 2005). This helped us see new paths to healthcare innovation and led us to the adoption of *Lean*. Once we decided on a new direction, then we hired a consultant to help us operationalize it.

A useful approach to major change is to visit an existing example of what you are trying to achieve. This can convert a nay-sayer. Before a trip to Fed-Ex one physician leader said, "Our patients aren't packages." After the trip he said, "If we knew as much about our patients as Fed-Ex does about its packages, we would transform care" (Gabow and Goodman, 2015).

Thought Exercise

Where do you look to decide to lay new tracks?
The key aspects of laying new tracks are to:

■ Use others for models.
■ Seize opportunities.
■ Be bold.
■ Create a logical progression of steps.
■ Grasp that one success creates the opportunity for the next step.
■ Understand that your transformation often requires others to change.
■ Establish allies and partners.
■ Know the time horizon is not short.

Several examples at Denver Health illustrate these approaches and steps:

■ Create a new financial model.
■ Become an independent entity.
■ Adopt and adapt *Lean*.
■ Change the care delivery model.

Create a New Financial Model

Denver Health, like many safety net institutions, was in the red to the tune of $39 million. It quickly became apparent that being a poor institution was like being a poor person in our society—many people assumed our debt was due to incompetence. The Mayor wanted to sell Denver Health. Fortunately, no buyers lined up.

The solution to debt is money—no surprise, but where to find it without abandoning the core mission of caring for everyone, including the uninsured. Looking at other safety net healthcare systems and other states offered a solution, Disproportionate Share Funding (DSH). While DSH is commonly used now, at the time Colorado was not availing itself of this source of funding. As is often the case with transformation, the solution necessitated convincing others outside our organization to make some significant changes. In this case, it was convincing the chairperson of the State's powerful Joint Budget Committee. He labeled DSH "the cocaine of public hospitals." It was his goal to keep us from getting addicted. One useful approach in influencing others is to meet them where they are, both positionally and geographically. The latter involved a trip to the chairperson's district in the extreme southeastern corner of the state. At lunch in the town's only restaurant, he asked, "Why are you here?" When we said to discuss DSH, he informed us, "I hate DSH." Our response, "By the end of lunch, you will love it as much as we do." He did. This meeting was not our first with him on the subject, but this one was in his territory, a long way from our home base. (Remember the rule, never make an ask on your first meeting; Chapter 7.) In the next legislative session he introduced major DSH legislation that enabled us to create a new financial model capitalizing on our care of the uninsured, rather than an often-used approach of decreasing access to the uninsured.

Become an Independent Entity

Sustainability, growth, and innovation required Denver Health to be freed from the numerous governmental constraints that limited agility and flexibility (Gabow, 1997). A transformational journey, like any risky trip, needs a good road map. When you are making a radical change, it is useful to have a local example to help create the roadmap and use the other's success to build faith in the process and outcome. Colorado General Hospital had become an independent governmental authority, the University of Colorado Hospital, several years earlier. Their leadership helped us with many aspects of our transformation. While others can be a model, you will likely need to adapt the approach to varying degrees to your own circumstances. Denver Health's adaption of the University of Colorado Hospital's approach reflected it being a city entity rather than a state institution, and Denver Health being an integrated delivery system with many components rather than simply one hospital.

If the organizational transformation affects a public asset or one that the public highly identifies with, you need a powerful champion and advocates. Our champion was the Mayor. Our supporters were employees and many others in the community, including the business community. Any transformation will have nay-sayers. Involve them in the process early—better to have them inside than outside. Even smaller changes within an organization benefit from internal champions and the inclusion of nay-sayers in the process. This organizational transformation benefited Denver Health, the city, the community, and the patients. When an initiative at any level in the organization has a positive outcome, widely share it. That creates trust and makes future efforts easier.

Adopt and Adapt Lean

This example illustrates looking outside of healthcare for approaches to improve our care. When Denver Health began its *Lean* journey only two hospital systems had their toes in that water. Neither were safety net institutions nor were they integrated delivery systems that included everything from the paramedic services to jail healthcare. They had not instituted the model of training the middle managers as Black Belts as leaven for change. There were many consultants who had implemented *Lean* in industry, but there was a paucity of expertise in how one could do this in healthcare. This was truly laying new tracks, and the benefits were enormous. Over seven years we realized the power of harnessing the expertise of the frontline workers; we had tremendous employee engagement; we attained outstanding quality of care; we realized over $194 million of financial benefit (Gabow and Goodman, 2015). Other industries have much to teach us, so we need to scan the horizon when we lay new tracks.

Change the Care Delivery Model

The final example underscores seizing an opportunity. In 2010 as part of the Affordable Care Act, the Center for Medicare and Medicaid Innovation (CMMI) was created. The Center initially provided grant funding of up to $20 million for an innovation project. Pursuing such opportunities not only provides funding for a transformative effort, but also requires you to clarify your thinking about the problem, the solution, and the evaluation. We applied for a $20 million CMMI grant. We were awarded almost that amount. Implementing the grant changed our primary care model to match patients' needs (Johnson et al., 2015). If you are successful, your innovations not only help your organization, but they can serve as models for others.

Another important point of this example, particularly for women, is don't aim too low. This grant, my NIH Program Project grant, Denver Health's goal and motto, all underscore aiming high. When my first NIH application was turned down, my mentor, Dr. Schrier said it wasn't bold enough. I then submitted a large program project grant that was awarded and sustained for 15 years. Denver Health's motto was "Level I Care for All," not for some. Our goal was to be the model for the nation—quite audacious for a safety net hospital. When my father-in-law's home in Aspen wasn't selling, he raised the price, and it promptly sold—apparently aiming too low matters even in real estate. A local woman author I recently met wrote a short story that she could not get published so she turned it into a successful book.

Changing Landscape and Risk

Laying new tracks requires looking outside of healthcare for innovation and radical changes. A leader must always be scanning the horizon. Where are societal changes happening? What are the next decade's challenges and opportunities? At this time leaders need to ask how healthcare should respond to globalization, changing demographics, augmented intelligence, and climate change. These current issues will continue to impact every aspect and domain of healthcare so no leader can ignore them. When a leader sees such changes in the landscape, she should ask two questions:

How can I utilize these changes to create opportunities to improve the healthcare system and the health of the population?
How do I mitigate the risk inherent in the change?

The importance of assessing risk is underscored by the number of sessions on catastrophic risk at the Davos Economic Forum. They went from a few sessions in the 1990s to half the sessions in the 2010s. Leaders need disciplined and defined approaches to identify risk. There are available tools that permit assessment of financial, market, environmental, technological, physical, cyber, and reputational risk. In considering approaches to risk a leader needs to balance the likelihood of its materializing, the impact on the institution or her area if it does occur and the cost of mitigating any risk. Risk assessment should occur not only at the organizational level but to some extent in the relevant domains in your area of responsibility.

Keeping the trains running on time and laying new tracks guarantee that a leader, no matter how large the organization she manages, will never have a dull day! The challenges and the opportunities to improve what we currently do and create better health for tomorrow are what make many women step up to lead.

Chapter 9

Sharing and Receiving Lessons Learned

As discussed in the previous chapters, our healthcare system has many problems rang-ing from cost, access, disparities, and quality to barriers to the advancement of women and minorities, including bias and sexual harassment. The systems are complicated and complex. Every leader struggles to see and understand the issues and implement solutions. None of us should have to reinvent every wheel. Therefore, a leader should view sharing what she has learned as part of her responsibility to improve healthcare. Sharing helps those who receive new insights as well as those who give them. It enables others to see a path they might not otherwise have discovered and can help them avoid pitfalls that are costly in time, money, and patient outcomes. Also, when we share our learnings, others can scrutinize our work. They can identify flaws in our thinking, show us improvements to our path, and we can learn from them.

Sharing Your Lessons Learned

Barriers to Sharing

While the case for sharing is strong, there are three barriers to sharing:

- Time and effort
- Expectation
- Competition

In order to share, we need to reflect on what we have learned, realize that what we learned can be valuable to others, and develop approaches and venues for sharing.

This involves more than a casual conversation at the coffee pot, a phone call, or an email. It takes time and effort—both in short supply. These are reasons why leaders may not share as often as they should.

Of note, the barrier of expectation does not apply in academic medicine. You cannot achieve a leadership role in that domain without sharing your learnings. You must have publications to become a Section Chief, Division Head, Department Chair, or Dean. The expectation is clear for these roles. However, it is not the standard expectation for many administrative leadership positions, most C-suite roles, or CEO positions. It is not considered a core part of making the trains run on time or laying new tracks. Few, if any, of our many bosses outside of academic medicine hold us accountable for sharing. Since it is not an expectation, it falls off our to-do list. If it is not your own priority, this important leadership function won't happen.

The competitive environment in healthcare, particularly at a local or regional level, inhibits sharing freely. While people may be willing to offer a big picture concept such as documenting patients' social and community issues in order to provide comprehensive care, they don't get down to the "nitty gritty." Often gaining the competitive edge makes people keep good ideas and their implementation within their walls.

Thought Exercise

What problem have you solved that would be useful for others to know about?

How to Share

When we do commit to sharing, we often think of it as something with an external focus, some big speech, or large event. It certainly can be those, but you don't need to start there or even end there. Teaching your own team is an important and relevant aspect of sharing.

One of the most obvious ways to teach is in orientation sessions. As CEO, I always was the lead speaker at new employee orientation. There is no better way to introduce yourself to employees and to share the culture and mission of the organization. After I retired, I would meet someone who would say, "Dr. Gabow, I remember your talk at new employee orientation 10 years ago"—pretty good reinforcement.

You don't have to be the CEO to engage in orientation. Nurses seem to do this routinely in an organized and structured manner. When I was Director of Medicine, I did orientation every month with the new rotation of students, interns, and residents. It gave me an opportunity to share the importance of safety net healthcare institutions, and to provide the perspective that caring for vulnerable patients can give us in our profession and in our lives. I told them that they were being given the opportunity to see a different America than the one they lived in. Having seen it, they would be able to decide what responsibility they had in practicing their profession. Again, decades later, a physician would remind me of those sessions. Whatever group you lead, there are always new people joining your team. Don't miss the opportunity to start them off on the right foot.

Thought Exercise

How are you sharing your learnings within your organization?

Many organizations see training as a human resource function. Often external groups are hired to deliver specific education. This is appropriate and useful, but training is also a leadership function—it is a part of mentoring. One example of this at Denver Health was the expectation for the *Lean* Black Belts. They had been given training, and they were expected to become *Lean* teachers. They led RIEs, spoke at the quarterly Black Belt meetings, and often presented to outside visiting groups. This particular effort underscored the importance of mid-managers' roles.

One of my mentors, Dr. Schrier, told me the best way to crystallize my thinking was to give a presentation or write a paper. I found this to be true. People differ on whether they are more comfortable with speaking or writing (for some both are equally hard). There are many available training courses for both skills, often at your institution. Take advantage of them. You can also get feedback from your colleagues and mentors. If sharing your learning is new terrain for you, start small. Speak or write about what you know first-hand: something you have improved, why you pursued the issue, how you approached the problem, and what the outcomes were. You may think what you accomplished is unimportant and not worth sharing, but if it was a problem you encountered, others have likely encountered the same problem, and they may not have found a solution. One of my most memorable examples of this is two young faculty members who published an article in a major journal on how they helped evacuate the Denver Veteran's Administration Hospital in the middle of the night (Blaser and Ellis, 1985). You never know where such a beginning leads. Dr. Blaser went on to become Chair of a distinguished Department of Medicine.

Start your sharing in the "safest" environment by giving a presentation in your own organization. It can be as simple as sending an email to your peers that you would like to share, over a brown bag lunch, the outcome of a problem you tackled, or the "hot" items from a meeting you attended.

The next step can be addressing local groups. In the current environment, healthcare issues are top of mind for many, and people have gaps in their knowledge and want to learn. Also, the range of experiences women have had in their careers is of interest to many groups. These venues can be schools, clubs, and not-for-profit organizations. These groups are always searching for speakers. They offer a way to teach, interact, create relationships, and educate those political and community "bosses" that we all have (Chapter 7). If you are a beginning speaker, it may be helpful to have someone you know in the audience who will give you honest feedback. Someone from your communications group can be a good choice, especially if they helped arrange the lecture. This will help you improve content and style. Remember to add these lectures to your CV.

Your next stop can be a national stage. Many of us belong to professional or trade organizations. Consider being part of the planning committee for these groups' meetings, volunteering to speak, or submitting an abstract for a presentation or poster. Utilize your mentor and/or sponsor to direct you to these opportunities. This is especially important for women to establish themselves as thought leaders. If you are a scientist, consider adding your name to "Request a Woman Scientist" (Chapter 2).

Don't volunteer if you do not have the time to prepare a well-organized and well-presented lecture. It is worse to present a rambling talk than to be silent. You will spend more time and effort recovering from a poor impression than you would have invested in doing a great job. Remember a poor impression reflects not only on you, but on your organization.

Lecturing and writing are areas in which physician leaders have more experience than most leaders from administrative career paths. Similarly, individuals with significant research backgrounds tend to be comfortable in both these areas. So, they have few excuses for not doing this!

Thought Exercise

How are you sharing your learnings externally?

Many leaders have their communications group prepare their speeches. Certainly, it saves you time, but I never found that approach useful. Unless a person knows you very well, it is hard for someone to authentically capture your thinking and speaking style. However, if you find preparing and delivering a lecture difficult, your communications group can be very helpful in providing instruction and guidance.

For those new to lecturing, and even those who are experienced, practicing a lecture is worth the time. Saying it out loud can lead to a different impression of your words than reading them. When I was training fellows, and even when preparing our leadership team for key events, we practiced the presentations—no one's final version was ever the one they started with. Practice does make perfect—well, at least better. Critiquing your presentations is an appropriate function for your mentor.

Speakers debate whether to use slides or not. I have always been a slide person. Making the slides organizes my thoughts. Never put up a slide saying, "I know you can't see this," or "I know this is a busy slide." If you know it, why are you doing it? Never put up a slide and then say something completely different. The audience doesn't know whether to read the slide or listen to you. If you are using slides, only use as many as you can comfortably discuss in the time allotted. Racing to the finish line doesn't convey an organized, prepared person. While these guidelines are obvious, in my experience they are often not followed. Always save time for questions unless the event sponsor does not want a question period. The questions help you see areas you could clarify in the future and identify which points were of most interest.

An interview may seem easier than a lecture or writing a piece. It can be a bridge between a lecture and written piece, since what you say is often written for publication by the interviewer. There are a variety of interview opportunities, from your local radio station and newspapers to national news outlets and publications. Your sponsor and/or communications group can help identify and arrange these opportunities. At first glance, it seems an easy way to get your voice heard. But if you don't know what you will be asked and if you haven't organized your thoughts, it can be a challenge. Even after years of doing interviews, when I see the printed version, I often have concerns that my comments may have been too casual.

While lectures demand time and thought, published articles require more of both. As a result, they may provide a better opportunity to clarify your message. Moreover, they often have a broader reach. One approach to facilitate writing articles for publication is to do them as a team project. Many, if not most published articles have multiple authors.

Published articles can run the gamut from your own institution's newsletters, to blogs, letters to the editor and op-eds in your local paper, professional society newsletters, trade journals, peer-reviewed publications, and yes, even books. Local newsletters and trade journals, like local organizations, are often looking for interesting pieces. The benefit of peer-reviewed publications, and to a lesser extent trade journals, is that they provide feedback on both the substance and the presentation. Publications add weight to any resume. They show that you can examine questions, communicate with others, are willing to share your learnings, and are a thought leader.

Don't expect to see your work on a bestsellers list. In fact, be prepared for rejections. Don't let this upset or deter you. The first article I sent to a journal was rejected. My chief, Dr. Schrier, read the same negative reviews (and believe me they were negative) and responded, "They loved it. Call the editor and asked why he rejected it." Being a young faculty member, I did what I was told. Surprisingly, the editor not only took my call, but suggested I resubmit, and it was accepted. This little vignette underscores the important role of a mentor and willingness to persevere. However, don't expect the same result. I have had to send articles to more than one journal to get them published—but, if you keep at it, you will succeed.

Grant proposals are often viewed simply as a way to get project funding, but they also are a way to crystallize your thinking, particularly about laying new tracks (Chapter 8). Since they often involve a team, new ideas and approaches bubble up. This certainly was the case with our CMMI proposal. The submitted version was much more robust than the initial concept. Proposals also disseminate your learnings to the influencers who are evaluating the submissions. Some granting agencies have pre-submission meetings that offer an opportunity to network. Some funding agencies have follow-up meetings at which the grant recipients present their work.

Some funders publish and disseminate the results of the work on their websites or as white papers.

Another dissemination approach for your learnings that we often forget is applying for awards or prizes for yourself or your organization. Individual awards can range from local business awards to membership in honorary societies, to national or international awards. Almost all communities have a range of awards for business and community leaders. Given the role healthcare plays in the economy of communities, these are opportunities for women leaders.

If you are a woman leader or an aspiring leader, look for potential awards and ask your mentor or sponsor to nominate you. If you are in a leadership role, nominate others. I find it helpful to have the nominee write a draft nomination. They know what they have accomplished. Tell them not to be afraid to "toot their own horn." You must edit it. It needs to be your nomination.

Asking individuals to do the first draft brings up the fact that you may be asked to do such a draft. This is one reason why you must keep an updated and complete CV (Chapter 5).

Thought Exercise

What awards would you be eligible to receive? Have you asked your mentor or sponsor to nominate you?

Trade organizations often have organization-level awards. These are generally easy to submit. In the 20 years that I was CEO, Denver Health never missed submitting to the National Association of Public Hospitals' awards (now America's Essential Hospitals). While we didn't win every year, each year two or three Denver Health employees learned to write an award submission, and many saw their submission in print. Major national awards are more work and require a team effort, but they make a bigger splash, and your innovation reaches more people.

Clinical leaders, especially physician leaders at the section-head, division, or department level, have an obligation and expectation that they will continue to share their learnings in their discipline at meetings, invited lectures, and in publications. This often requires devoting less, if any, time to examining and sharing information regarding more traditional management or organization innovations. While this is challenging, it is worth doing.

Another effective way to share your organization's learning and spread innovations is to offer formal courses in areas of excellence. Denver Health started a *Lean* Academy to share our approach and successes with *Lean*. Unlike lectures or publications, these efforts give attendees a chance to see the innovation in action. If a picture is worth a thousand words, seeing the actual work being done is worth a million words. This gives your team a chance not only to develop the course and present the lectures, but also to shine—the latter is worth its weight in gold.

If you are leading from where you stand, or if you have achieved a leadership position, you have something to share. That sharing helps you and others to grow and learn. Every time you put the effort into sharing, you learn. It makes you a thought leader and can lay a path to positional leadership. Moreover, the affirmation you receive from kudos at lectures, the satisfaction of seeing your name in print, and the pride you feel from obtaining a competitive grant or receiving an award, can be potent prevention and a remedy for burnout and imposter syndrome.

Receiving Lessons Learned

The flip side of the coin of sharing what you learn is garnering learning from others. If you want to be an effective leader, you must keep learning. You can't be a great or even a good leader in 2022 with 2012 knowledge. In many ways receiving learnings from others is easier than sharing what you have learned. It primarily requires four components:

■ Curiosity
■ Commitment to life-long learning
■ Openness to a wide range of knowledge
■ Making the time

Karen DeSalvo captured these when she said, "I just love to learn." Undoubtedly this allowed her to transition from clinical leadership to be the National Coordinator for Health Information Technology.

However, as with sharing, time and effort present barriers to learning. Fortunately, the paths to life-long learning are numerous and accessible. They include blogs, online tutorials, videos, journal articles, print and audiobooks, book clubs, lectures, podcasts, professional meetings, formal courses, and visits to other institutions, or even other countries. If you are working at an academic or other large institution, lectures and courses are readily available. As discussed in Chapter 5, leadership training, including that tailored to women, is available at many institutions and professional organizations. One can also pursue advanced degrees. Denver Health's COO who had many years of experience pursued an MBA—what a role model for life-long learning.

Thought Exercise

How are you continuing to learn not only about your specific discipline, but also about healthcare and leadership?

If you are in a leadership role, there are ways to help others in this endeavor of life-long learning. Any time I came across something that I thought would be interesting to someone on my team or in the organization, I sent it to them. I was notorious for constantly sending out articles.

My team cringed whenever I attended a meeting because I would return full of information to share and ideas to pursue. In some organizations if you attend a meeting, you are expected to share a brief presentation or written report on the key learnings. This serves two purposes. It requires you to formulate what you learned, and it gives the information to those who didn't attend. If it was a meeting which several people from the organization attended, an informal brown bag lunch can be a sharing session between attendees and for your colleagues who did not attend.

Another way for a leader to facilitate learning opportunities for others is to encourage and nominate them to participate in leadership experiences. For example, we always nominated employees for the National Association of Public Hospitals' (now America's Essential Hospitals) fellowship which enabled them to learn and network. There are many such fellowships that vary in substance and time commitment. If you are an aspiring leader, ask your sponsor to nominate you for a fellowship that fits your needs.

A standard and useful approach to learning is to invite individuals to speak to your team or organization. This not only enables more people to be exposed to new ideas and a range of opinions, but familiarizes the speaker with you, your area of responsibility, and the organization. As women leaders, we must remember to have an equitable representation of women and minorities among our invited speakers. Seeing others like you as thought leaders provides encouragement for all of us.

Just as offering training at your institution gives others a chance to see innovation, going to other institutions can provide new perspectives. Several of us traveled to Sweden to see their care innovations. Of course, being able to visit another country is not something available to most of us, but there are bright spots locally and around the country (Chapter 8).

Sharing your learning and being a life-long learner should be on every leader's to-do list. This part of leadership is especially important for women—it makes them visible, gives them a place at many tables, develops them as thought leaders, and opens a path to positional leadership.

Chapter 10

Remember the Obvious

The strange contradiction about the obvious is that it is often hidden, unseen, and elusive. G. H. Hardy, a famous Cambridge University Mathematics Professor, writing a long proof on the board, began the next step with the words "It is obvious," then paused and asked, "Is it really obvious?" He left the podium for 15 minutes (remarkably the students stayed) and returned with the declaration, "Yes, it is obvious." I will adopt a more direct approach and point out what seems obvious to me after many years in healthcare leadership. Three of the most obvious aspects of life and leadership are balance, appearance, and behaviors.

Balance

Throughout a healthcare career and especially when you take on the mantle of leadership, you focus on what you need to learn, and what you need to accomplish. You are dealing with myriad tasks and many demands on your time, making it is easy to overlook other aspects of life. A phrase that has come into vogue in the last several decades to capture this tension is "work–life balance." Its intent is to remind all of us, men and women, that we should not only focus on work, but we should have time and energy for other aspects of living that make us fully human. To achieve this balance, we need to understand the value of both work and the other aspects of life and operationalize having the appropriate time for each.

Work, particularly the work those of us in healthcare are privileged to do, adds purpose and meaning to our lives and is a component of self-worth, happiness, and well-being. Work holds a particularly meaningful place for women because we have struggled collectively and individually to have equal access to this work. Yet, as women we shoulder other demands that challenge us in achieving balance.

157

When I was at an event with women who did not work outside the home, they asked me, "What do you do for yourself?" My answer was, "My work is something I do for myself." I believed that. But I think the question they were asking was if there was something else in my life that was equally important. Did I have a work–life balance? Honestly, sometimes yes and sometimes no.

The question that women often ask is, "Can I have it all?" I think the answer is, "You can have it all—a profession including leadership roles and all the other components of a happy, healthy, and rewarding life." Many women have done it and are doing it now. But it doesn't just happen. The important part in the "work–life balance" phrase is balance. Just like the gymnast who keeps her balance while doing amazing feats, it takes focus, practice, and a support team. Leah Devlin emphasized this: "It is important for women to build and create a support team around them, so they can do it all."

Over the last decades fathers are spending more time in childcare and doing household chores (Pew Research Center, 2013). However, gender equality still has not been achieved in family responsibilities. This is a challenge for women trying to achieve balance. Women, even professional women, still carry most of the household and caregiving duties (Chapter 2). A survey of over 1000 early career pediatricians revealed that women were more likely than men to have primary responsibility for 13 of 16 household chores and were less satisfied with their share of responsibilities (Starmer et al., 2019). However, neither women nor men felt they were very successful at achieving work–life balance (women, 15 percent; men 19 percent, $p = 0.05$).

Most of us who have partners in our lives want an equal partnership. What that means and how it plays out does not conform to a simple recipe, but ideally each partner in a relationship would have the same understanding. A friend once asked me how my husband and I made sure all the household responsibilities were shared 50–50 every week. I never did such a calculation. Fortunately, for us the division of labor seemed to happen naturally. But this is not always the case.

A recent *Time Magazine* poll showed that men underestimate the unpaid work that women do in managing the household and children (Barone, 2019). Men estimated that women did 20 to 40 percent more of the unpaid work. (The good news is that men acknowledged that women did more work). Women's estimate of 60 to 80 percent greater amount of work is more in line with the 67 percent estimated by the OECD (Barone, 2019). A woman physician leader and her husband tried to do a calculation of household responsibilities because he (like the men surveyed by *Time Magazine*) was unconvinced that she was doing most of the tasks. After a couple of weeks, the data clearly supported her view. But the solution was not a new division of tasks. Rather, it was to stop keeping count. It is telling and helpful to know that even Melinda and Bill Gates and Michelle and Barack Obama had this discussion (Gates, 2019; Obama, 2018). As a result, Bill shared driving the children to school, and Michelle hired some help to cook meals.

Women, both those with families, spouses, or partners, and those who are single, understand the "work" of living has many components. There are all those pesky things we all need to do: grocery shopping, laundry, and cleaning the bathroom. I started out using my working mother as an example, thinking scrubbing floors was something I personally had to do. It took several years on the balance beam to abandon that idea. If you have a spouse or partner, certainly chores can be shared. Fortunately, many professional women have the luxury of being able to pay others to help. If you can afford it, do it. As Lilly Marks has pointed out, "What you are buying is time."

One twist in the healthcare professional work–life balance is dual-career families. Overall, the number of dual-earner and dual-career families has increased in the United States over the last decades (Bureau of Labor Statistics, 2019; Career Research, 2019). This is also true in the physician workforce. A sample of over 47,000 physicians demonstrated that almost 50 percent of physicians were married to other physicians. Among male physicians, 17 percent were married to physicians, 8 percent to nurses, and 3.3 percent to other healthcare professionals; among female physicians, 31 percent were married to physicians, 0.6 percent to nurses, and 2.4 percent to other health professionals (Ly et al., 2018). For dual-physician households the balancing can start with the choice of residencies and fellowships. The complexity of dual choices (hopefully, not dueling choices) for internship and residency has been eased by the availability of couples matching (Ferrante and Mody, 2019). An examination of data on dual-physician couples from the American Community Survey showed that women, but not men, in these dual-physician families with children worked fewer hours than women in dual-physician households without children (Ly et al., 2017). While households with dual-healthcare careers have challenges, they may share a greater understanding of the demands of being a healthcare professional. Data on the frequency and implications of other dual-healthcare professionals and on same-sex healthcare professional couples are not readily available.

An important component of achieving work–life balance is to actually evaluate it (Raja et al., 2014; Schrager, 2016). Define what balance looks like for you and set goals. Step back intermittently (maybe once a month), look at your calendar and assess the balance, plan your time, ask what you could/should stop doing, and don't expect perfect balance every week or every month.

Thought Exercise

Look over your calendar for the next month. Do you think that it demonstrates work–life balance?

Children

Here is some breaking news—we are the ones who get pregnant and have the babies. You need to take care of yourself during pregnancy. Don't get exhausted—you will have that experience after the baby comes. Maternity leave was not "a thing" when

I had my children, but I was able to piece together about a month off. Fortunately, maternity leave is more common now, especially for professional women, but it is still far from universal. For example, there is a critical gap in the availability of maternity leave for those in medical training (Chapter 3). In fact, we are the only HIC that does not have paid maternity leave (Livingston, 2016). This is unlikely to change soon, as the public ranked it 21 out of 21 priorities for the administration and Congress in 2017 (Horowitz et al., 2017). If you have maternity leave, use it. If your spouse's or partner's job offers parental leave, have them take it. A new baby takes at least two FTEs!

Among the general population, mothers with household incomes greater than $75,000 per year took a median maternity leave of 12 weeks. However, among fathers who took any paternity leave the median time was only one week (Horowitz et al., 2017). But 53 percent of mothers and 59 percent of fathers wished they had taken more time off after the birth or adoption of a child. So, don't wish for after the fact, do it!

One question that arises with maternity leave is whether it hurts her career? A Canadian study examined the question comparing 12 months' leave (the norm in Canada) to 1 month. There are some data that the longer period of time off did have a negative impact on a woman's career, but there were ways to lessen that impact, such as programs for keeping connected (Hideg et al., 2018). However, the United States is very far from this time frame. It would be a step in the right direction if women in the United States had to worry about the work implications of their taking 12 months of paid leave!

For me and probably many other women, the real balancing act came when we had children. They need loving care 24/7. So how can you do that? You can't, not by yourself. There are many solutions for childcare, from extended family to live-in help to day care. If you have children, you have already explored the options. But for those who are in the stage of planning a family, it is worth detailing the choices.

One of my professional colleagues and her husband made the decision to find positions in the city where her family lived, and the grandparents provided much of the childcare. My colleague said this was the best personal and professional decision she ever made. There is another way to get to the same end—have the grandparents move to where you are. Several of my retiring colleagues have moved to the cities where their children live to help with the grandchildren. Having lived with my grandparents for much of my early life, the intergenerational bond is one of life's treasures. It is noteworthy that overall 27 percent of childcare in the United States is provided by relatives and one in five of these is a grandparent (Gerencer, 2015). How often this alternative is utilized by women in the healthcare professions or in healthcare leadership is not known.

When I moved to Colorado, one of the few women faculty members gave me the following advice, "Hire someone to come into your home, pay them a living wage, and treat it like a real job." We had one grandmotherly type for six years until my second child was three, and another wonderful woman who stayed with us until my second child went to college. I once asked my husband if we should have another child to justify this long-term support. His answer was, "Just keep her." Having a wonderful, reliable person as a constant removed so many of the stresses of balancing a demanding career with other desires and needs. It was a perfect solution for us, but again not available to everyone. Others have found that au pairs offer both in-home childcare and exposure to other cultures and languages.

Of course, there are a wide variety of day care options. If you are fortunate enough to have a day care option at your institution, that offers the great advantages of ease of bringing the children to day care and being able to "drop in."

We are seeing changes in the workplace and in society that offer new solutions. One change for spouses in the same discipline is job sharing so that one parent is always at home. Job sharing can also occur with a colleague and provide you with more flexibility. Another option is the male partner being the primary stay-at-home parent. There is growing support for full-day kindergarten which offers a partial solution for older children.

A woman can also decide to take time out of her career path. This clearly has the challenge of re-entry. While there has been some effort towards developing approaches for re-entry into the workforce for both nurses and physicians, there does not seem to be either a robust, broad-based approach or specific approaches that relate to the reason for the period of inactivity (Mark and Gupta, 2002; Varjavand et al., 2015).

All of these options (except grandparents) come at a considerable cost; some of it is direct cost, some of it is indirect in foregoing income. The direct costs are extremely high. For example, the average cost for a child in a day care center is $14,960 per year; in California it is $16,542 per year (Child Care Aware of America, 2019). This is significantly above the federal childcare tax credit. Fortunately, many women in healthcare leadership positions can afford some, if not all, of these options. For us it becomes a matter of prioritizing how to use the financial resources. Unfortunately, many of those who work in healthcare do not have such a straightforward choice. The need for and the cost of childcare is one reason why gender pay inequity, including the Motherhood Penalty is so problematic (Chapters 2 and 3). Women are better at negotiating for others than for themselves. So, when you are negotiating for salary (if you are in an institution where that is the process) think that you are negotiating for your current or future children!

The part of the mother-balancing act that was most challenging for me was school and extracurricular activities. Comparing myself to mothers who did not work outside the home (probably such comparisons are something one should not do), I never researched every aspect of my children's school to find which school was the perfect fit, or which teacher was the best, or intervened in potential or actual problems as other mothers did. These are things in which I wish I had been more engaged. I certainly was not at every soccer game or performance. It's hard not to worry about those omissions and absences.

Beyond Children

Another challenge that women face is caring for other family members, which is a role we assume more often than men (Chapter 2). Nearly half the individuals between the ages of 40 and 59 are in the sandwich generation, having financial, caregiving, and emotional support obligations to both young children and aging parents (Parker and Patten, 2013). Thirty-one percent of those with these dual responsibilities say they feel rushed all the time—no surprise there. This is precisely the age range in which many women are either preparing for or ascending to leadership positions—one more balancing trick. As with childcare, as women we need to spread the responsibility and use other resources. One resource is family medical leave which can enable you and/or your partner to care for an ill family member.

Most women who are in a leadership role or who are aspiring to that role have worried more than once (probably more than once a day) that someone who depends on her is getting short-changed—her children, her partner, or her boss. Lilly Marks observed, "If you have responsibilities for a job, spouse, and children and yourself, on any given day two or three will be underserved, but over the long term it is appropriate." A relevant testimonial on this came from my son as he was leaving for college: "Mom, I am glad you spent your life trying to help others instead of playing bridge or golf." That assuaged years of concern. We should all post a version of this above our desks.

Support

One challenge that women face regarding equity is affinity and networking (Chapter 3). Men often develop relationships through sports activities, membership in non-professional groups, and serving on Boards. Often, they have this opportunity because their wife is doing the household activities. Organized sports have been less available to women than men in the past. Although this is improving, it can be another drain on time. While participating in activities, membership in groups, and serving on Boards have value, choose such activities carefully, make certain they fit with what is important to you, and you have the support you need to give the time and energy for these.

We all need friends, especially other women, with whom we can relate and share. When I was growing up, Sunday dinner at my paternal grandparents' home was where that happened. All the grown children, their spouses, and children were there. After dinner, the men played cards and talked, and the women adjourned to another room (after they did the dishes) and shared what was on their minds. What extended families offered is rare nowadays, so we need other solutions. For me, and I expect for many professional women, our friends are our work colleagues. Spending the last 10 to 15 minutes at the end of many a day just chatting with the COO was a time to wind down with a colleague and friend. Your colleagues share a big part of your life, and they are right there. Build those relationships and supports.

Another approach is participating in women's groups with regular meetings where participants can confidentially share successes, concerns, and ask advice. The value of this is documented by Ellen Daniell in her book, *Every Other Thursday* (Daniell, 2006; Chapter 5). These groups can take some pressure off a partner to provide all the advice and support.

Thought Exercise

What is the support team that you have built for yourself? Is it sufficient?

Well-Being

There are aspects to well-being beyond balancing work with other obligations. Achieving physical, mental, and spiritual well-being are integral parts of being fully human. Doing those things that keep us healthy and whole are important. Our professional life certainly engages our minds. As discussed in Chapters 6 and 8, leaders need to be out and about, not always sitting in the office. You can rack up a lot of steps doing this. Integrating physical activities into your daily routine can help—riding a bike to work, taking the stairs, and making family time physical activities. Many institutions have on-site gyms or wellness centers. When Risa Lavizzo-Mourey was CEO at Robert Wood Johnson Foundation she often did "walking meetings," even on side-by-side treadmills!

For many of us, sleep is something we think we can cut down on without any major negative consequences. Those of us in the clinical disciplines are used to being up all night on call or working the night shift. In fact, it may have started with all-nighters in college. We think we can extend this regularly into our day-to-day adult lives. Recent information from the National Health Interview Survey revealed that lack of adequate sleep occurs in 36 percent of Americans (Khubchandani and Price, 2019). The healthcare workforce had the second-highest level of short sleep duration at 45 percent. This is not without consequences. There is a growing body of data to support the importance of adequate sleep to our physical, mental, and emotional well-being (Walker, 2017). Walker provides abundant data on the effects of inadequate sleeping on physical performance, productivity, learning, memory, agreeability, behavior control, and depression. We need to consider how this might link to harassment and burnout. Among the many startling facts provided is that drowsy driving is the cause of more vehicle accidents than those caused by alcohol or drugs combined.

Don't forget vacation. As healthcare professionals we are fortunate to have paid time off—use it and make it really time off. In the early years of my leadership career, even when I was away, I was not really gone. I kept in constant touch. Today we stay connected 24/7. At some point I gained insight. When I was on vacation I would disconnect. I would tell my team, "If the building is burning down and I am the only one who knows where the water valve is, call me. Otherwise I will hear about when I get back."

Sometimes the parts of a robust life need to be compartmentalized not by the hours of the day, or days of the month, but by years or decades. In Hindu philosophy life has four stages: the student stage where one is engaged in acquiring knowledge; the householder stage where one is focused on occupation and family; the retired stage where one is more centered on the spiritual; and the renunciation or forest stage where one detaches from material things. Unfortunately, many of the issues of balance are in stage two. For me, retirement did offer that period of spiritual growth, although I am not planning to transition into the forest hermit stage. Perhaps, those of us in the West would find life less stressful if we didn't try to pack everything into the same decade and realized there can be at least two halves of life.

If women are going to achieve balance in their lives, we need to know what balance looks like for us. We need to advocate for federal and institutional mandates for maternity and paternity leave, flexible work hours, programs for re-entering the workforce, better and more affordable childcare options, universal kindergarten, and equal pay to enable women to pay for the needed support team.

Appearance

Talking about appearance is a sensitive subject, in large part because women see this as a topic that is more often directed at them than at men and they are measured by how they look more than men are. Just think of the comments about Hillary Clinton during her presidential campaign, Serena Williams' outfits on the tennis court, or Mark Zuckerberg giving a talk in his tee-shirt and jeans while Sheryl Sandberg wears a dark suit, hose, and high heels for her TED talk. Despite the tricky ground, I am going to tread into this terrain. How we, men and women, choose to look sends a statement. We should consciously decide what statement we want to send. My grandfather told my husband and me early in our careers, "You need to dress the part." Fortunately, what it means to look the part has become more flexible in the last decades. Professional roles for women and men no longer require a dark suit and a white blouse or a starched shirt.

For both women and men, attire and appearance are linked to their role, the occasion, and the place. If you are the head of surgery or the nurse manager for the operating room, scrubs are appropriate, but they are not if you are the CFO. A man going to a black-tie event in khakis would likely draw negative comments just as would a woman in casual clothes. Even Mark Zuckerberg abandoned his hallmark hoodie for a suit and tie when he testified before Congress. Similarly, you would not want to go to the organization's picnic in a business suit. Neither a woman nor a man should go to an interview looking as if they didn't care about their appearance. A great resume can be undone by looking as if you just rolled out of bed.

How you present yourself goes beyond clothes—think hair, make-up, perfume, tattoos, and body piercings. Lilly Marks pointed out that a woman may be willing to spend for a suit, but never pay for a good haircut. She notes you "wear" your hair every day and everywhere—more than you can say for that suit! Thankfully, make-up and perfume are not as much in use as in the past, but tattoos are very common. Covering tattoos or revealing them depends upon their size, location, message, as well as with whom you will be interacting and the organization's rules and culture.

Your organization has its culture and part of that culture is an expectation about appearance. It can span from whether the workforce is required to wear uniforms to whether body piercing is acceptable. Desired appearance for physicians, other professionals, and leaders presented an interesting issue for me at Denver Health. Most of Denver Health's patients were poor, many were homeless, clothes could not be a priority for them. My question was, "What is the most respectful to the patients?" The culture had drifted to less business and more casual attire—sometimes really casual. One of my early efforts was to raise the bar, both by establishing a dress code and by example. Dress Down Fridays disappeared (Chapter 6). Costumes on Halloween were for after work except for those working in pediatrics. Job-specific uniforms became the expectation, and much to many people's dismay, no Broncos T-shirts (well, I did give in for Super Bowl appearances). I went a little too far in the early days by having women wear stockings (the men wore socks). After several years, I came in line with the rest of the culture and relented on the stockings. One role which your children can play for you in leadership is keeping you in touch with societal norms—they are always up to date.

My personal guideline was to dress in a way that presented the best face for the organization. I didn't want to embarrass myself or the organization if I was called to the Governor's office, to a press conference, or to a family at the bedside of a loved one. Just as the other managers read the books that the leadership read for our book club, the women and men managers modeled the Executive's appearance.

Thought Exercise

What is the message you want to give with your appearance?

Behaviors

Leaders' behaviors have always been important, but in today's environment of rapid and ubiquitous information sharing, it is even more important. Whether you are a male or female leader, your behavior reflects on the institution. If you are an Executive, especially the CEO, President, or Dean, the public conflates you and the institution. If you are a leader or an aspiring leader, what you say, how you say it, what you do and don't do are all relevant (Chapter 6).

Behavior both at and away from work matters. As leaders we need to remember that because something is legal doesn't mean it is appropriate. Drinking and using legal marijuana come to mind. Few would argue against a glass of wine or a cocktail at an event but being intoxicated or high crosses a line. When an employee or leader does that, we need to intervene. That intervention can be both therapeutic and disciplinary (Chapter 6).

As a leader it is important to support camaraderie and that means participating in celebrations and parties. However, there are some venues where it is better not to go.

What gets posted online matters. We have many recent, dramatic examples that illustrate that not only what you do today, but what you did 20 years ago can have an impact. In fact, it can cost you your position. You can control what you do today, but the past is gone. If there is something in your past that you should not have done or wished you hadn't done, you need to think about how to deal with it. An option is to reveal it yourself to the right people, in the right venue, at the right time, rather than wait for it to be discovered. One thing you should never do is lie about it. As my grandmother said, "Lies have short legs." They can't get very far before someone catches them. Neither should you sugar-coat it or gloss over it. If the behavior should not have happened, a genuine apology should be given, and you should be able to demonstrate that you have indeed turned over a new leaf. Your role and the circumstances will dictate to whom and when the apology should be given.

Unfortunately, many of us don't know how to apologize. Given that none of us are perfect, it is an important skill to acquire. However, like many obvious aspects of life, we see daily examples of people's inability to effectively apologize. One of the most popular books in our leadership book club was *On Apology* (Lazare, 2005). Lazare points out that a genuine apology has four parts:

- Correctly identifies who should apologize and to whom the apology must be directed
- Provides details on the offending behavior
- Recognizes the impact of the behavior
- Acknowledges that the behavior broke a moral or social contract

How often have we heard an apology that starts out, "If you were offended …"? As Lazare points out, this redirects the problem to the person to whom you are apologizing—they are thin-skinned. You did nothing wrong.

There is no denying that caring for patients and being a leader can be stressful at times. It is easy to be short with others, use inappropriate language, or lose your temper. I have done all of these. In fact, I managed to do all of them at the same time in one stressful point during the second intense day of the first national disaster drill focused in Denver. This is when understanding both apology and personal improvement can come into play. Learning to minimize or eliminate these behaviors not only made me a better leader, but also a better spouse, parent, and person.

As leaders, not only must we be aware of and manage our behaviors, but we must also observe behaviors in those we lead. When those behaviors deserve praise, we should freely give it. When those behaviors are out of line, inappropriate, wrong, unethical, or illegal, we must intervene (Chapter 6). Your intervention can range from counseling to termination, depending on the behavior. As discussed in Chapter 3, young women are looking to senior women to see how to react in situations of sexual harassment and microaggression. The first time I had to intervene with a resident who used bad language to a patient, I wondered where the line was between being a mother and a leader. Sometimes there is no line and we just need to help people see their behavior.

As leaders we have access to confidential information. We find out aspects of others' lives that can be shocking and not public knowledge. If these behaviors are inappropriate, unethical, or illegal, we cannot ignore them. We must act. However, as tempting as it may be to share this information with a close colleague or friend, it is inappropriate. Keeping this kind of information to yourself is one reason that it can feel lonely at the top.

The growing lack of civility and increased violence in society can put caregivers and their leaders into abusive and even dangerous situations. De-escalation training is useful and should be provided. On the other hand, no healthcare workers should tolerate physical violence against them. We have arrested patients and visitors in these circumstances. Sadly, healthcare institutions have been the sites of gun violence, injuries, and deaths of healthcare professionals. As leaders we must see this risk and put in place measures to help protect our workers and ourselves. One of our first steps many years ago was to add metal detectors at the entrance to the Emergency Department. We confiscated guns that otherwise would have been in the institution. Many organizations have areas of restricted access for both patient and worker protection. We must also provide both expert and peer support for the workforce after an actual or potential event.

As leaders, we must advocate for policies that address the root causes of these societal issues. These are public health issues and addressing them not only protects healthcare workers, but also our patients and the population.

Leaders need to focus on the many tasks and obligations, but we must strive for balance. There are times we will lose our balance, but if a 15-year-old gymnast can recover her balance, so can we. What would life be without challenges and opportunities to improve? Achieving balance, becoming good or even great leaders, and happy, healthy human beings requires that we remember the obvious.

Chapter 11

Reflections of Women Leaders

This book grew out of my experiences as a woman healthcare leader, but I am only one woman. There are hundreds of other women healthcare leaders in this country. Each has had her own experiences, reflections, insights, and guidance to offer to others. These varied perspectives provide more richness than any one person could provide. Therefore, I asked 12 successful women who became leaders by different paths, and who have held a broad range of roles in healthcare to share their perspectives and guidance (Table 11.1). Every woman I asked eagerly accepted.

Each leader received a list of questions in advance of the interview. Some questions were those that I was frequently asked by other women, and some were ones I thought would flesh out certain topics. I did not expect every woman to address each question and I have not provided every response from each woman. I tried to capture both their unique perspectives and their common ground. Where it seemed useful, I integrated some of their comments into the other chapters.

In what ways can women uniquely contribute to solving healthcare problems and improving the system?

These leaders held a common view that women can uniquely contribute to healthcare. They underscored many skills, talents, and experiences of women that will lead to better health and a better healthcare system when women are at the tables of leadership. Women's managing the care of their families give them a critically needed perspective. Women are masters of relationship building that facilitates solving complex healthcare problems.

"Women's role in our current society gives us a unique perspective. We see the impact of the system in its entirety. We are responsible for well care and prevention.

Table 11.1 Senior Women Leaders

Nancy Howell Agee
Current: President and CEO, Carilion Clinic
    Past: Past Chair, American Hospital Association

Kim Bimestefer
Current: Executive Director, Colorado Department of Health Care Policy and Financing
    Past: President & General Manager, Cigna Mountain States
          Board Chair & President, Cigna Healthcare of Colorado
          President, General Manager & Founder, Cigna's Taft-Hartley & Federal Business
          Segment

Evalina Burger, M.D. (B. Med. Sc.; MB Ch B.; M Med (Ortho))
Current: Professor and Robert D. Ambrosia Chair of Orthopedics, University of Colorado
          School of Medicine Anschutz Medical Campus

Linda Burnes Bolton, DrPH, RN, FAAN
Current: Senior Vice President and System Chief Health Equity Officer, Cedars Sinai
          Health System
    Past: Senior Vice President and System Chief Nursing Executive, Cedars Sinai Health
          System

Carrie L. Byington, M.D.
Current: Executive Vice President, University of California Health
    Past: (held concurrently): Jean and Thomas McMullin Professor and Dean of the College
          of Medicine and Senior Vice President for Health Sciences, Texas A&M University
          Vice Chancellor for Health Services, Texas A&M System

Karen DeSalvo, M.D.
Current: Chief Health Officer, Google Health
    Past: Acting Assistant Secretary for Health, US HHS
          National Coordinator for Health Information Technology, US HHS
          Health Commissioner, City of New Orleans

Leah McCall Devlin, DDS, MPH
Current: Professor of the Practice, UNC Chapel Hill Gillings School of Global Public Health
          Chair of the CDC Foundation Board
    Past: State Health Director for Public Health, NC Department of Health and Human
          Services

Hale Fischer-Wright, M.D., MMM, FAAP, FACMPE
Current: President & Chief Executive Officer, MGMA

Risa Lavizzo-Mourey, M.D., MBA
Current: University Professor of Population Health & Health Equity, University of Pennsylvania
    Past: CEO and President, Robert Wood Johnson Foundation

Donna Lynne
Current: CEO Columbia Doctors and COO Columbia University Medical Center
    Past: Lt.-Governor of the State of Colorado
          EVP Kaiser Foundation Health Plans

Lilly Marks
Current: Vice President for Health Affairs, University of Colorado Anschutz Medical Campus
    Past: Executive Vice Chancellor, Anschutz Medical Campus
          Senior Associate Dean, Finance & Administration, University of Colorado
          School of Medicine
          CEO, CU Medicine (formerly University Physicians, Inc.)

Nanette Santoro, M.D.
Current: Professor and E. Stewart Taylor Chair of Obstetrics and Gynecology, University
          of Colorado School of Medicine Anschutz Campus

We are the caregivers for those with chronic disease and the ones most involved with long-term care. We are the primary healthcare decision-makers. Over our lifetime we see the good and bad in healthcare from all perspectives ... Women see two generations of care. Two generations of challenges help us see the need for longer term solutions. We have less of a tendency to see only one part of it. These societal roles give us a more comprehensive perspective than others may have" (Risa Lavizzo-Mourey).

"There are differences between men and women in how they communicate, how they lead, how they use power, how they solve problems, and how they collaborate. This is not to say it is better, but it is different. Women are more collaborative and are more detail- and issue-oriented and focused. Women are the primary purchasers and coordinators of care for the family. This gives them a broader perspective on the healthcare system and the issues of access and coordination. They have an important view of the pathways of care, and where those pathways get interrupted. They see the gaps" (Lilly Marks).

"Women are the CMO, the CFO, and Chief Transportation Office. When it comes to a family's healthcare decisions—they chose the health plan; they chose the doctors; they take people there and back; they take the notes; they make the decisions. When you are leading a healthcare corporation, you better recognize that women are in charge at the customer level. If you are not meeting the needs of women, then you are missing the boat. If you are not hiring women who have walked in those shoes, then you are missing a great opportunity to understand your market" (Kim Bimestefer).

"[We] think about how pressing on one part of the system might affect another part of the system. It is not unique to women, but it is part of how we were raised and how we experience the world. Maybe it's why we are good at finding not only system-level solutions but multi-sector solutions. I don't want to overgeneralize about gender, [but] women have the humility and the capacity to see the big picture. We are good collaborators. We listen well. We find common ground not by shared solutions but by coming to shared values and principles. I have had male mentors ... who can do this, but it comes more naturally to women. We feel that if people win or the system wins, we win" (Karen DeSalvo).

"Our health system has a lot of complex issues. Women are particularly well-suited to address some of these issues because we are collaborative ... I do think women are raised to be more collaborative and to work together more cooperatively than perhaps men are raised. Our collaborative nature is important in solving the problems that we have now. They are large and diffuse problems that are deep-seated and [we] need new ways of looking at them. They need individuals and organizations to cooperate and work together. I do think that women bring that to the table in a way that is somewhat unique" (Carrie Byington).

"Women are particularly good at relationship building. We understand on some different level the importance of relationships, the significance of verbal and non-verbal communications. We have a knack for assessing problems and opportunities and putting things together. Women are especially good at giving support to and credit to others without regard for ourselves. In today's environment we need creative solutions where disparate teams come together. Women have a natural and well-honed skill in bringing people together in a positive way" (Nancy Agee).

"Women are the caregivers and the caretakers in the family. They bring that perspective to the table ... they anticipate problems and are better multi-taskers. Women have better listening skills. That ability to listen allows women to bring something different to the table in negotiations and problem-solving" (Evalina Burger).

"Part of leading is connecting with those you lead, showing compassion and concern. This is a skill that women have" (Donna Lynne).

"Most women are both passionate and compassionate and are driven to be of use to others. I believe that empowers women to engage others in the heavy-lifting work of human caring. We are committed and are willing to stand up, speak up, and reach out to achieve improvement" (Linda Burnes Bolton).

"Many times, women are the glue in families including making healthcare decisions, caring for aging parents and children. Women juggle multiple priorities all the time. That is what we have to do. Because of the need to juggle many priorities, women have developed a team-based approach to help them. This goes into the workplace. They are used to working in teams and that is where we are moving in healthcare. Many times, but not always, women are more about the work and getting the job done and less about who gets the credit" (Leah Devlin).

"All the storied institutions that are at the crossroad of change want to maintain their status. Change is an area that women handle well. Because of who we are, change has always been part of our life journey. They are capable of balancing each perspective. They can skillfully navigate different interests. Women skillfully manage the interest of partners. Seventy percent of the people in the healthcare industry are women, but only 10 percent of the Executives are, so we are an underrepresented voice in healthcare. If we keep putting the same people in the same positions, we will keep getting the same outcomes" (Halee Fischer-Wright).

"Women are uniquely disadvantaged by our healthcare system because it tends to ignore or minimize the importance of reproductive healthcare. I see tremendous opportunity ... for not only enhancing women's ability to choose when they have babies, but also in addressing their healthcare needs in advance of pregnancy. This radical model of healthcare improves women's health and the health of all their children. This would provide the biggest bang for the buck because it is the purest form of prevention and population health" (Nanette Santoro).

What made you move into a leadership role?

Some women were at the front of the parade early in life. Others grew into leadership. They were all motivated by the desire to serve more broadly and to improve both health and the healthcare system. None were motivated by money, position, or power.

"I was the eldest of 12 children so my commitment of being of use to others started at home ... I have actively engaged others on the journey [of] being of use to society and other human beings" (Linda Burnes Bolton).

"I often found myself leading. I always wanted to make things better and learn. The one time I really pressed hard for a leadership role was when Katrina occurred. I felt driven to lead because I had a clear sense of where the community should be heading, and who the actors should be, and what it would take to get there. Much of that leadership was as an influencer rather than as someone with line authority. You can lead from behind. I do leadership because I enjoy it. I like to see improvement and change. I get very energized by making something better" (Karen DeSalvo).

"I never aspired to be a leader. I had a passion to make things better and improve lives. As a medical student I did mission trips into Lesotho ... I set up a clinic in an area that was off limits to white people. I never thought of it as leadership. I thought I was just doing the right thing. When someone asked for something, I always volunteered. Over time I realized who I was and embraced it. I knew I was a leader and I started to concentrate on that" (Evalina Burger).

"My path to leadership wasn't obvious. I was always a highly opinionated kid and had disdain for people who made excuses for not getting things done. Early in residency I realized that I would be a successful physician. I was made Chief Resident, and I started to feel responsible for teams. I'm not sure I would have initially tolerated myself in a leadership role, but my residency director, and then my Chair saw leadership in me and encouraged me. When I began to see how I could leverage [my] talents to do good, I began to embrace leadership more fully and [took] on being a Chair" (Nanette Santoro).

"I never aspired to a leadership role. I have a natural inclination to get things done and to take charge of a situation. People asked me to take on an acting role as a local health officer and then as a state health officer, and then [they] asked me to take on the role permanently. I was asked to step up, and doors were opened ... [I went through them] even though I didn't think I was ready" (Leah Devlin).

"As I had more responsibility, I realized that moving up was the way to have increased impact and use my knowledge and experience. I did not seek leadership for title or power" (Lilly Marks).

"I was quite happy as an investigator and clinician ... but as I advanced through academic medicine, I realized that there were many inequities ... There were any number of issues that I felt were impacting women, and there came a point where I did not feel comfortable sitting on the sidelines, and realized that if I wanted to see change, I needed to be part of making that change happen, and that meant taking on different responsibilities and different roles. The only reason I feel compelled to enter into a leadership role is to make things better for patients, for my colleagues, for those in the pipeline" (Carrie Byington).

"Like a lot of women, I had to fight for the notion that I was a leader. Seeing problems and lack of opportunity for people. I was frustrated that people weren't seeing the problems and taking them seriously. This frustration compelled me to be a leader. It wasn't a big decision. Small decisions to step up, to take something on— it grew organically and led to leadership opportunities" (Risa Lavizzo-Mourey).

"The things that influenced me the most [were] restlessness and wanting to accomplish more than I could one patient at a time, and the notion that I could improve care on a broader scale. My experience gave me a perspective about patient care that is incredibly important" (Nancy Agee).

"I have always been a leader, even in medical school. I always said if you have a complaint, do something about it. I thought I could make more impact as an administrator than as a general pediatrician" (Halee Fischer-Wright).

"I have always felt comfortable in leadership roles—from being a [sport's team] captain as a youth ... to climbing the corporate ladder ... I preferred to be in charge. I trust my judgment. I trust myself to surround myself with people smarter than me ... I trust myself to bring the diversity I need to make decisions. When I worked for a boss ... I [was] the one raising my hand and saying I will take that on ... I wanted to make a meaningful difference. Being a leader was the way to achieve that" (Kim Bimestefer).

What helped you most on your leadership journey?

The support of others helped women on their leadership journey. Their mothers were often important role models and support for them. Mentors and colleagues played an important role as did a passion for the work.

"I had great mentors along the way who cared about what I was doing, who were encouraging, but also gave an expectation for learning and that made me a better leader. Being part of a great community of people whom I admire so much and working with them fuels my energy and passion to be an effective leader. The fact that I had taken care of patients gave me 'street cred'" (Nancy Agee).

"My mother was a wonderful role model. She loved everyone unconditionally and saw value in everyone. I watched her and she taught me. Hard work helped me. People who work hard get the baton. I can see over the horizon ... having vision helped me to be a leader. Willingness to collaborate helped me bring good ideas to the table. Approachability. People feel they can talk to me" (Karen DeSalvo).

"Mentors are essential and can provide information and support when needed. The leadership path is filled with potholes, twists, and turns. I was blessed to have several mentors early in my career, including my mother. They helped me along the leadership path. There are very few experiences in one's professional career that haven't occurred to others prior to your personal journey. Having a broad network of individuals and mentors from diverse backgrounds is essential for leaders" (Linda Burnes Bolton).

"The encouragement of mentors helped me the most. They tolerated my missteps and took the time and trouble to point them out to me, rather than let them go. They expected better of me, and that made me want to deliver. There is a thrill and reinforcement to simply getting things done and getting your team to do a great job" (Nanette Santoro).

"Having enough courage to get out of my comfort zone. Being willing to tack against convention, not always take mentors' advice. Every time I was willing to go off the standard path, I was helped in becoming a leader. Serving on corporate boards which were largely composed of men, I saw how they interacted" (Risa Lavizzo-Mourey).

"What helped me most on my leadership journey ... was being willing to take risks. If you don't take risks, you will never advance. I have been successful because I took risks. People ask me if I regret running for Governor of Colorado. The answer is definitely, no. What a great opportunity to learn" (Donna Lynne).

"Mentors and a strong team that complement you and your skills helped me in leadership. Leadership training was very helpful. The first was a ... program of 50–60 public health officers from around the country. It was transformative. It created a life-long network that was very helpful over time. The other program was for new state health officers. As part of the program you were assigned a senior state health officer to work with. I stayed connected with this woman for 20 years. These healthcare leadership jobs are rocky. It is great to have mentors and peers you can call on" (Leah Devlin).

"What helped me most was finding a peer group. I found that peer group when I became a member of ELAM, and we were assigned into learning communities. Our group was formed in 2007, and it exists today still. We have every-other-week phone calls, and we meet together in person once a year. With these seven other women going through the challenges we all face in leadership and having people to talk with and to share ideas, to get inspiration from, and get support from ... was absolutely vital on my journey. That community ... was transformational in my life" (Carrie Byington).

"I was helped most by mentors. I had advocates who supported me—[gave me] the right push at the right time. I found the other women in the ELAM leadership training ... helpful and supportive. All six people in my study group are now Chairs" (Evalina Burger).

"The most help to me has been a group of women and men who served as counselors and who served as sounding boards and strategic advisers. These are people I can go to with questions. They are invested in me, and I am in them. I didn't have mentors. I don't think mentors are helpful, but sponsors are" (Halee Fischer-Wright).

"An internal passion for the work. Having a passion for what you are doing is a great propellant over the long arc of a career. Believing in what you are doing helps you through the inevitable difficult times. Having high energy and high tolerance for stress, and being comfortable juggling competing interests. Being curious and always reaching beyond my expertise. This really propelled my career. Building credibility. I was not always the smartest person in the room, but I was always the most prepared. Over time this led people to turn to me. This made me a thought leader before I was a positional leader. Being strategic about the positions I took. I worked for people who realized my talents and gave me running room to develop them" (Lilly Marks).

"Attitude. I was always an athlete. So, I always worked hard ... play until the whistle blows ... never give up trying to win ... we win or lose as a team. My definition of 'no' was pulling more people into the room until you find your way to 'yes'. Confidence and persistence to drive change, to do things differently and creatively" (Kim Bimestefer).

What are the most important barriers for women?

Every woman leader faced barriers, both external and internal. The external barriers ranged from overt bias to cultural norms of accepted behavior. The internal barriers reflect self-doubt. Many of these women came from families they described as poor, creating financial barriers for them.

"For me the most important challenges were financial, and the strong biases in the culture I grew up in and in the medical profession against women in the medical professions in general and in the surgical disciplines in particular. There were only 3 medical schools in South Africa, and they each only took 20 women a year. I wanted to do general surgery, but I was told, 'A woman is not suited for a career in general surgery.' I only got into orthopedics on a probationary status. During this training I had taken six weeks off due to complications with the birth of my son, and I had to repeat the year. On the other hand, men took off 30 weeks for national guard duty during the five years of training and didn't have to do any extra training. In the United States the barriers occur when women get to a high level. They hit a glass ceiling in academics at the Chair and Dean level" (Evalina Burger).

"Barriers are a complicated picture. On one hand women have innate characteristics as leaders ... and being a woman had advantages sometimes. Early in my academic career, I was often the only woman in the room, so I got noticed. In retrospect, I recognize that there were subtle and not so subtle barriers I was able to overcome or didn't see. My first job offer was for a salary below the level of others. When I asked my adviser about it, he told me that since my husband was a doctor and will make plenty of money, I didn't have to worry about it. These signals make women feel not quite comfortable ... they get into your head that you are not as valuable as others. Women internalize more—women think they are not good enough. Men's activities, golf, etc., give them access to people who help them and sponsor them. This doesn't happen as much for women. On the one hand women don't have a culture of helping one another. On the other hand, we create special women's groups that can be helpful, but it can actually keep us out of the mainstream. We need to work in the mainstream" (Karen DeSalvo).

"Where I thought there were barriers, I realized many of these barriers were of my own making. There certainly are external barriers, but women often shoot themselves in the foot. One area is salary. Every job I interviewed for I was told, 'Your husband is a physician.' Every man to whom I have offered a position and quoted a salary, negotiates; women almost never do. In the business world what you are paid reflects the value that business puts on you. Ageism is much more brutal for women than for men. When women are moved out of their positions in mergers and acquisitions, if they are over 60 years old, they have much more difficulty finding a position than a man does. The leadership journey for physicians is harder than for nursing. In nursing there is a structure for leadership training and development. The physician culture is more competitive. Other physicians are a barrier. Every step I have taken in leadership, I heard, 'You are not a real physician anymore.' We get told to play down our femininity. We struggle with authenticity because we have been told we need to be a 'badass.' Part of the external problem is that there are not enough role models for the current generation" (Halee Fischer-Wright).

"Stereotypes are still a barrier to women. There is still a belief that women are not willing to work as hard as men because they have a family. Times are changing both in the workplace and in the home. There is more willingness for flexible hours, working from home, and paid family leave—making the workplace a more level playing field. But our work in breaking stereotypes and barriers is not done. Some men realize this and are helping elevate women. On the other hand, some women don't help other women. It is hard to get off the leadership path and get back on. The pay differential remains a problem. Sexuality in the workplace [remains a problem]" (Leah Devlin).

"Being somewhat invisible to the organization, or if not invisible underestimated [as] to what you can bring to the organization. One of the things I tell young women, and all women who are trying to advance, is to make sure that their boss knows what they want to do and knows what they can do. Make it explicit. I have had many men say to me, you have far exceeded my expectations, and I wonder to myself why were your expectations so low? I don't think it is conscious. I think it is an unconscious evaluation we make as human beings. We have cultural expectations of what our behavior should be like that is definitely different for men and women. I think that affects how we lead" (Carrie Byington).

"The barriers are on both sides. Women don't get called on to lead often enough. When they do get called on, they often shy away from leadership or make an excuse—I have no time; my kids need me; I can't move. So, they miss opportunities early and aren't tapped again. Women have narrower guardrails for their behavior. The higher I have moved in organizations, the narrower the guardrails. Agentic women tend to be punished for that. Women have to navigate the inherent conflict between their desire and ability to lead and the dissonance it causes in others. This double standard is difficult and damaging. Most of my women faculty are still doing more than half the housework and childcare. Women need to actively and consistently support other women. This doesn't always happen. But we also need to let women know it is OK not to be a leader" (Nanette Santoro).

"Often women are alone in a room of men as they move up the corporate ladder or they are a severe minority in the leadership team. Women lead differently and that is a good thing. However, that diversity of perspective and style is not always welcomed … Sometimes that shocks the status quo. Women have to learn to deal [effectively] with the frustration when they are not being recognized or when their voices are not being heard" (Kim Bimestefer).

"Some barriers women make for themselves. We need to be honest about that. They self-eliminate themselves from leadership. I have been on search committees where women have been the first choice and they withdrew because they felt there was a risk, or the conditions weren't perfect, or that they hadn't checked all the boxes. You have to be willing to take a risk and be comfortable with discomfort. All the other responsibilities you bear are not equally distributed. Even well-intentioned men who are committed to gender equity don't see the daily lived experience of their women colleagues. You have to organize your life and your psyche to deal with that reality and not feel guilty about pursuing a career and (not) cheating your family. Many structural barriers for getting into professions are being addressed. Women coming out of professional schools can get a job. The glass ceiling is higher but still there. Implicit bias is a now a barrier. If a woman loses a position because she was considered unsuccessful, she has more trouble bouncing back than a man does. A man can fail at multiple positions and still get another job and even a promotion" (Lilly Marks).

"When women are looking at a job if they don't have 100 percent of the criteria they won't apply. If the job asks for 10 years of experience and they have nine, they won't go for it. If men meet 60 percent of the criteria and have five years of experience, they'll go for it. One of the main challenges women face is finding the balance between being forceful and showing emotion. Women still fear expressing their emotions. They think it makes them appear weak or feminine. We perseverate in our head about how other people perceive us. Emotional intelligence is important in leadership and it is a skill woman have" (Donna Lynne).

"Many women face the barrier of underestimating their ability to make meaningful contributions in life. This self-imposed limitation often leads women to accept less … [in] where they work, go to school, or see opportunities to use their knowledge and skills in different ways within their communities and the nation. Sometimes women will limit their opportunities to lead outside their comfort zone. Women and men leaders must be willing to reach back and pull women forward who have demonstrated a willingness to lead and the capacity to do so. We need to provide support for individuals to spread their wings and soar as active members of society" (Linda Burnes Bolton).

"There is a dearth of role models, mentors, and sponsors over one's professional lifetime. It is rare for women to [have someone with a] deep commitment and belief in you. Too often we are told why something won't work for us. Even women in powerful positions still don't have the same deep network of influential people that men do. They are a notch down in the connection with real influencers. These are real barriers for women to have positions they should have" (Risa Lavizzo-Mourey).

"Women don't see as many role models, so it is hard for young women to see themselves in leadership roles. People with clinical expertise worry that they don't understand the balance sheet or the financial language, so they get intimidated" (Nancy Agee).

What are the most important leadership characteristics and skills? Are they different for men and women?

These women underscored that we have different skills and talents. They believed you need to be authentic—be who you are and be the best "you." Living your values is what enables you to lead. You must be willing to take risks. While the leadership skills may be the same for men and women, how these are manifested is different.

"Good leaders are the same regardless of gender, color, or race. The most important characteristic is honesty. You need to be honest and transparent. This is how you establish trust. If people don't trust you, you are done. Whether the news is good or bad is not the issue. Is it the truth? You need perseverance, grit, sacrifice, and you need to embrace who you are" (Evalina Burger).

"The skills are the same for men and women, but they may not have the same understanding of them. Transparency is important for trust and trust is critical. Being a good communicator is important—being able to connect the dots for people. Being able to exercise influence is a needed skill. Women don't understand this as well as men, because they haven't been in the inner sanctum. Having diverse teams. Having a willingness to solve problems—run into the fire when others are running away. The ability to inspire people" (Lilly Marks).

"Earn the trust of your people. People follow those they trust. Invest in your people, and they will invest in you. I believe my people are my greatest asset. I can't run a company alone. Clarity and concise communication around vision and priorities. Set the example for others … hard work, be prepared, master your craft. Be bold. Innovation is risky. Anyone can do more of the same. These skills are not different between men and women. Their approaches may be" (Kim Bimestefer).

"Leadership skills for men and women are mostly similar. Acknowledge your strengths and take opportunities to lead. Get out of your comfort zone. The most important skill for a female leader is learning to appreciate [your]self and your contributions to humankind. Be a giver and receiver of knowledge and skills. Be authentic … Be an active societal leader. Learn balance. You need personal refueling to prevent burnout. Maintain a sisterhood network. Be supportive and respectful of other opinions" (Linda Burnes Bolton).

"I have a brass turtle on my desk that reminds me that she needs to stick her neck out to get anywhere, and that is OK to do. Lead with your head and your heart. We are in a human business. Genuine compassion makes you stronger, not weaker. But being caught up in emotion without leading doesn't make you stronger. Be authentic and care more about what you are doing than about yourself. I am from the South, and I have a concept of magnolia leadership. A steel magnolia is someone who has a tenderness for the work but whose values are as strong and as unbendable as steel. I ascribe to servant-leadership—you are serving others so they can do their job well. I don't know that it has to be different for men and women" (Nancy Agee).

"Part of leading is connecting with those you lead, showing compassion and concern. Women should not model their behavior after men in all aspects. The most important characteristic for any leader is being willing to take a risk. If you don't take risks, you will never advance. You may be successful, or you may fail, but you will learn from failing" (Donna Lynne).

"Hard work, integrity, being ethical by design. Be collaborative and approachable. Have a vision. Be evidence-driven. Make sure people know what is expected of them. Bad experiences can teach you what not to do" (Karen De Salvo).

"I believe leaders have to be values-driven. You need to know your own values and adhere to those values. It is true for men and women. I think having integrity is vital. Your word should mean something. It is really important to have a vision for your organization or for your program ... try to build something that meets and matches your vision. I definitely look at leadership as service. These leadership skills are similar for men and women but [how they] bring these things into reality might be different for men and women" (Carrie Byington).

"You have to have a vision but be able to modify it with input from others. Inspire others. Build a team. Set an example by doing what needs to be done. Not being afraid to do whatever needs to be done yourself. Communication. Acknowledge the work of others. Remember it is about the work; it is not about you; don't take things personally. Have a sense of humor" (Leah Devlin).

"Have a clear vision and be able to articulate it with how to get there. Have a genuine commitment to improve yourself and the organization. Give others space to be creative and thrive. You can't do it all yourself. Have empathy" (Risa Lavizzo-Mourey).

"High achievement drive, high tolerance for frustration, a coherent ethical and moral stance. Charisma is important. If you start to walk in one direction, do people follow you?" (Nanette Santoro).

"Being able to see where the opportunities are. Women have much better listening skills than men. I think this makes them better strategists. You can't be a great leader without authenticity" (Halee Fischer-Wright).

What are the biggest leadership challenges and landmines? Are they different for men and women?

Every woman could identify clear challenges but the biggest challenges for these women differed, often stemming from their path to leadership.

"Building a team and driving for outcomes while you are still learning to be a CEO. The biggest landmine for men and women is around communication. It is letting expediency truncate communication" (Halee Fischer-Wright).

"My biggest challenge throughout my entire career was imposter syndrome and what it took to overcome that. [I had a] sense from the very first day of medical school that somehow a mistake was made, and I didn't really belong with this group. It would be easy for me to lose confidence. If a paper wasn't accepted … to question whether I was really smart enough or really belonged and should I keep trying. I cannot say that I was over imposter syndrome until I was a Full Professor and understood what it was and began to … realize that I had equivalent or better credentials than these people who I admired so greatly and really felt that they belonged" (Carrie Byington).

"One of my biggest challenges was accepting an Executive role when I was approached by senior leaders. I was doing quite well as a clinician and felt like the proverbial fish out of water accepting an Assistant Director role. It was difficult for me to move from serving as a peer with other clinicians to becoming their boss. I overcame this [by] being forthright and open. [A landmine is] stating or acting on a position where you are the lone wolf" (Linda Burnes Bolton).

"East coast behavior—being direct, being in a hurry was off-putting in Colorado. Becoming a Chair and winning over the department. Women tend to be more under-resourced for the job more often than men. It may be because they ask for less. One of the things that helped avoid landmines is to give senior faculty coaching" (Nanette Santoro).

"A challenge for me and for women, especially for women of color is keeping in balance all the multiple constituencies and their concerns, other women, people of color, mainstream groups, small and big political groups. Balancing these constituencies and keeping things moving is a challenge. [The biggest landmine is] taking reputational hits whether deserved or not. [It is] very hard especially for women to recover from. It happens when you are arrogant. Everyone needs to understand, protect, and enhance the reputation of the organization" (Risa Lavizzo-Mourey).

"My biggest challenge is managing myself—having self-awareness. Being aware of how you are coming across helps build relationships. Managing your own confidence level … Remember the environment can change around you and you need to be aware and understand how you fit in changing times and environment. The biggest landmine for men and women is to lose trust. Being transparent, being true to the mission of the organization, not getting pulled into your own issue. Holding the organization accountable. Recognizing that relationships are everything. Building relationships and trust are the most important part of dealing with the consequences of landmines" (Leah Devlin).

"My biggest challenge is frustration—being a strategist and other people can't see it; being a risk-taker and other people are afraid of change. You have to get really good at bringing people along. How do you bring people along so they can see everything you see?" (Kim Bimestefer).

"For me as a leader the biggest challenges have been two-fold and they are related. Not knowing what I don't know and how to find out. That is the second part. Leadership can be isolating. You may not be the first to know something; in fact, you may be the last to know. How do you make sure you are in touch and have good communication channels? That you know where potential issues are and [having] people willing to bring them to you. As you get farther from the point of the spear, there are more opportunities for things to go awry. Another challenge or landmine is when you want to brainstorm, and you are thinking out loud with a group and the next thing you hear is that someone assumes that is the direction. It is hard for a leader to just muse about something" (Nancy Agee).

"[My biggest challenge] was not having a terminal degree in an academic center and building my credibility. How can I show I have value although I wasn't in the M.D. club? [The biggest landmine is] not understanding the politics of power and control. You can understand the problem but are not able to execute on your plan because [of not] understanding human behavior. Not dealing with problems in a timely way. You need to understand not only individual but also institutional conflicts of interest and act on that" (Lilly Marks).

What do you look for in hiring a team?

Successful leaders place great weight on individuals with shared values, a sense of mission, and a cultural fit. They looked for those who could complement their skills and those of the team.

"They must resonate with the vision and values of the organization. [They need to be] smarter than me in some ways and complement my weaknesses. You have to be able to trust that they will have good judgment when it matters. They need to believe in teams and be willing to work in a team" (Risa Lavizzo-Mourey).

"Integrity is foundational. Passion, value system, energy, courage, willingness to disagree with me, challenge my thinking. I am not so concerned about past experience that fits in a box, but rather do they have the inherent characteristics that will make them successful no matter what the job" (Lilly Marks).

"Smart—smarter than me, values, mission-driven, love to learn. [They] may not be the very best X, but they want to be the best. I love to hire people who are unsung or unrecognized talent. They bring a fresh vision. If you shine a light on them, you can watch them bloom. I have an intentional goal for diversity, especially for people of color. If I don't have the right network, I find the right network. Put your mind to make the organization look like the country and the people they serve" (Karen DeSalvo).

"I look for people who are incredibly smart. I look for people who have experience and actually made things happen, doers, people who can show a record of completing things, doing things … people who are willing to work as part of a team, and to really respect others on the team and to work together. We need to broaden our perspective on credentials. We have to recognize that those very straight trajectories are not open to women and minorities. Those candidates will have other experiences that … might have given similar growth opportunities" (Carrie Byington).

"Proven record of experience in the area where I need [their] skills. Time tested. Can-do attitude and ethics. I can teach a lot of things. I can't teach good attitude. Ethics is the same. I want individuals who will stick around, become part of the team, invest in themselves, in our organization and our mission. Passion—I want them … to see themselves making a difference" (Kim Bimestefer).

"Work experience and track record matter. Complement my strengths and weaknesses. Complement and add value to the team. Interpersonal skills—are they someone you want to work with? Reference checks including social media" (Leah Devlin).

"Cultural fit. I ask three questions: Can they do the job—do they have the skills and maturity? Will they do the job—do they have the motivation? Can I stand to work with them?" (Halee Fischer-Wright)

"I look for communication skills, maintenance of technical knowledge, and negotiating skills. We are in highly matrixed organizations and everything is a negotiation" (Nanette Santoro).

"I look for people who are smart, talented, experienced, more importantly curiosity, courage to do the right thing, being life-long learners, no yes-people. I need people to tell me what they are really thinking but when we walk out of the room, we walk out as a team. I want people who have passion and joy in their work, who have a sense of humor, who understand that we take our work seriously, but ourselves not so much. I want people who take a risk without being reckless. I used to pride myself on being agnostic to color and gender, but I am now more intentional about diversity. Seek out more candidates for a position so I can find diversity. The only way we can make progress is ... to become more intentional" (Nancy Agee).

How do you create institutional change?

Healthcare institutions are large, complex organizations and changing their direction is not easy. Experienced leaders realize it takes a well-thought-out approach and that it doesn't happen quickly. They emphasized the importance of having the right people and getting people on board with the change. Communication and dialogue play a central role in helping people to embrace change.

"The right vision, the right path, and the right people. Being consistent, keep focused, be disciplined. One of the hardest things I did [was] letting people go— people who did their job for many years but didn't want to change. [Changing an institution] takes five to seven years" (Halee Fischer-Wright).

"You need a three-pronged approach. Your team—committed to change. No mixed messages from the leadership team. You need to move change from the middle. The middle [managers] are important in giving feedback to the Executives, and they influence those who report to them. You need metrics that give insight into what is going on. The bigger the organization the more important this is. You need to take a long view—10 years is about right" (Risa Lavizzo-Mourey).

"Create a culture for the important work to be done. A paradox for me has been that healthcare providers can change ... in a nanosecond if the patient's condition warrants but ask them to change ... their office—oh, my goodness. You need to connect the dots for them—connect the why with the how. Engaging people ... to make things better. Leadership takes patience, appreciating where people are. Communicate, communicate, communicate. Find ways for people to really hear you. It is powerful to have some champions. Celebrate small victories and give people credit so they have the confidence to move forward" (Nancy Agee).

"Start by figuring out where people think the organization is and where they think they are going. Why does the organization exist? Why does the organization matter? Talk to people at all levels of the organization. Find out who understands that the organization needs change—where the bright stars are in the organization because you are going to need them. Find out who wants to go with you. You need a strategic plan and metrics. You need to help the people who aren't on board to exit in the least disruptive way. Most of the people who had to leave, I still had a good relationship with. Make sure there are people coming in behind them to do the work" (Karen DeSalvo).

"You need to look at what is good and what is bad. The way to change is through structure, process, and culture. You need to meet with people. You need to get to change piece by piece. You need to give people expectations and the tools to be successful" (Evalina Burger).

"It took a small crowd of loyal faculty, multiple visioning exercises, and then just plodding forward, dragging the nay-sayers with us, and coping with some inevitable loss of faculty and staff along the way" (Nanette Santoro).

"You need to engage the members of the organization in a focused effort to answer five questions: Why is change necessary? What is the anticipated benefit to the team and our customers? How long will it take to implement the change? What are the potential advantages and disadvantages? How will we know if a successful change has been adopted by all?" (Linda Burnes Bolton).

"Hire a few key people. Timing is important—take advantage of the honeymoon period. Change can be evolutionary and incremental or revolutionary. In evolutionary change you ... need to say this is where we are going and then talk about how we are going to get there. Be content with small incremental change that takes you along the path. Be ready to go the distance. We were in it for the long haul. Focus on what you want to be remembered for" (Leah Devlin).

"Trust and integrity are the foundation for everything you want to do. They are the great enabler for change. Be transparent, be a good communicator, and be a good educator. If you give people good information that is accurate, consistent, reliable, understandable and relevant, you can have a real conversation about the problem and the solution. Most people want to do the right thing. Getting people to change is to help them understand reality. Don't make the problem so big that people can't grasp it. By breaking the problem into small steps, you can deliver a lot of change. It is not a grand slam; it's a bunch of base hits" (Lilly Marks).

"Change is vital for the evolution of organizations. It is very uncomfortable sometimes, yet necessary ... having data that are reliable and open for people to examine and to become comfortable with I think can help drive the change. If we can see a problem, and people agree that it is an issue, and we have data that we can track, and show that we are making progress I think that goes a long way towards enabling change or getting people ready for change. The other thing ... is the socialization of the change and … that takes time. Winning over champions for change that people trust … is really important. Build those relationships and help people come along with you together. There always are … casualties with change" (Carrie Byington).

"Invite everyone to be part of the solution, empowering them and recognizing that they had answers. Communicating where we are going and how they fit in. Consistency, communication, valuing everybody, making the plan together, and constant communication of where we are against that plan. Hiring [is important]—the right people, in the right place. I don't believe in firing people. I believe everybody has gifts, and we can find the right place for them. [But] there are people who do things that are not tolerable" (Kim Bimestefer).

"Leadership is not about preserving how the organization has operated. You need to look at whom you are serving and ask what they want. You have to ask that question. The things that have been useful to me have been … data. One of the important approaches to use to create change … is to look outside the organization. Always look at what your competitors are focusing on. Organizations die because they didn't watch their competitors. While they were doing things the same way, their competitors evolved. If you are staying the same and [others] are moving ahead, you will be left behind" (Donna Lynne).

Appendix

Denver Health was established in 1860 when Denver was only a mining camp. Over the ensuing decades, the city leaders built it into a model safety net institution serving not only Denver but all of Colorado. In 1997 Denver Health became an independent governmental entity governed by a Board appointed by the Mayor.

The following statistics are from the last available year (2018 or 2019).

Denver Health is a highly integrated public safety net healthcare system. Its components include:

- 555-bed hospital with Level I trauma center, neonatal intensive care, inpatient adult and adolescent psychiatric units—24,621 admissions
- Nine federally qualified community health centers—585,263 visits
- Eighteen school-based clinics
- Denver public health department—65,690 visits
- Denver paramedics and ambulance service—117,630 emergency responses and 76,000 patient transports
- 100-bed non-medical detoxification center—38,924 encounters
- Poison and drug call center—113,898 calls
- Healthcare services for City/County jail
- HMO serving Denver Health and Denver city employees, Medicaid, Medicare, Child Health Plan, and the Health Exchange

Denver Health provides care to a large percentage of Denver's population:

- 220,000 patients served; 930,000 total visits.
- 72 percent of patient encounters are to patients from minority communities.
- One third of Denver population (adults and children) receive care in the system.
- One third of Denver's babies were born at Denver Health.

Denver Health delivers high-quality care:

- 97% trauma survival
- 0.58 Observed-to-expected mortality (i.e. 42% lower than expected)

- 65% Blood pressure control among patients with hypertension
- 83% Childhood immunization (19 vaccines before age 3 years)
- 88% Adolescent immunization (3 vaccines age 13-17)
- 0% Early elective delivery between 37-39 weeks gestation

Denver Health is a major community anchor institution:

- $1 billion operating budget.
- Gross revenue is distributed across Medicaid (46%), Medicare (21%), Commercial/contracts (18%), Unsponsored (14%), Correctional (1%).
- Unsponsored care—$230 million.
- 7,000 employees, including 422 fulltime physicians.

Denver Health is a major teaching institution:

- All physicians have academic appointments at the University of Colorado School of Medicine.
- 970 interns, residents and fellows.
- 781 nursing students have clinical rotations.
- 120 other student trainees have clinical rotations.
- Training in 34 different health professions.

References

Adesoye, Taiwo, Christina Mangurian, Esther K. Choo, Christina Girgis, Hala Sabry-Elnaggar, and Eleni Linos. "Perceived discrimination experienced by physician mothers and desired workplace changes: A cross-sectional survey." *JAMA Internal Medicine* 177, no. 7 (2017): 1033–1036.

Aguilar, Aurora. "Editorial: How this congress might redefine women's issues." *Modern Healthcare.* January 10, 2019.

Amazing Women in History, s.v. "Elizabeth Blackwell, M.D., America's first female doctor." October 31, 2012. https://amazingwomeninhistory.com/elizabeth-blackwell-first-female-doctor/. Accessed June 19, 2018.

American Academy of Pediatrics and Pediatric Policy Council. "Leading pediatric groups call for congressional action on paid family leave." 2017. https://www.aap.org/en-us/about-the-aap/aap-press-room/Pages/AAPPPCFamilyLeaveAct.aspx. Accessed July 17, 2019.

American Association of Colleges of Nursing. "Nursing fact sheet." 2019. https://www.aacnnursing.org/News-Information/Fact-Sheets/Nursing-Fact-Sheet. Accessed May 25, 2019.

American Association of Medical Colleges. *AAMC Data Book: Medical Schools and Teaching Hospitals by the Numbers.* Washington, D.C.: AAMC, 2017.

American Association of Medical Colleges. "U.S. medical school faculty, 2018." 2019. https://www.aamc.org/data/facultyroster/reports/494946/usmsf18.html. Accessed May 26, 2019.

American Association of University Women. "The simple truth about the gender pay gap." *Fall 2018 Edition.* https://www.aauw.org/research/the-simple-truth-about-the-gender-pay-gap/. Accessed July 12, 2019.

American College of Healthcare Executives. "A comparison of career attainments of men and women healthcare executives." November, 2018. https://www.ache.org/learning-center/research/about-the-workplace/gender-studies/a-comparison-of-the-career-attainments-of-men-and-women-healthcare-executives. Accessed July 12, 2019.

AMN Healthcare. "2017 Survey of registered nurses: Viewpoints on leadership, nursing shortages, and their profession." 2017. https://www.amnhealthcare.com/uploadedFiles/MainSite/Content/Campaigns/AMN%20Healthcare%202017%20RN%20Survey%20-%20Full%20Report.pdf. Accessed May 25, 2019.

Anderson, Gerard F., Peter Hussey, and Varduhi Petrosyan. "It's still the prices, stupid: Why the US spends so much on health care, and a tribute to Uwe Reinhardt." *Health Affairs* 38, no. 1 (2019): 87–95.

Anderson, Gerard F., Uwe E. Reinhardt, Peter S. Hussey, and Varduhi Petrosyan. "It's the prices, stupid: Why the United States is so different from other countries." *Health Affairs* 22, no. 3 (2003): 89–105.

Anderson, Timothy S., Chester B. Good, and Walid F. Gellad. "Prevalence and compensation of academic leaders, professors, and trustees on publicly traded US healthcare company boards of directors: Cross sectional study." *BMJ* 351 (2015): h4826.

American Organization of Nurse Executives (2016). AONE Salary and Compensation Study | 2016. Chicago, IL: American Organization of Nurse Executives. Accessed June 25, 2019.

Artiga, Samantha, Julia Foutz, Elizabeth Cornachione, and Rachel Garfield. "Key facts on health and health care by race and ethnicity." *Kaiser Family Foundation* 7 (2016). https://www.kff.org/.../key-facts-on-health-and-health-care-by-race-and-ethnicity/ Accessed May 20, 2019.

Auerbach, David, P. Buerhaus, D. Staiger, and L. Skinner. "Data brief update: Current trend of men in nursing." *Centre for Interdisciplinary Health-Workforce Studies* (2017). http://healthworkforcestudies.com/publications-data/data_brief_update_current_ trends_of_men_in_nursing.html. Accessed June 25, 2019.

Bannow, Tara. "Detailed rules, transparency should define health system CEOs' outside directorships." *Modern Healthcare*. December 8, 2018.

Barone, Emily. "Many American men have a skewed view of gender inequality, Time poll finds." *Time*. September 26, 2019. https://time.com/5667397/gender-equality-opinions/. Accessed September 29, 2019.

Bazelon, Emily. "A seat at the head of the table." *The New York Times Magazine*. February 24, 2019.

Beard, Myron, and Alan Weiss. *The DNA of Leadership: Creating Healthy Leaders and Vibrant Organizations*. New York: Business Expert Press, 2017.

Bertakis, Klea D., and Rahman Azari. "Patient-centered care: The influence of patient and resident physician gender and gender concordance in primary care." *Journal of Women's Health* 21, no. 3 (2012): 326–333.

Berwick, Donald M. "Elusive waste: The Fermi paradox in US health care." *JAMA* 322, no. 15 (2019): 1458–1459.

Besser, Richard, and Patricia Gabow. "Commentary: Health systems should look within to address social determinants." *Modern Healthcare*. December 13, 2018.

Blaser, Martin J., and Richard T. Ellison III. "Rapid nighttime evacuation of a veteran's hospital." *The Journal of Emergency Medicine* 3, no. 5 (1985): 387–394.

Bloomberg Gender Equity Index. 2019. https://data.bloomberglp.com/company/sites/46 /2019/01/20094_2019_GEI_brochure_revamp_V15-2.pdf. Accessed June 26, 2019.

Boozary, Andrew S., Yevgeniy Feyman, Uwe E. Reinhardt, and Ashish K. Jha. "The Association Between Hospital Concentration and Insurance Premiums in ACA Marketplaces." *Health Affairs* 38, no. 4 (2019): 668–674.

Bradley, Elizabeth H., Maureen Canavan, Erika Rogan, Kristina Talbert-Slagle, Chima Ndumele, Lauren Taylor, and Leslie A. Curry. "Variation in health outcomes: The role of spending on social services, public health, and health care, 2000–09." *Health Affairs* 35, no. 5 (2016): 760–768.

Brooks Jr., Frederick P. *The Mythical Man-Month: Essays on Software Engineering, Anniversary Edition, 2/E*. India: Pearson Education, 1995.

Brotherton, Sarah E., and Sylvia I. Etzel. "Graduate medical education, 2015–2016." *JAMA* 316, no. 21 (2016): 2291–2310.

Brown, S. Max. "Real leadership: The power of humility." In *Character Based Leader: Instigating a Leadership Revolution …One Person at a Time*, eds. Tara Alemany, Deb Costello, and Don Shapiro. Indianapolis: Dog Ear Publishing, 2012.

Bureau of Labor Statistics. *Health Care*. November 2009. https://www.bls.gov/spotlight/2009/health_care/. Accessed August 8, 2019.

Bureau of Labor Statistics. "BLS Reports. Highlights of women's earnings in 2016." 2017. https://www.bls.gov/opub/reports/womens-earnings/2016/home.htm. Accessed July 3, 2018.

Bureau of Labor Statistics. "Employee Benefits." July 20, 2018. https://www.bls.gov/news.release/pdf/ebs2.pdf. Accessed August 8, 2019.

Bureau of Labor Statistics. "Families by presence and relationship of employed members by family type, 2017–2018." *Economic News Release*. Accessed September 29, 2019.

Carayon, P., Christine Cassel, and Victor J. Dzau. "Improving the system to support clinician well-being and provide better patient care." *JAMA*. Published online October 23, 2019.

Career Research. "Two career relationships." http://career.iresearchnet.com/career-development/two-career-relationships/. Accessed September 25, 2019.

Carnes, Molly, Patricia G. Devine, Linda Baier Manwell, Angela Byars-Winston, Eve Fine, Cecilia E. Ford, Patrick Forscher et al. "Effect of an intervention to break the gender bias habit for faculty at one institution: A cluster randomized, controlled trial." *Academic Medicine: Journal of the Association of American Medical Colleges* 90, no. 2 (2015): 221.

Carter, Patrick M., Maureen A. Walton, Douglas R. Roehler, Jason Goldstick, Marc A. Zimmerman, Frederic C. Blow, and Rebecca M. Cunningham. "Firearm violence among high-risk emergency department youth after an assault injury." *Pediatrics* 135, no. 5 (2015): 805–815.

Castellucci, Maria. "Women still a rarity in high-paying surgical specialties." *Modern Healthcare*. July 28, 2018.

Castellucci, Maria. "Healthcare leaders continue to overlook assault and discrimination." *Modern Healthcare*. August 12, 2019.

Catalyst. "The bottom line: Connecting corporate performance and gender diversity." 2004. info@catalystwomen.org. Accessed May 22, 2019.

Center for American Women and Politics. "Women in elected office 2019." https://cawp.rutgers.edu/women-elective-office-2019. Accessed January 17, 2019.

Centers for Disease Control and Prevention. "Achievements in public health, 1900–1999: Healthier mothers and babies." *Morbidity and Mortality Weekly Report* 48, no. 38 (1999): 849–858. https://www.cdc.gov/mmwr/preview/mmwrhtml/mm4838a2.htm. Accessed May 23, 2019.

Cervantes, Lilia, Delphine Tuot, Rajeev Raghavan, Stuart Linas, Jeff Zoucha, Lena Sweeney, Chandan Vangala et al. "Association of emergency-only vs standard hemodialysis with mortality and health care use among undocumented immigrants with end-stage renal disease." *JAMA Internal Medicine* 178, no. 2 (2018): 188–195.

Chetty, Raj, Michael Stepner, Sarah Abraham, Shelby Lin, Benjamin Scuderi, Nicholas Turner, Augustin Bergeron, and David Cutler. "The association between income and life expectancy in the United States, 2001–2014." *JAMA* 315, no. 16 (2016): 1750–1766.

Child Care Aware of America. "The US and the High Cost of Child Care 2018 Report." https://cdn2.hubspot.net/hubfs/3957809/COCreport2018_1.pdf. Accessed October 3, 2019.

Clance, Pauline Rose, and Suzanne Ament Imes. "The imposter phenomenon in high achieving women: Dynamics and therapeutic intervention." *Psychotherapy: Theory, Research & Practice* 15, no. 3 (1978): 241–247.

Collins, Francis. "Time to end the manel tradition." *The NIH Director.* June 12, 2019. https://www.nih.gov/about-nih/who-we-are/nih-director/statements/time-end-manel-tradition. Accessed June 29, 2019.

Colorado Department of Labor and Employment. https://www. colorado.gov/cdle. Accessed October 19, 2018.

Conant, Eve. "The best and the worst countries to be a woman." *National Geographic.* October 2019. https://www.nationalgeographic.com/culture/2019/10/peril-progress-prosperity-womens-well-being-around-the-world-feature/#feature. Accessed October 17, 2019.

Connelly, Maureen T., Amy M. Sullivan, Manuel Chinchilla, Margaret L. Dale, S. Jean Emans, Carol Cooperman Nadelson, Malkah Tolpin Notman, Nancy J. Tarbell, Corwin M. Zigler, and Eleanor G. Shore. "The impact of a junior faculty fellowship award on academic advancement and retention." *Academic Medicine: Journal of the Association of American Medical Colleges* 92, no. 8 (2017): 1160–1167.

Correll, Shelley, and Caroline Simard. "Vague feedback is holding women back." *Harvard Business Review* 94 no 4 (2016):2-5.

Correll, Shelly, Stephen Benard, and In Paik, "In getting a job; Is there a motherhood penalty?" *Gender Action Portal Harvard Kennedy School.* http://gap.hks.harvard.edu/getting-job-there-motherhood-penalty. Accessed September 11, 2018.

Council on Foreign Relations. "Women's participation in peace processes." *CFR Interactives.* January 30, 2019. https://www.cfr.org/interactive/womens-participation-in-peace-processes. Accessed August 11, 2019.

County Health Rankings and Road Map. (2019). *Robert Wood Johnson Foundation.* http://www.countyhealthrankings.org/. Accessed May 21, 2019.

Crandall, Carolyn J., and Edward Livingston. "Women's Health: A New JAMA Clinical Insights Series." *JAMA* 321, no. 17 (2019): 1676.

Cua, Santino, Susan Moffatt-Bruce, and Susan White. "Reputation and the best hospital rankings: What does it really mean?" *American Journal of Medical Quality* 32, no. 6 (2017): 632–637.

Curtin, Melanie. "25 Oprah Winfrey quotes that will empower you (and make you laugh)." *Inc. This Morning.* https://www.inc.com/melanie-curtin/25-oprah-winfrey-quotes-that-will-empower-you-and-make-you-laugh.html. Accessed July 28, 2019.

Dahrouge, Simone, Emily Seale, William Hogg, Grant Russell, Jaime Younger, Elizabeth Muggah, David Ponka, and Jay Mercer. "A comprehensive assessment of family physician gender and quality of care." *Medical Care* 54, no. 3 (2016): 277–286.

Daniell, Ellen. *Every Other Thursday: Stories and Strategies from Successful Women Scientists.* New Haven: Yale University Press, 2006.

DeChant, Paul, and Diane W. Shannon. *Preventing Physician Burnout: Curing the Chaos and Returning Joy to the Practice of Medicine.* North Charleston: CreateSpace Independent Publishing Platform, 2016.

Desmond, Matthew. *Evicted: Poverty and Profit in the American City.* New York: Broadway Books, 2016.

DeWolf, Mark. "12 stats about working women." *U.S. Department of Labor Blog.* March 1, 2017.

Diamond, Dan. "Women make up 80% of the health care workers-but just 40% of executives." *Daily Briefing Blog Advisory Board.* August 26, 2014. https://www.advisory.com/daily-briefing/blog/2014/08/women-in-leadership. Accessed July 5, 2018.

Diaz, Monica. "Exploring integrity and leadership." In *Character Based Leader: Instigating a Leadership Revolution …One Person at a Time*, eds. Tara Alemany, Deb Costello, and Don Shapiro. Indianapolis: Dog Ear Publishing, 2012.

Donnelly, Laura. "NHS hospital bosses given pay rises worth more than a nurse's annual salary." *Daily Telegraph.* January 2, 2016. https://www.telegraph.co.uk/news/health/12077917/NHS-hospital-bosses-given-pay-rises-worth-more-than-a-nurses-annual-salary.html. Accessed May 14, 2019.

Donovan, Sarah. "Paid family leave in the United States." *Congressional Research Services.* 2019. https://crsreports.congress.gov. Accessed July 17, 2019.

Doximity. "2019 physician compensation report: Third annual survey." 2019. https://s3.amazonaws.com/s3.doximity.com/press/doximity_third_annual_physician_compensation_report_round4.pdf. Accessed May 27, 2019.

Dyer, Owen. "US life expectancy falls for third year in a row." *BMJ* 363 (2018): 5118.

Dyrbye, Liselotte N., Sara E. Burke, Rachel R. Hardeman, Jeph Herrin, Natalie M. Wittlin, Mark Yeazel, John F. Dovidio et al. "Association of clinical specialty with symptoms of burnout and career choice regret among US resident physicians." *JAMA* 320, no. 11 (2018): 1114–1130.

Dzau, Victor J., and Paula A. Johnson. "Ending sexual harassment in academic medicine." *New England Journal of Medicine* 379, no. 17 (2018): 1589–1591.

Equal Rights Amendment. ERA. https://www.equalrightsamendment.org/. Accessed June 29, 2019.

Executive Leadership in Academic Medicine. "Fast facts." https://drexel.edu/medicine/academics/womens-health-and-leadership/elam/. Accessed July 31, 2019.

ExploreHealthCareers. "Health administrator." https://explorehealthcareers.org/career/health-administration-management/health-administrator/. Accessed August 13, 2019.

Family Caregiver Alliance. "Caregiver statistics: Demographics." 2019. https://www.caregiver.org/caregiver-statistics-demographics. Accessed June 15, 2019.

Ferrante, Lauren, and Lona Mody. "Dual-physician households: Strategies for the 21st century." *JAMA* 321, no. 22 (2019): 2161–2162.

Fleming, Geoffrey M., Jill H. Simmons, Meng Xu, Sabina B. Gesell, Rebekah F. Brown, William B. Cutrer, Joseph Gigante, and William O. Cooper. "A facilitated peer mentoring program for junior faculty to promote professional development and peer networking." *Academic Medicine: Journal of the Association of American Medical Colleges* 90, no. 6 (2015): 819.

Freudenberger, Herbert J. "Staff burn-out." *Journal of Social Issues* 30, no. 1 (1974): 159–165.

Freudenberger, Herbert J., and Geraldine Richelson. *The High Cost of High Achievement.* New York: Paperback-Bantam Books, 1980.

Gabow, Patricia A. "Life is a series of useful lessons." In *Women in Medicine and Management: A Mentoring Guide*, ed. Deborah M. Shlian. Tampa: American College of Physician Executives, 1995.

Gabow, Patricia A. "Perspective: Denver Health: Initiatives for survival." *Health Affairs* 16, no. 4 (1997): 24–26.

Gabow, Patricia A. "From the bedside to the boardroom." *Seminars in Nephrology* 19, no. 2 (1999): 109–114.

Gabow, Patricia A. "Life is a series of useful lessons." In *Lessons Learned: Stories from Women in Medical Management*, ed. Deborah M. Shlian. Tampa: American College of Physician Executives, 2012.

Gabow, Patricia A., and Philip L. Goodman. *The Lean Prescription: Powerful Medicine for Our Ailing Healthcare System.* Boca Raton: CRC Press, 2015.

Gabow, Patricia A., Sheri Eisert, Amit Karkanis, and Andrew Knight. "A toolkit for redesign in health care." *Agency for Healthcare Research and Quality* (2005).

Gabow, Patty. "The ability to see the truth." In *The Heart of Leadership: Inspiration and Practical Guidance for Transforming Your Health Care Organization*, eds. M. Barbara Balik, and Jack A. Gilbert. Chicago: AHA Press, 2010.

GAO. "Drug safety: Most drugs withdrawn in recent years had greater health risks for women." 2001. https://www.gao.gov/assets/100/90642.pdf. Accessed May 24, 2019.

Gates, Melinda. *The Moment of Lift: How Empowering Women Changes the World*. New York: Flatiron Books, 2019.

Gawande, Atul. *Checklist Manifesto: How to Get Things Right*. New York: Metropolitan Books. Henry Holt and Company, LLC, 2010.

Gerencer, Tom. "The exploding cost of childcare in the U.S." *Money Nation*. September 1, 2015. Accessed October 22, 2019.

Ginther, Donna K., Shulamit Kahn, and Walter T. Schaffer. "Gender, race/ethnicity, and National Institutes of Health R01 research awards: Is there evidence of a double bind for women of color?" *Academic Medicine: Journal of the Association of American Medical Colleges* 91, no. 8 (2016): 1098–1107.

Goddu, Anna P., Tonya S. Roberson, Katie E. Raffel, Marshall H. Chin, and Monica E. Peek. "Food Rx: A community–university partnership to prescribe healthy eating on the South Side of Chicago." *Journal of Prevention & Intervention in the Community* 43, no. 2 (2015): 148–162.

Gonzales, Selena, Marco Ramirez, and Bradley Sawyer. "How does U.S. life expectancy compare to other countries?" *Peterson-Kaiser Health Tracker*. April 4, 2019. https://www.healthsystemtracker.org/chart-collection/u-s-life-expectancy-compare-countries/ Accessed July 7, 2019.

Goodwin, Doris Kearns. *Team of Rivals: The Political Genius of Abraham Lincoln*. London: Penguin UK, 2009.

Gottlieb, Amy S., and Elizabeth L. Travis. "Rationale and models for career advancement sponsorship in academic medicine: The time is here; the time is now." *Academic Medicine: Journal of the Association of American Medical Colleges* 93, no. 11 (2018): 1620–1623.

Greenwood, Brad N., Seth Carnahan, and Laura Huang. "Patient–physician gender concordance and increased mortality among female heart attack patients." *Proceedings of the National Academy of Sciences* 115, no. 34 (2018): 8569–8574.

Grundy, Quinn, and Elissa Ladd. "'Nurse ambassadors': A new 'Fulcrum' of pharmaceutical marketing." *Health Affairs Blog*. January 4, 2019.

Han, Shasha, Tait D. Shanafelt, Christine A. Sinsky, Karim M. Awad, Liselotte N. Dyrbye, Lynne C. Fiscus, Mickey Trockel, and Joel Goh. "Estimating the attributable cost of physician burnout in the United States." *Annals of Internal Medicine* 170, no. 11 (2019): 784–790.

Harvey, Sheila, Diane Rach, M. Colleen Stainton, John Jarrell, and Rollin Brant. "Evaluation of satisfaction with midwifery care." *Midwifery* 18, no. 4 (2002): 260–267.

Hechtman, Lisa A., Nathan P. Moore, Claire E. Schulkey, Andrew C. Miklos, Anna Maria Calcagno, Richard Aragon, and Judith H. Greenberg. "NIH funding longevity by gender." *Proceedings of the National Academy of Sciences* 115, no. 31 (2018): 7943–7948.

Heinemann, Linda V., and Torsten Heinemann. "Burnout research: Emergence and scientific investigation of a contested diagnosis." *Sage Open* 7, no. 1 (2017): 2158244017697154.

Henderson, Jillian T., and Carol S. Weisman. "Physician gender effects on preventive screening and counseling: An analysis of male and female patients' health care experiences." *Medical Care* 39, no. 12 (2001): 1281–1292.

Hideg, Ivona, Anja Krstic, Raymond Trau, and Tanya Zarina. "Do longer maternity leaves hurt women's careers?" *Harvard Business Review*. September 14, 2018.

Horowitz, Juliana Menasce, Kim Parker, Nikki Graf, and Gretchen Livingston. "Americans widely support paid family and medical leave, but differ over specific policies." *Pew Research Center*, March 23, 2017.

Horrocks, Sue, Elizabeth Anderson, and Chris Salisbury. "Systematic review of whether nurse practitioners working in primary care can provide equivalent care to doctors." *BMJ* 324, no. 7341 (2002): 819–823.

Hu, Yue-Yung, Ryan J. Ellis, D. Brock Hewitt, Anthony D. Yang, Elaine Ooi Cheung, Judith T. Moskowitz, John R. Potts III et al. "Discrimination, abuse, harassment, and burnout in surgical residency training." *New England Journal of Medicine* 318 (18) (2019):1741–1752.

Institute of Medicine and National Research Council. *U.S. Health in International Perspective: Shorter Lives, Poorer Health*. Washington, D.C.: National Academies Press, 2013.

Jaffe, Aniela. *Memories, Dreams, Reflections by CG Jung*. New York: Vintage, 1989 (1961).

Jagsi, Reshma, Kent A. Griffith, Rochelle Jones, Chithra R. Perumalswami, Peter Ubel, and Abigail Stewart. "Sexual harassment and discrimination experiences of academic medical faculty." *JAMA* 315, no. 19 (2016): 2120–2121.

Javadi, Dena, Jeanette Vega, Carissa Etienne, Speciosa Wandira, Yvonne Doyle, and Sania Nishtar. "Women who lead: Successes and challenges of five health leaders." *Health Systems & Reform* 2, no. 3 (2016): 229–240.

Jee, Eunjung, Joya Misra, and Marta Murray-Close. "Motherhood penalties in the US, 1986–2014." *Journal of Marriage and Family* 81, no. 2 (2019): 434–449.

Jefferson, Laura, Karen Bloor, Yvonne Birks, Catherine Hewitt, and Martin Bland. "Effect of physicians' gender on communication and consultation length: A systematic review and meta-analysis." *Journal of Health Services Research & Policy* 18, no. 4 (2013): 242–248.

Jena, Anupam B., Andrew R. Olenski, and Daniel M. Blumenthal. "Sex differences in physician salary in US public medical schools." *JAMA Internal Medicine* 176, no. 9 (2016): 1294–1304.

Jena, Anupam B., Dhruv Khullar, Oliver Ho, Andrew R. Olenski, and Daniel M. Blumenthal. "Sex differences in academic rank in US medical schools in 2014." *JAMA* 314, no. 11 (2015): 1149–1158.

Johnson, Steven R. "The rise of physician MBA programs creates opportunities, challenges for business schools." *Modern Healthcare*. October 6, 2018.

Johnson, T.L., D.J. Rinehart, J. Durfee, D. Brewer, H. Batal, J. Blum, C.I. Oronce, P. Melinkovich, and P.A. Gabow. "For many patients who use large amounts of health care services, the need is intense yet temporary." *Health Affairs* 34, no. 8 (2015): 1312–1319.

Jolly, Shruti, Kent A. Griffith, Rochelle DeCastro, Abigail Stewart, Peter Ubel, and Reshma Jagsi. "Gender differences in time spent on parenting and domestic responsibilities by high-achieving young physician-researchers." *Annals of Internal Medicine* 160, no. 5 (2014): 344–353.

Kaiser Family Foundation. "Key facts about the uninsured population." 2018. https://www.kff.org/uninsured/fact-sheet/key-facts-about-the-uninsured-population/. Accessed February 25, 2019.

Kaiser Family Foundation. "Professionally active physicians by gender." *State Health Facts Data*. 2019. https://www/kff.org/other/state-indicator/physician-by-gender/. Accessed June 26, 2019.

Kaiser Family Foundation. "Total number of nurse practitioners by gender." *State Health Facts Data*. 2019. https://www.kff.org/other/state-indicator/total-number-of nurse-practitioners-by-gender/. Accessed July 5, 2019.

Kaiser Family Foundation. "Total number of physician assistants by gender." *State Health Facts Data*. 2019. http://www.kff.org/other/state-indicator/total-physician-assistants/. Accessed July 5, 2019.

Kaiser Family Foundation. "Total number of professionally active nurses by gender." *State Health Facts Data*. 2019. https://www.kff.org/other/state-indicator/total-number-of -professionally-active-nurses-by-gender/. Accessed July 5, 2019.

Kamal, Rabah, and Cynthia Cox. "How do healthcare prices and use in the US compare to other countries." *Peterson-Kaiser Health System Tracker*. May 8, 2018. Accessed May 10, 2019.

Kane, L. "Medscape national physician burnout, depression & suicide report 2019." medscape. com/slideshow/2019-lifestyle-burnout-depression-6011056(2019). Accessed June 26, 2019.

Karlsson, Per-Ola, Martha Turner, and Peter Gassmann, "Succeeding a long-serving legend in the corner office." *Strategy+Business*. May 15, 2019 / Summer 2019 / Issue 95. https://www.strategy-business.com/article/Succeeding-the-long-serving-legend-in-the-corner-office? Accessed July 28, 2019.

Karpowitz, Christopher F., and Tali Mendelberg. *The Silent Sex: Gender, Deliberation, and Institutions*. Princeton: Princeton University Press, 2014.

Kaufman, Steven, Nadia Ali, Victoria DeFiglio, Kelly Craig, and Jeffrey Brenner. "Early efforts to target and enroll high-risk diabetic patients into urban-community-based programs." *Health Promotion Practice* 15, no. 2_suppl (2014): 62S–70S.

Khubchandani, Jagdish, and James H. Price. "Short sleep duration in working American adults, 2010–2018." *Journal of Community Health* 44 (2019): 1–9.

Khullar, Dhruv, Daniel Wolfson, and Lawrence P. Casalino. "Professionalism, performance, and the future of physician incentives." *JAMA* 320, no. 23 (2018): 2419–2420.

Kirch, Darrell. "A landmark for women in medicine." *AAMC News*. December 18, 2017. https://news.aamc.org/medical-education/article/word-president-landmark-women-medicine/. Accessed August 17, 2018.

Knowles, Megan. "5 top-paid hospital, health system executives." *Becker's Hospital Review*, November 20, 2018. https://www.beckershospitalreview.com/compensation-issues/5-top-paid-hospital-health-system-executives.html. Accessed May 14, 2019.

Korenstein, Deborah, Maha Mamoor, and Peter B. Bach. "Preventive services offered in executive physicals at top-ranked hospitals." *JAMA* 322, no. 11 (2019): 1101–1103.

Korn Ferry Institute. "Women CEOs speak: Strategies for the next generation of female executives and how companies can pave the road." *Korn Ferry Institute* (2017). https://engage.kornferry.com/womenceosspeak. Accessed March 2, 2019.

Landivar, Liana Christin. *Men in Nursing Occupations: American Community Survey Highlight Report*. US Census Bureau, 2013. https://www.census.gov/newsroom/blogs/random-samplings/2013/02/men-in-nursing-occupations.html. Accessed May 27, 2019.

Lazare, Aaron. *On Apology.* Jericho: Oxford University Press, 2005.

Leisher, Craig, Gheda Temsah, Francesca Booker, Michael Day, Leah Samberg, Debra Prosnitz, Bina Agarwal et al. "Does the gender composition of forest and fishery management groups affect resource governance and conservation outcomes? A systematic map." *Environmental Evidence* 5, no. 1 (2016): 6.

Levitin, Daniel J. *A Field Guide to Lies: Critical Thinking in the Information Age.* London: Penguin, 2016.

Lima, Luciana, and Eduardo Vieira Barnes. *Indigenous Women: Keepers of the Amazon Rainforest.* Nature Conservancy, August 4, 2019. https://www.nature.org/en-us/ what-we-e-/our-insights/perspectives/indigenous-women-xikrin-amazong-rainforest. Accessed August 11, 2019.

Liu, Katherine A., and Natalie A. Dipietro Mager. "Women's involvement in clinical trials: Historical perspective and future implications." *Pharmacy Practice* 14, no. 1 (2016): 1–9.

Livingston, Gretchen. "Among 41 Nations, U.S. is the outlier when it comes to parental leave." *FactTank: News in the Numbers.* September 21, 2016. Pew Research Center. Accessed September 21, 2019.

Liz Cornwall. "RNnetwork 2018 portrait of a modern nurse survey." *Nurse life.* December 12, 2018. http://rrnetwork.com/blog/rrnetwork-2018-portrait-of-a-modern-nurse-survey/. Accessed June 13, 2019.

Lukela, Jennifer Reilly. "What's in a name?" *JAMA* 322, no 3 (2019): 211–212.

Lurie, Nicole, Jonathan Slater, Paul McGovern, Jacqueline Ekstrum, Lois Quam, and Karen Margolis. "Preventive care for women—does the sex of the physician matter?" *New England Journal of Medicine* 329, no. 7 (1993): 478–482.

Ly, Dan P., Seth A. Seabury, and Anupam B. Jena. "Hours worked among US dual physician couples with children, 2000 to 2015." *JAMA Internal Medicine* 177, no. 10 (2017): 1524–1525.

Ly, Dan P., Seth A. Seabury, and Anupam B. Jena. "Characteristics of US physician marriages, 2000–2015: An analysis of data from a US census survey." *Annals of Internal Medicine* 168, no. 5 (2018): 375–376.

Macy, Beth. *Dopesick: Dealers, Doctors and the Drug Company that Addicted America.* London: Head of Zeus Ltd, 2018.

Madera, Juan M., Michelle R. Hebl, Heather Dial, Randi Martin, and Virgina Valian. "Raising doubt in letters of recommendation for academia: Gender differences and their impact." *Journal of Business and Psychology* 34, no. 3 (2019): 287–303.

Magnan, Sanne. "Social determinants of health 101 for health care: Five plus five." *NAM Perspectives.* 2017.

Magrane, Diane, and Page S. Morahan. "Fortifying the pipeline to leadership: The international center for executive leadership in academics at Drexel." In *Forward to Professorship in STEM*, ed. Rachelle S. Heller, Catherine Mavriplis and Paul Sabila. San Diego: Academic Press, 2016.

Magudia, Kirti, Alexander Bick, Jeffrey Cohen, Thomas SC Ng, Debra Weinstein, Christina Mangurian, and Reshma Jagsi. "Childbearing and family leave policies for resident physicians at top training institutions." *JAMA* 320, no. 22 (2018): 2372–2374.

Maranz, Felice and Rebecca Greenfield. "Men get the first, last and every other word on earnings calls." *Bloomberg Business News.* September 13, 2018. https://www.bloomberg. com/news.articles.2018-09-13/men-get-the-first-last-and-every-other-word-on-earnings-calls. Accessed August 8, 2019.

Mark, Saralyn and Jhumka Gupta. "Reentry into clinical practice: Challenges and strategies." *JAMA* 288, no. 9 (2002): 1091–1096.

Martinson, Brian C., Melissa S. Anderson, and Raymond De Vries. "Scientists behaving badly." *Nature* 435, no. 7043 (2005): 737.

Maslove, David M. "Limitations concerning the association of physician sex and patient outcomes." *JAMA Internal Medicine* 177, no. 7 (2017): 1056.

Mathews, T. J., Danielle M. Ely, and Anne K. Driscoll. "State variations in infant mortality by race and Hispanic origin of mother, 2013–2015." NCHS Data Brief. No 295. January 2018. https://www.cdd/gov/nchs/data/databriefs/db295.pdf. Accessed May 23, 2019.

McCullagh, Elizabeth A., Katarzyna Nowak, Anne Pogoriler, Jessica L. Metcalf, Maryam Zaringhalam, and T. Jane Zelikova. "Request a woman scientist: A database for diversifying the public face of science." *PLoS Biology* 17, no. 4 (2019): e3000212.

McGlynn, Elizabeth A., Steven M. Asch, John Adams, Joan Keesey, Jennifer Hicks, Alison DeCristofaro, and Eve A. Kerr. "The quality of health care delivered to adults in the United States." *New England Journal of Medicine* 348, no. 26 (2003): 2635–2645.

McHugh, Matthew D., Ann Kutney-Lee, Jeannie P. Cimiotti, Douglas M. Sloane, and Linda H. Aiken. "Nurses' widespread job dissatisfaction, burnout, and frustration with health benefits signal problems for patient care." *Health Affairs* 30, no. 2 (2011): 202–210.

Medicare Payment Advisory Commission (MedPAC). "Report to the Congress: Medicare and health care delivery." June 2018.

Mehnert, Robert and Kathy Cravedi. "Papers of Florence R. Sabin added to National Library of Medicine's Profiles in Science / United States National Library of Medicine." National Institutes of Health. 2003. https://profiles.nlm./gov/RR. Accessed May 23, 2019.

Menegatti, Michela, and Monica Rubini. "Gender bias and sexism in language." In *Oxford Research Encyclopedia of Communication*, 2017. https://oxfordre.com/communication/view/10.1093/acrefore/9780190228613.001.0001/acrefore-9780190228613-e-470. Accessed June 12, 2019.

Millman, Jason. "A knee replacement surgery could cost you $17k or $61k. And that's in the same city." *Washington Post.* January 12, 2015.

Modern Healthcare a. "Health care hall of fame." *Modern Healthcare.* March 4, 2019.

Modern Healthcare b. "Modern healthcare top 25 emerging leaders." *Modern Healthcare.* October 14, 2019.

Modern Healthcare c. "Modern healthcare top 25 women leaders." *Modern Healthcare.* July 29, 2019.

Morahan, Page S., Katharine A. Gleason, Rosalyn C. Richman, Sharon Dannels, and Sharon A. McDade. "Advancing women faculty to senior leadership in US academic health centers: Fifteen years of history in the making." *NASPA Journal About Women in Higher Education* 3, no. 1 (2010): 140–165.

Moran, Victoria. "Word for the Day." *A Network for Grateful Living.* December 27, 2018.

Muench, Ulrike, Jody Sindelar, Susan H. Busch, and Peter I. Buerhaus. "Salary differences between male and female registered nurses in the United States." *JAMA* 313, no. 12 (2015): 1265–1267.

Mullangi, Samyukta, and Reshma Jagsi. "Imposter syndrome: Treat the cause, not the symptom." *JAMA* 322, no. 5 (2019): 403–404.

Mylona, Elza, Linda Brubaker, Valerie N. Williams, Karen D. Novielli, Jeffrey M. Lyness, Susan M. Pollart, Valerie Dandar, and Sarah A. Bunton. "Does formal mentoring for faculty members matter? A survey of clinical faculty members." *Medical Education* 50, no. 6 (2016): 670–681.

National Academies of Sciences, Engineering, and Medicine. *Taking Action Against Clinician Burnout: A Systems Approach to Professional Well-Being.* Washington, DC: The National Academies Press, 2019. doi:10.17226/25521. Accessed October 31, 2019.

National Academies of Sciences, Engineering, and Medicine. *Sexual Harassment of Women: Climate, Culture, and Consequences in Academic Sciences, Engineering, and Medicine.* Washington, DC: The National Academies Press, 2018.

National Health Expenditure Data. 2018. https://cms.gov/Research-Statistics-Data -and-Systems-Reports/NationalHealthExpendData/downloads/highlights.pdf. Accessed April 22, 2019.

National Institute for Occupational Safety and Health. "Healthcare workers." 2017. https://www.cdc.gov/niosh/topics/healthcare/default.html. Accessed June 27, 2018.

"National Institutes of Health Office of Research on Women's Health: US Department of Health and Human Services b: 'Report to the Advisory Committee on Women's Health FY 2015–2016'." https://orwh.od.nih.gov/sites/orwh/files/docs/ORWH_Biennial_ Report_WEB_508_FY-15-16.pdf. Accessed May 24, 2019.

"National Institutes of Health Office of Research on Women's Health: US Department of Health and Human Services a: Report of the NIH Advisory Committee on Research on Women's Health Fiscal Years 2013–2014." https://orwh.od.nih.gov/sites/orwh/ files/docs/2-ORWH-ACRWH-Biennial-Report-FY13-14.pdf. Accessed May 28, 2019.

NIH Databook. 2019. https://report.nih.gov/nihdatabook/report/173. Accessed May 24, 2019.

Nittrouer, Christine L., Michelle R. Hebl, Leslie Ashburn-Nardo, Rachel CE Trump-Steele, David M. Lane, and Virginia Valian. "Gender disparities in colloquium speakers at top universities." *Proceedings of the National Academy of Sciences* 115, no. 1 (2018): 104–108.

Nohria, Nitin. "You are not as virtuous as you think." *Washington Post.* October 15, 2015.

Noland, Marcus, Tyler Moran, and Barbara R. Kotschwar. "Is gender diversity profitable? Evidence from a global survey." *Peterson Institute for International Economics Working Paper,* 2016. https://piie.com/publications/working-papers/gender-diversity-profitable-evidence-global-survey. Accessed March 4, 2019.

Nunes, Debra A., and Jane Stevenson. "The new roadblock for women: Performance reviews." *Korn Ferry Institute Reports & Insights.* October 22, 2019. https://www. kornferry.com/institute/vague-performance-reviews-women-leaders?utm_campaign= 10-24-19-twil&utm_source=mailjet&utm_medium=email. Accessed October 25, 2019.

Nurse.com. "Nursing salary research report." 2018. http://mediakit.nurse.com/wp-content/ uploads/2018/06/2018-Nurse.com-Salary-Research-Report.pdf. Accessed May 27, 2019.

Obama, Michelle. *Becoming.* New York: Crown Publishing Group, 2018.

OECD iLibrary. "Health at a Glance 2017." 2018. http://www.oecd.org/about/publishing/ Corrigendum_Health_at_a_Glance_2017.pdf. Accessed July 20, 2019.

Oliveira, Diego F.M., Yifang Ma, Teresa K. Woodruff, and Brian Uzzi. "Comparison of National Institutes of Health grant amounts to first-time male and female principal investigators." *JAMA* 321, no. 9 (2019): 898–900.

Olson, Alexandra. "Women in workplace-catalyst CEO story." *AP News.* August 21, 2018. https://www.apnews.com/fc24ccabc38e4c7a8d1532a19ef256. Accessed June 27, 2019.

Ornstein, Charles, and Katie Thomas. "Top cancer researcher fails to disclose corporate financial ties in major research journals." *New York Times.* September 8, 2018.

Papanicolas, Irene, Liana R. Woskie, and Ashish K. Jha. "Health care spending in the United States and other high-income countries." *JAMA* 319, no. 10 (2018): 1024–1039.

Parker, Kim, and Eileen Patten. "The sandwich generation: Rising financial burdens for middle-aged Americans." *Pew Research Center, Social & Demographic Trends Project,* 2013.

Patton, Elizabeth W., Kent A. Griffith, Rochelle D. Jones, Abigail Stewart, Peter A. Ubel, and Reshma Jagsi. "Differences in mentor-mentee sponsorship in male vs female recipients of National Institutes of Health grants." *JAMA Internal Medicine* 177, no. 4 (2017): 580–582.

Penn Nursing. "American nursing: An introduction to the past." https://www.nursing.upenn.edu/nhhc/american-nursing-an-introduction-to-the-past/. Accessed June 20, 2018.

Petersen, Emily E., Nicole L. Davis, David Goodman, Shanna Cox, Nikki Mayes, Emily Johnston, Carla Syverson et al. "Vital signs: Pregnancy-related deaths, United States, 2011–2015, and strategies for prevention, 13 states, 2013–2017." *Morbidity and Mortality Weekly Report* 68, no. 18 (2019): 423. https://www.cdc.gov/vitalsigns/maternal-deaths/index.html. Accessed August 19, 2019.

Pew Research Center. "Modern parenthood: Roles of moms and dads converge as they balance work and family." *Numbers: Facts and Trends Shaping Your World.* March 14, 2013. Pew Research Center. https://www.pewsocialtrends.org/2013/03/14/modern-parenthood-roles-of-moms-and-dads-converge-as-they-balance-work-and-family/. Accessed September 29, 2019.

Pinker, Steven. *Enlightenment Now: The Case for Reason, Science, Humanism, and Progress.* New York: Viking, 2018.

Pololi, Linda H. *Changing the Culture of Academic Medicine: Perspectives of Women Faculty.* Hanover: University Press of New England, 2010.

Rabatin, Joseph, Eric Williams, Linda Baier Manwell, Mark D. Schwartz, Roger L. Brown, and Mark Linzer. "Predictors and outcomes of burnout in primary care physicians." *Journal of Primary Care & Community Health* 7, no. 1 (2016): 41–43.

Radley, David, Douglas McCarthy, and Susan Hayes. *Scorecard on State Health System Performance 2018 Edition.* The Commonwealth Fund, 2018. https://www.commonwealthfund.org/publications/fund-reports/2018/may/2018-scorecard-state-health-system-performance. Accessed May 21, 2019.

Raja, Siva, and Sharon L. Stein. "Work–life balance: History, costs, and budgeting for balance." *Clinics in Colon and Rectal Surgery* 27, no. 02 (2014): 071–074.

Ranji, Usha, Caroline Rosenzweig, Ivette Gomez, and Alina Salganicoff. *Executive Summary: 2017 Kaiser Women's Health Survey.* The Henry J. Kaiser Family Foundation, March 2018. https://www.kff.org/womens-health-policy/issue-brief/overview-2017-kaiser-womens-health-survey/. Accessed September 20, 2018.

Regenstein, Marsha, Jennifer Trott, Alanna Williamson, and Joanna Theiss. "Addressing social determinants of health through medical-legal partnerships." *Health Affairs* 37, no. 3 (2018): 378–385.

Riano, Nicholas S., Eleni Linos, Erin C. Accurso, Dawn Sung, Elizabeth Linos, Julia F. Simard, and Christina Mangurian. "Paid family and childbearing leave policies at top US medical schools." *JAMA* 319, no. 6 (2018): 611–614.

Rockey, S. "Women in biomedical research." *Extramural Nexus. National Institutes of Health, Office of Extramural Research.* April 14, 2017 (2014). https://nexus.od.nih.gov/all/2014/08/08/women-in-biomedical-research/. Accessed May 24, 2019.

Rockwell, Dan. "Leading yourself into humility." In *Character Based Leader: Instigating a Leadership Revolution …One Person at a Time,* eds. Tara Alemany, Deb Costello, and Don Shapiro. Indianapolis: Dog Ear Publishing, 2012.

Roser, Max, and Hannah Ritchie. "Maternal mortality rates." Our World Data. https://ourworldindata.org/maternal-mortality. Accessed October 1, 2019.

Ross, David A., Dowin Boatright, Marcella Nunez-Smith, Ayana Jordan, Adam Chekroud, and Edward Z. Moore. "Differences in words used to describe racial and gender groups in Medical Student Performance Evaluations." *PloS one* 12, no. 8 (2017): e0181659.

Rotenstein, Lisa S., Matthew Torre, Marco A. Ramos, Rachael C. Rosales, Constance Guille, Srijan Sen, and Douglas A. Mata. "Prevalence of burnout among physicians: A systematic review." *JAMA* 320, no. 11 (2018): 1131–1150.

Roter, Debra L., Judith A. Hall, and Yutaka Aoki. "Physician gender effects in medical communication: A meta-analytic review." *JAMA* 288, no. 6 (2002): 756–764.

Ruzycki, Shannon M., Sarah Fletcher, Madalene Earp, Aleem Bharwani, and Kirstie C. Lithgow. "Trends in the proportion of female speakers at medical conferences in the United States and in Canada, 2007 to 2017." *JAMA Network Open* 2, no. 4 (2019): e192103.

Sadek, Salwa. "The women who helped bring down Sudan's President." *Vox.* April 11, 2019. https://www.vox.com/world/2019/4/11/18305358/omar-al-bashir-sudan-president-military-coup-protests-women. Accessed April 20, 2019.

Sakulku, Jaruwan, and James Alexander. "The imposter phenomenon." *International Journal of Behavioral Science* 6, no. 1 (2011): 75–97.

Sandberg, Daniel J. "When women lead, firms win." *S & P Global.* 2019. www.spglobal.com. Accessed October 22, 2019.

Sandberg, Sheryl. *Lean In: Women. Work and the Will to Lead.* London/New York: Alfred A. Knopf, 2013.

Saralyn, Mark, and Jhumka Gupta. "Reentry into clinical practice: Challenges and strategies." *JAMA* 288, no. 9 (2002): 1091–1096.

Schaufeli, Wilmar B. "Burnout: A short socio-cultural history. " In *Burnout, Fatigue, Exhaustion* ed. Sighard Neckel, Anna K. Schaffner and Greta Wagner, 105–127. Cham: Palgrave Macmillan, 2017.

Scheffler, Richard M., Daniel R. Arnold, and Christopher M. Whaley. "Consolidation trends in California's health care system: Impacts on ACA premiums and outpatient visit prices." *Health Affairs* 37, no. 9 (2018): 1409–1416.

Schmittdiel, Julie A., Ana Traylor, Connie S. Uratsu, Carol M. Mangione, Assiamira Ferrara, and Usha Subramanian. "The association of patient-physician gender concordance with cardiovascular disease risk factor control and treatment in diabetes." *Journal of Women's Health* 18, no. 12 (2009): 2065–2070.

Schor, Nina F. "The decanal divide: Women in decanal roles at US medical schools." *Academic Medicine: Journal of the Association of American Medical Colleges.* 93, no. 2 (2018): 237–240.

Schrager, Sarina B. "Beyond work-life 'balance.'" *Family Practice Management* 23, no. 2 (2016): 7.

Sege, Robert, Linley Nykiel-Bub, and Sabrina Selk. "Sex differences in institutional support for junior biomedical researchers." *JAMA* 314, no. 11 (2015): 1175–1177.

Shanafelt, Tait D., Sonja Boone, Litjen Tan, Lotte N. Dyrbye, Wayne Sotile, Daniel Satele, Colin P. West, Jeff Sloan, and Michael R. Oreskovich. "Burnout and satisfaction with work-life balance among US physicians relative to the general US population." *Archives of Internal Medicine* 172, no. 18 (2012): 1377–1385.

Sherman, Rachel. "The rich kid revolutionaries." *New York Times.* April 27, 2019.

Shrank, William H., Teresa L. Rogstad, and Natasha Parekh. "Waste in the US health care system: Estimated costs and potential for savings." *JAMA* 322 no 15 (2019): 1501–1509.

Slomski, Anita. "Why do hundreds of US women die annually in childbirth?" *JAMA* 321, no. 13 (2019): 1239–1241.

Starmer, Amy J., Mary Pat Frintner, Kenneth Matos, Chloe Somberg, Gary Freed, and Bobbi J. Byrne. "Gender discrepancies related to pediatrician work-life balance and household responsibilities." *Pediatrics* 144 no 4(2019): e20182926.

State of Colorado. *Acceptance of the Statue of Doctor Florence Rena Sabin.* Washington, D.C.: United States Government Printing Office, 1959.

Stoll, Barbara J. "Reflections on leadership: Seizing and embracing opportunities—holding up half the sky." *JAMA* 321, no. 22 (2019): 2165–2166.

Stone, T., B. Miller, E. Southerian, and A. Raun. *Women in Healthcare Leadership 2019.* Oliver Wyman, 2019. https://www.oliverwyman.com/content/dam/oliver-wyman/v2/publications/2019/January/WiHC/WiHCL-Report-Finadf. Accessed May 28, 2019.

Tahhan, Ayman Samman, Muthiah Vaduganathan, Stephen J. Greene, Gregg C. Fonarow, Mona Fiuzat, Mariell Jessup, JoAnn Lindenfeld, Christopher M. O'Connor, and Javed Butler. "Enrollment of older patients, women, and racial and ethnic minorities in contemporary heart failure clinical trials: A systematic review." *JAMA Cardiology* 3, no. 10 (2018): 1011–1019.

Tecco, Halle. "Women in healthcare 2017: How does our industry stack up?" *Rock Health* (2017). https://rockhealth.com/reports/women-in-healthcare-2017-how-does-our-industry-stack-up/. Accessed August 6, 2018.

Thibault, George E. "Women in academic medicine." *Academic Medicine: Journal of the Association of American Medical Colleges* 91, no. 8 (2016): 1045–1046.

Travis, Elizabeth, Leilani Doty, and Deborah Helitzer. "Sponsorship: A path to the academic medicine C-suite for women faculty?" *Academic Medicine: Journal of the Association of American Medical Colleges* 88, no. 10 (2013): 1414–1417.

Trix, Frances, and Carolyn Psenka. "Exploring the color of glass: Letters of recommendation for female and male medical faculty." *Discourse & Society* 14, no. 2 (2003): 191–220.

Tsugawa, Yusuke, Anupam B. Jena, Jose F. Figueroa, E. John Orav, Daniel M. Blumenthal, and Ashish K. Jha. "Comparison of hospital mortality and readmission rates for Medicare patients treated by male vs female physicians." *JAMA Internal Medicine* 177, no. 2 (2017): 206–213.

Unger, Laura, and Caroline Simon. "Which states have the worst maternal mortality." *USA Today.* November 1. 2018. https://www.usatoday.com/list/news/investigations/maternal-mortality-by-state/ Accessed July 11, 2019.

UN-Water. "Gender, water, and sanitation: A policy brief." *Interagency Task Force on Gender and Water.* May 26, 2006. https://www.unwater.org/publications/gender-water-sanitation-policy-brief/. Accessed August 11, 2019.

U.S. Census Bureau. "Male nurses becoming more commonplace." *Newsroom*. February 25, 2013. https://www.census.gov/newsroom/press-releases/2013/cb13-32.html. Accessed July 13, 2019.

Varda, Briony K., and McKinley Glover. "Specialty board leave policies for resident physicians requesting parental leave." *JAMA* 320, no. 22 (2018): 2374–2377.

Varjavand, Nielufar, Nigel Pereira, and Dipak Delvadia. "Returning inactive obstetrics and gynecology physicians to clinical practice: The Drexel experience." *Journal of Continuing Education in the Health Professions* 35, no. 1 (2015): 65–70.

VCU Center on Society and Health. "Measuring healthy places: The metropolitan Washington healthy places index." *VCU Center on Society and Health*. 2018. https://societyhealth.vcu.edu/work/the-projects/measuring-healthy-places-the-metropolitan-washington-healthy-places-index.html. Accessed May 21, 2019.

Walker, Matthew. *Why We Sleep: Unlocking the Power of Sleep and Dreams*. New York: Scribner, 2017.

Wallis, Christopher J.D., Bheeshma Ravi, Natalie Coburn, Robert K. Nam, Allan S. Detsky, and Raj Satkunasivam. "Comparison of postoperative outcomes among patients treated by male and female surgeons: A population based matched cohort study." *BMJ* 359 (2017): j4366.

Westfall, Brian. "The open office concept failed. So, what now." *Talent Management*. November 15, 2018. https://blog.capterra.com/articles/talent-management/. Accessed September 17, 2019.

Wikipedia a, s.v. "Clara Barton." https://en.wikipedia.org/wiki/Clara_Barton. Accessed May 29, 2018.

Wikipedia b, s.v. "Eleanor Roosevelt." https://en.wikipedia.org/wiki/Eleanor_Roosevelt. Accessed March 21, 2019.

Wikipedia c, s.v. "Margaret Sanger." https://en.wikipedia.org/wiki/Margaret_Sanger. Accessed March 21, 2019.

Wikipedia d, s.v. "Phyllis Schlafly." https://en.wikipedia.org/wiki/Phyllis_Schlafly. Accessed July 14, 2019.

Willis, Jay. "The 30 most influential Deans of Nursing in the United States." *Mometrix Media*. March 17, 2015. https://www.mometrix.com/blog/the-30-most-influential-deans-of-nursing-in-the-united-states/. Accessed June 20, 2018.

Winsor-Games, Kathleen. "Why you should align your values with work—and how to do it." *Denver Post*. July 7, 2019.

Zenger/Folkman. "A study in leadership: Women do it better than men." *Zenger/Folkman*. 2012. http://zengerfolkman.com/media/articles/ZFCo.WP.WomenBetterThanMen.033012.pdf. Accessed March 2, 2019.

Index